MORE
CHRISTIANITY

MORE CHRISTIANITY

Dwight Longenecker

Our Sunday Visitor Publishing Division
Our Sunday Visitor, Inc.
Huntington, Indiana 46750

Copyright © 2002 by Our Sunday Visitor Publishing Division, Our Sunday Visitor, Inc.

All rights reserved. With the exception of short excerpts for critical reviews, no part of this book may be reproduced in any manner whatsoever without permission in writing from the publisher. Write:
Our Sunday Visitor Publishing Division
Our Sunday Visitor, Inc.
200 Noll Plaza
Huntington, IN 46750

ISBN: 1-931709-35-1 (Inventory No. T22)
LCCCN: 2002107147

Cover design by Rebecca Heaston
Interior design by Sherri L. Hoffman
PRINTED IN THE UNITED STATES OF AMERICA

In memory of Keith Charles Jarrett, K.S.G.,
Secretary of the St. Barnabas Society, 1992-2000

"He was a good man, full of the
Holy Spirit and of faith"
(Acts 11:24).

Table of Contents

Acknowledgments

More Christianity was developed from a series of radio scripts I was commissioned to write for London's Premier Radio. The fact that C. S. Lewis's *Mere Christianity* also grew from a radio series prompted my shameless title. The radio series on Premier, like this book, sought to explain the Catholic faith to an Evangelical audience in a sympathetic way. The series was the brainchild of Francis Holford. He got me on board, raised the finances, and steered the whole series through to completion. I have to thank Francis for his friendship, encouragement, patience, and good humor throughout the process.

Through the wonders of the Internet I met Bob Trexler of the New York C. S. Lewis Society. Bob read many of these chapters and made numerous helpful comments and suggestions. The Internet also put me in touch with Gregg Terrell and David and Jill Kalinski. Both Gregg and Jill were on their own journey toward the Catholic Church at the time and they kindly read the manuscript and gave me their comments. Stratford Caldecott of the Centre for Faith and Culture in Oxford also sampled the text and encouraged me to carry on. I must also thank Cyprian Blamires, my colleague at the St. Barnabas Society, whose father was a student of C. S. Lewis. Cyprian read the opening chapters and helped direct my attention to my real audience. Joe Pearce also took time to read, comment, and encourage. I must also thank Marcus Grodi — and the staff of the Coming

9

Home Network — who published some of the first chapter versions in the *Coming Home Journal*. However, the person who read the book with the most attention, and made the best and most numerous suggestions, is David Gustafson, an old acquaintance whom God very providentially brought back into my life after an absence of over twenty years. David's intelligence, breadth of learning, tact, and wisdom have influenced every chapter for the best. He approached my words with a lawyer's objectivity and offered incisive comments and new angles to my argument even when he disagreed with my point.

I need to thank Professor John Saward, who kindly read the manuscript and corrected my sometimes errant theology. Thanks also go to Tom Howard, who said he liked the book enough to write the foreword, Mike Dubruiel of Our Sunday Visitor, who thought it ought to be published, and Henry O'Brien, also of Our Sunday Visitor, who edited the manuscript with care, tact, and a professional touch. Finally, I thank my wife, Alison, who thinks it is more fun having a husband at home writing religious books than one going out to a "sensible" job.

— Dwight Longenecker
Chippenham
November 22, 2001

Foreword

One of the conundrums of modern Church history attaches to the ecclesiology of the most widely read Christian apologist of our epoch: Why did C. S. Lewis never become a Roman Catholic?

The question is asked over and over. The question itself is intriguing, since one might reply, "But why ask the question to begin with? You don't ask that about Billy Graham." But there is something at work in the whole fabric of Lewis's vision of reality that seems to push things in the direction of Catholicism. For one thing, of course, he not only takes the sacraments seriously (he speaks of "the Blessed Sacrament," and made a practice of auricular confession), but his work, most notably his fiction, is unmistakably "sacramentalist." It is doubtful whether *The Chronicles of Narnia* could ever have been written by a full-blown Protestant, since Protestantism is quintessentially a verbalist, propositionalist, discursive handling of the faith, whereas Catholicism is profoundly narrative, dramatic, and participatory (for example, the fifteen mysteries of the rosary, and the Mass itself). The sacraments are the physical points at which eternity touches time — the Incarnation itself, of course, being the Sacrament of all sacraments.

Readers may justifiably object here, "But Lewis was a Protestant: what do you mean, it is doubtful whether a Protestant could have written the Narnia tales?" A fair question. Lewis stoutly and stolidly insisted that he was a Protestant, and an Ulsterman into the bargain. Nothing Romish about him. But attentive readers, with the greatest trepidation, may find themselves in the awkward position of wishing to quarrel, ever so meekly, with Lewis. "You are not as Protestant as you think, sir." The point, of course, is that he was an Anglican, for a start, and that Church has never quite made up its mind whether it is Protestant or Catholic (we are in a minefield here, and must tiptoe along with fearful caution). The Anglican Church is episcopal, hierarchic, sacramentalist, and claims to be apostolic. These categories are very far from being the common currency of Protestantism. Furthermore, one gets the impression that Lewis wore his Protestantism like a cockade in his hat, or perhaps closer to the mark, like a helmet and body armor, ready for battle.

The most important remark here remains to be put forward: Lewis loathed ecclesiology because ecclesiology is the topic *par excellence* that divides Christians, and Lewis wanted most earnestly to speak as a "mere Christian." He stuck rigorously to the creedal matters upon which all serious Christian believers are agreed, and eschewed like the black pestilence any topic at all that would excite Christians to bickering with each other. He avoided all discussion as to the mode of baptism, for example, and anything that concerned itself with the details of the *eschaton* (from the Greek for "the end" or "the end of the world"). Hence (and I speak as a partisan of Lewis who will champion him to the death — or at least to the mat, shall we say), Lewis's work cannot be said to encompass the whole substance of the Catholic faith. His Christianity (or more exactly, his published Christianity) while robust, wise, and ardent, is incomplete.

It would be a very rare breed of browser among books who will not recognize instantly Dwight Longenecker's explicit and calculated debt to Lewis in the title of the present work: *More Christianity*. "Forsooth!" we might cry. "Are we to understand that you have set yourself the task of improving on Lewis's best-known theological work? Come. It won't do." Mr. Longenecker is wise enough to steer clear of any such claim. What he does bring to our attention in this work is the titanic matter of the Catholic Church, which topic Lewis sedulously avoided. Lewis was a loyal churchman but did not wish to be drawn into any discussion of the matter. He was Anglican because that happens to have been the sector of the Church into which he was baptized. He simply "went to church," as any Christian ought to do, he would have urged. But holding to such a minimalist position, he would have had some heavy sledding if he had found himself in a conversation with Peter, Clement, Ignatius, Polycarp, Cyprian, Irenaeus, Justin, or any of a score of others.

These gentlemen would have wanted to know how it came about that Lewis claimed to be a "mere Christian" and yet had attached himself to a body that had cleaved itself from the only authentically apostolic Church known to them. They would have wondered why Lewis avoided certain "extras" that they considered essential parts of the Christian faith. These "extras" are the topics that inevitably arise in Catholic-Protestant discussion century after century: the Marian dogmas, the papacy, the Mass, purgatory, the communion of the saints, and such practices as penance, the rosary, and so forth.

To touch on only one of these (since Mr. Longenecker treats the topic magnificently in the body of the book), the ancient Church increasingly became aware that Mary had been granted a dignity, by God's grace, unparalleled by any other creature in the universe, including the seraphim. There were patriarchs, prophets, kings, apostles, the Fathers, the martyrs, and all the angelic orders. All of these bear witness to the Word: Mary bore the Word. No seraph has ever been drawn into the mystery of Redemption in even a remotely analogous manner. In the early Church the right doctrine and the right devotion concerning the mother of our Lord was inextricably linked with the right doctrine and devotion toward Jesus himself. As such, for the early Christian, devotion to the Blessed Virgin Mary was not an extra but an essential.

The title of Longenecker's book reveals the theme, and it would be a highly interesting business to ask whether Lewis himself might not be given pause, and, then possibly even applaud, were he given the chance to read the chapters that follow. He was aware that he was sticking rigorously to the "mere" aspects of the faith (and gigantically mere they were, to be sure). He was certainly aware that the Church herself, from the beginning, most notably in the Fathers, discovered and took into her worship, confession, and doctrine, all of the matters that constitute this "more" of which Mr. Longenecker speaks. The "more" does not stand over against the "mere," much less does it cast the "mere" into question: It is, quite simply, the "more" that developed organically as the ancient Church reflected on the Scriptures and the tradition handed down from the apostles. Instead of the "more" being something different from the "mere," the "more" turns out to be of one fabric with the "mere" of which Lewis so eloquently spoke. It is to be most sedulously urged that all believers (Catholics who have not much reflected on their own *Catechism of the Catholic Church*, and Protestants who have approached all these matters only as points to be refuted) ponder with open minds and open hearts what follows here.

Dwight Longenecker has not written a Catholic diatribe. This is not a Catholic attack on Protestants. Rather, with immense tact, clarity, sagacity, and learning, he takes us the rest of the way along the road charted in *Mere Christianity*. Again, it must be stressed that Longenecker is not presuming to piggy-back, or cash in on, Lewis's work, nor to set himself up as Lewis's successor. There is no hint of this in the book. We find here all of the questions that arise *vis-à-vis* the doctrine of the Church, and the fullness of doctrine that she teaches. It is a beautiful book, and one that any believer serious about the ancient Faith ought to find vastly rewarding.

— Thomas Howard

C. S. Lewis and the Fullness of Faith

One day on a railway platform C. S. Lewis picked up a copy of George MacDonald's book *Phantastes*. Years later, in his introduction to MacDonald's work, Lewis describes the effect the little book had on him:

> A few hours later I knew that I had crossed a great frontier. I had already been waist deep in Romanticism; and likely enough, at any moment, to flounder into its darker and more evil forms, slithering down the steep descent that leads from the love of strangeness to that of eccentricity, and thence to that of perversity. . . . I was only aware that if this new world was strange, it was also homely and humble; that if this was a dream, it was a dream in which one at least felt strangely vigilant; that the whole book had about it a sort of cool morning innocence. . . . What it did was to convert, even to baptize my imagination.[1]

Lewis himself has had a similar effect on a whole generation. Through his imaginative fiction, and his Christian apologetics he has rescued the minds and hearts of millions. I count myself among the rescued. During my college years I was already wallowing in the fragrant lowlands of romantic eccentricity, and was close to being swallowed in the quicksand of perversity. Lewis's commonsense approach to faith and his robust morality made Christianity seem new and attractive. The fresh air and brisk showers of Lewis's humor and common sense woke me up and introduced me to a Christianity that was invigorating and real. It made my effete inclinations seem sordid, small, and sad. How could snootiness over church, chasubles, and china teacups compare with the bracing possibilities of goodness that Lewis offered?

Lewis rescued Evangelical Americans of my generation in another way. Many of us were the first generation of Evangelicals who had gone all the way through university. Our grandparents had been brought up within various Protestant sects that were suspicious of higher education. Our parents may have gone to college, but we finished and went on to graduate school. In the process we were introduced to the wider world of literature, classical music, art, and architecture. We were introduced to the classics of theology and philosophy, and if we went far enough in our religious studies we had to struggle with the rigors of biblical criticism, modernist theology, and the whole "liberal agenda." In the midst of these challenges C. S. Lewis offered a lifeline. He was an intellectual giant, but he wrote with a clear common sense that our grandparents would have appreciated. His Christianity was orthodox, yet it was educated and cultured, intelligent and witty. We knew we could trust him to preach the "mere Christianity" that we wanted to retain, and yet we were happy that he challenged us, broadened that Christianity, and made it big enough to accommodate all the other learning and culture we were hungry to absorb.

The baby boomer generation in America were also the first to travel widely. The elite may have visited Europe in earlier generations, and our fathers may have gone to Europe to fight in the war, but we jumped on planes and were the first to backpack across Europe. Visiting the great centers of European Christianity made us think. In America our Christian forefathers were the Puritans, Brethren, Presbyterians, and Baptists, so our history went back no further than a few hundred years. In Europe everything from the cathedrals and parish churches, to the music, literature, and art spoke of a Christianity that was integrated into culture. We discovered a form of Christianity that was deeper, broader, and more ancient than anything we had encountered before. C. S. Lewis offered an expression for our faith that provided connections into that venerable and attractive world. As an Anglican academic, Lewis gave us a bridge from revivalist religion to the heart of Christian European culture.

Like many others I jumped in headfirst. As an undergraduate American I became sick with the sweet illness of Anglophilia. I started attending a little Anglican church and was immediately taken with candles, musty prayer books, decent hymns, and kneeling to pray. Someone gave me a picture book called *The World of C. S. Lewis*. It was full of soft-focus photographs of Oxford quadrangles and people punting at Cambridge. There were black-and-white photos of Lewis and his chums swilling dark beer in dark English pubs. There were shots of Lewis's home in Ireland, his rooms at Magdalen, and his house in Headington. The book was all misty fields, quiet English rivers, the green and gold of the English countryside, roaring fires in Oxford common rooms, the heavenly glories of college chapels, and the homely glories of Anglican country churches. As an undergraduate at Bob Jones University, I ducked from the rowdy preacher boys who wanted to "shoot the gospel gun" and escaped into the world of Lewis and his Inkling friends.

One summer I visited Britain with a Baptist mission team. I spent the summer street preaching and handing out tracts. Wearing my all-American smile and my white shirt and tie, I spent weeks knocking on the doors of dour Scottish villagers, inviting them to talk religion. But while I was busy being mistaken for a Mormon, I was all the time eyeing the Scottish Episcopal church on the hill, with its spire and overgrown churchyard, and wondering if I could ever be the minister of such a church. When I got back to Bob Jones, I was finally baptized and confirmed as an Anglican. I then began to nurture a dream that I might move to England and become a country parson like George Herbert. Americans believe their dreams can come true; so, fresh out of college, I taught school for a year and wrote to the only Anglican theologian I had heard of: the Evangelical J. I. Packer. I asked if he could recommend any places to study theology in England. One college on his short list was in Oxford, so I applied to Wycliffe Hall without a hope of getting in. I couldn't believe it when I was accepted. I was actually going to study for three full years at Oxford — the mecca of all Lewisean Anglophiles.

At Wycliffe it wasn't long before I realized my tastes in worship were "higher" rather than "lower." In other words, I gravitated to the incense, good music, and ritual of places in Oxford like Pusey House, New College, the cathedral at Christ Church, and Lewis's old college, Magdalen. It wasn't just the music and architecture I was going for. I surprised the people at the soundly Evangelical Wycliffe Hall by attending spirituality lectures with the Dominicans at Blackfriars, and used my vacation time to go to a nearby Benedictine abbey to learn more about the contemplative life.

Through all this, Lewis was a guiding light. Knowing he had worshiped at his college chapel every day allowed me to go to Magdalen for Evensong whenever I could. Believing Lewis was "high church" gave me permission to enjoy the smells and bells of Anglo-Catholic worship. When some modernist theologian tried to tell me theology was a science, Lewis assured me that theology was poetry as I had suspected all along. On the other hand, when another modernist suggested that theology was *only* poetry, Lewis insisted that it conveyed objective truth. When the other ordinands argued about the possibility of women's ordination, an essay of Lewis spoke more common sense in one page than the lot of them had spoken in two hours. When modern biblical critics tried to convince me that the Gospels were late embroidered fables and the Old Testament was a hodgepodge editing job, Lewis swept in, wearing his literary critic's hat, and showed them to the door. When the rationalists tried to disprove the reality of truth, Lewis showed how they were cutting off the branch they were sitting on. When the humanists tried to dispose of Christianity, Lewis proved that orthodox Christianity was more humane and optimistic than their shallow positive thinking. When the scientists tried to dismiss miracles, Lewis was there to rescue them. Over and over again Lewis helped me see that the orthodox faith I held to did not have to be ignorant and paranoid. He showed me that it was permissible to be skeptical of the skeptics. He also impressed me with the comforting fact that I was not cut out to be a theologian. Because he wrote as a layman, he could play the little child in the story of the emperor's new clothes and expose the arrogant delusion of contemporary professional Christianity. As a layman, Lewis spoke for me, and when he pulled the rug out from some pompous bishop or trendy theologian, I knew he was on my side.

Lewis's quick mind quickened mine. His ready wit made me ready to laugh. His imagination fired my own. His robust approach to life inspired me to put down my books and live a little. His commonsense approach to prayer and the Christian life made me believe that being a Christian in the real world was a possibility. If I have departed from Lewis's Anglican faith, I feel sure he would have approved of my reasons. Paradoxically it was Lewis's freshness of mind and critical facility that has enabled me to move on from Lewis's Anglicanism to something bigger and older and simpler. The title of this book is therefore not meant to be a parody of Lewis but a tribute. They say imitation is the sincerest form of flattery, so I hope Lewis will feel flattered that I've aped his title. If not, I hope he'll at least enjoy it as a mild joke — a little bow of gratitude and honor from an apprentice to his master.

C. S. Lewis and Anglicanism

The biographers tell us that Tolkien, who was so instrumental in Lewis's conversion to Christianity, tried to persuade Lewis to move on from Anglicanism to Catholicism. Besides Tolkien, Lewis counted Catholics like R. E. Havard and Dom Bede Griffiths among his friends. Despite his close friendships with Catholics, Lewis always resisted the step to Rome. A friend of Lewis's, Father Charles Smith, suggests why: "I never thought that Lewis ever contemplated conversion," Father Smith says, "because there was too much of the Northern Ireland Protestantism in him. There was always this anti-Romanism."[2]

Lewis might have been biased by an inborn anti-Romanism. Indeed his father had warned him never to trust a Roman Catholic.[3] Lewis may have been hesitant to "come home to Rome" because he felt he could serve God better by remaining neutral. Mere Christianity meant joining the most practical and most natural church, and for Lewis the Anglican Church was the Church on his doorstep. Furthermore, Lewis may have felt that through the Anglican Church he could better reach the English people. England in his time was very anti-Catholic and a large proportion of the population still considered themselves members of the Anglican Church. Lewis was probably right in thinking he could reach more people by remaining an Anglican layman. In the almost forty years since his death, however, England and the Church of England have changed beyond recognition. Furthermore, the changes in the Church of England are reflected in the rest of the mainstream Protestant churches in both England and the United States.

Lewis and his friends stuck up for the fundamentals of the faith, and believed they were best defended in the Anglican Church. Unfortunately, the Anglican Church, like the other historic Churches of the Reformation, has found it impossible to retain those fundamentals. The reasons for the decay of Western Reformed Christianity are complex, but in theological terms it is modernism that most undermined the essential Christianity Lewis found in the Anglican Church. In his day Lewis fought the forces of modernism. He defended a simple, supernatural form of the Christian religion. Lewis's satirical portrayal of the apostate bishop who believes "in a spiritual sense" and wants "nothing superstitious or mythological"[4] has become a sad portrait of the predominant tendency within Anglicanism and the other mainstream denominations.

As a result of nearly a century of modernism working its way through the system, the twenty-first-century clergyman is modernist without his even knowing it. In all the denominations there are a huge number of clergy who are like the vicar in *The Screwtape Letters*, who "has been so long engaged in watering down the faith to make it easier for a supposedly incredulous and hardheaded congregation that it is now he who shocks his parishioners with his unbelief and not *vice versa.*"[5] People wonder why things seem a bit empty. The problem is they have been given what Lewis called, "Christianity with water." It is bubble gum religion — something sweet to chew on but with no nutritional value and a tendency to rot the teeth.

The most insidious form of modernism retains traditional Christian language while disposing of traditional Christian belief. So the very typical Reverend Mr. Wooley stands up on Easter Sunday and says, "Today we thank God for the mighty resurrection of his Son, Jesus Christ, from the dead." The lady in the front row is pleased because her minister believes in the Resurrection. However, if she asks him what he means by "resurrection" he is very likely to say, "In some sort of way I would want to say that the teachings of Jesus continued to be relevant to his followers despite his tragic death." This theological sleight of hand has kept the pews relatively warm while the faith itself has gone cold.

In the Anglican Church, as in the other mainstream Churches of the Reformation, modernism has won the day, and produced the offspring called post-modernism. As a consequence, twenty-first-century Protestant Christianity has become a jumble of belief systems and worship styles. Everything is there from charismatic neo-fundamentalism to an urbane, agnostic activism. Within every denomination there is an increasing range of beliefs and styles of worship. Variety of style is also present in the Catholic Church, and it is not necessarily all bad. The mood of post-modernism is often curious, open-minded, and positive. It means Christianity is adapting to the real needs of modern men and women. It also means people are tolerant. They are open to new ideas and anxious to explore the truth. Toleration, open-mindedness, and exploration are good, but they are only possible if one believes there is actually a truth to explore. Styles and formulations may change legitimately, but the essential truths of the faith do not change. If the foundation is eroded too far, then nothing is left but personal choice, and toleration becomes the only virtue.

The answer to this predicament is not to run for cover and take refuge in fundamentalism or traditionalism — pretending that "mere Christianity" only exists in some past golden age. "Mere Christianity" is bigger than that. The Holy Spirit is not narrow-minded and he never leads backward — only forward. Somehow we must find an expression of the faith that is universal and open to various traditions while still retaining the essential beliefs — constantly reformulating them in a dynamic and fresh way. In a shrinking world we must find an expression of the faith that accepts the good things from every Christian tradition. We must find a Christianity that is also not afraid to engage with other religions — affirming the truths they offer without abandoning the unique and essential truths of Christianity. To do this we need a form of Christianity that is strong enough to take on these challenges — strong enough to be truly universal. The only way a church can be both universal and unique is for it to have an authority structure that can defend the core beliefs while still allowing cultural change, adaptation, and growth.

For Lewis the Anglican Church provided such a foundation. Within Anglicanism he found a modest, historical, and dignified expression of that basic universal faith that he called "mere Christianity." During Lewis's lifetime the Church of England was enjoying a golden age. On the literary front there was a little Anglican renaissance. Lewis was part of a vanguard of literary figures who championed an intellectually robust and creative faith. Along with Lewis, a number of other shakers and movers — including Dorothy Sayers, Charles Williams, and T. S. Eliot — made orthodox Anglicanism attractive and literate. Evelyn Underhill, Christopher Bryant, and Austin Farrer

brought scholarship and mysticism together while the leadership of the Church of England was made up of men who were
usually devout, educated, and cultured.

After two world wars the number of men in the priesthood
was higher than ever before in history. The Church was a valued institution in the establishment of England. The Anglo-
Catholics were feeling buoyant with strong leadership and
increasing loyalty among the rank and file. The Evangelicals
were rising in influence, and the overall picture looked good.
Lewis thought the universal had to be made particular in each
locality and so he saw the Church of England as the Church of
the English people.[6] In his day many more English people considered themselves Church members, and Church membership
often cut across class boundaries. You were as likely to find the
local butcher in church as the local banker. Lewis chose well,
and there is no denomination more beautiful, historic, and majestic than the Church of England.

But the strength of Anglicanism — its Englishness — is
also its weakness. Cut off from a universal authority structure
and with no contemporary shared belief, she has had to adapt
to a fast-changing world on her own through a system of trial
and error. In a multicultural and interracial society Lewis's Anglican Church, with its established status and quaint English
traditions, now seems archaic and small. Modernism has struck
a mortal blow to traditional belief systems and authority struc-
tures. At the same time forces of change around the Anglican
Communion have brought in extremes of charismatic sectari-
anism, sexual politics, and neo-paganism that would have made
Lewis shudder. While there are many "mere Christians" within
the Anglican Church, the present theological and cultural drift
makes Lewis's majestic and beautiful Church seem increasingly
alien to simple historic Christianity.

If the Anglican Church has changed over the last thirty years, the Catholic Church has changed even more. In Lewis's day, to become Catholic would have seemed foreign. Catholicism for him was anything *but* mere Christianity. It seemed top-heavy with strange customs and extraneous doctrines. But since Lewis's death nearly forty years ago the Catholic Church has changed in ways Lewis never could have dreamt of. She has simplified her liturgy, opened the door to worship in everyday language, and reformed herself without losing the historic faith. While the other mainstream denominations have crumbled under the onslaught of the "humanist" agenda, the Catholic Church has faithfully proclaimed the supernatural gospel of life in a culture of death. The Catholic Church struggles with the same destructive forces as the other churches, but with a centralized authority structure the erosion has been working on rock rather than shifting sand. The struggles of the last forty years have taken their toll in the Catholic Church too, but in many ways the conflict has made the Catholic Church leaner, more focused, and more aware of the central core of the faith. Now at the dawn of the twenty-first century, that simple Gospel that Lewis branded "mere Christianity" and that Evangelicals call the "old, old story" is more fully and universally presented in the Catholic Church than anywhere else.

'Mere Christianity'

Lewis is justly famous for his little book, *Mere Christianity.* But ironically in his sermon titled "Transposition," Lewis warns against the "merely mentality." The person who determines everything by "merely" or "only" or "nothing but" "sees all the facts but not the meaning."[7] Any attempt to reduce something great to something small should be resisted. For example, Lewis would fight against those who wish to explain human bad behavior as "merely the result of a chemical imbalance," or "merely the fruit of social conditioning." Things are always more than they seem, not less.

When the characters in Narnia meet Ramandu, the incarnation of a star, the obnoxious rationalist Eustace Scrubb says to him, "In our world a star is a huge ball of flaming gas." Ramandu replies, "Even in your world, my son, that is not what a star is, but only what it is made of."[8] While he commends "mere Christianity," Lewis was clear that a simple acceptance of the bare bones of the Christian faith was not enough. As Eustace must move past his chemical understanding of a star, so each new Christian must move beyond the basic beliefs of "mere Christianity" into the full experience of Christian discipleship with all its attendant joys and sorrows.

Lewis's *Mere Christianity* is good as far as it goes, and as a first step in Christian apologetics it probably has no equal. To be fair, Lewis denied that his use of "mere" in the title indicated the lowest common denominator. He took the phrase "mere Christian" from the seventeenth-century-Puritan preacher Richard Baxter who wrote, "You know not of what party I am of, nor what to call me; I am sorrier for you in this than for myself; if you know not, I will tell you, I am a Christian, a meer [mere] Christian."[9] As Timothy George has pointed out in a recent lecture, Lewis used the word "mere" to mean "real" or "true" or "sure." However, while Lewis argued valiantly that his "mere Christianity" was the "highest common factor" between Christians, it's not that easy to define just what that "mere Christianity" consists of. There must be a basic core of Christian belief to which all subscribe, but even the historic creeds are open to wild differences of interpretation among Christians. Just what are the basics that make up this "mere Christianity"? This difficulty is sensed in Dorothy Sayers's friend and biographer Barbara Reynolds's vague response when asked what those highest factors were: "Trinitarian and Incarnational. Those are absolutely indispensable fundamentals . . . *(pause)* . . . And Sacraments absolutely."[10] The clash is clear. Many Evangelicals would happily consider the sacraments dispensable extras, but for Reynolds they are indispensable essentials.

Like Lewis and his friends, Cardinal Newman also believed in an essential core of doctrine. It was the faith once delivered to the saints, which "ever existed in the church whole and entire, ever recognized as the faith, ascertainable as such and separable (to speak generally) from the mass of opinions."[11] Unlike Lewis, Newman didn't believe these fundamentals could be defined on their own. Ian Ker points out that the essential problem is that Lewis and other well-meaning non-Catholics believe the fundamentals can exist as objective truths outside the dynamic life of the Church. In this sense they are like Eustace who reduces a star to its chemical components. But Christianity, like a star, is more than what it is made of. The basic truths of the Christian faith cannot be separated from the wholeness of the Church. Catholics believe those basic truths can be most fully known within the bosom of the Church. Ker refers to an illustration of Newman's that makes the point: "I illustrated it by the contrast presented to us between the Madonna and Child, and a Calvary. The peculiarity of the Anglican theology was this — that it supposed the truth to be entirely objective and detached, not (as in the theology of Rome) lying hid in the bosom of the Church as if one with her, clinging to and lost in her embrace; but as being sole and unapproachable, as on the Cross . . . with the church close by, but in the background."[12] This exposes two fundamental problems often associated with Lewis's "mere Christianity" as it is popularly understood. First, Christianity is a life of faith, not just a set of beliefs with ethics attached. Second, without anyone to define just what that "mere

Christianity" is, each group and indeed each individual has to define his own version of "mere Christianity."

There are many Evangelicals who fervently wish to hold fast to Lewis's "mere Christianity." They also want to belong to a church where that simple faith is defined, defended, and lived faithfully. However, these "mere Christians" are increasingly homeless. They have been trained to regard the true Church as "invisible." Like Lewis, all they want is for their local church to simply be an outpost of "mere Christianity," no matter what the denomination. However, they see their once orthodox smaller denominations following the way of the mainstream Protestant groups into a shallow relativistic religion. At the same time they are too educated and aware to feel comfortable in a hard-line fundamentalist sect. Often they have acquired a taste for liturgy and historical Christianity but are not sure where to find it. Eastern Orthodoxy has an ancient appeal, but it doesn't travel well and lacks a unified teaching authority. Anglicanism looks good, but Evangelical Christians squirm at the Anglicans' theological and moral slipperiness.

True Churches and Perfect Churches

This book is intended to help non-Catholic Christians who are interested in historic Christianity to understand the modern Catholic Church more easily. It takes as a starting place a little point that Lewis makes in *Mere Christianity*. At the end of the introduction he says he is introducing the reader to simple Christianity with no frills or traditions. "However," Lewis writes, "I hope no reader will suppose that 'mere' Christianity is here put forward as an alternative to the creeds of the existing communions — as if a man could adopt it in preference to Congregationalism or Greek Orthodoxy or anything else. It is more like a hall out of which doors open into several rooms. If I can bring anyone into the hall I shall have done what I attempted to do. But it is in the rooms, not in the hall, that there are fires and chairs and meals. The hall is a place to wait in, a place from which to try the various doors, not a place to live in."[13]

In other words, you have to belong to a church if you want to be a Christian. Finding the right church is not always easy, and Lewis says sometimes one has to wait in the hall for some time before finding the right room. He also implies that some people have to visit various rooms before they find the right one. The quest may take a long time, and one may end up waiting during the search. Then he says:

> When you do get into your room you will find the long wait has done you some kind of good which you would not have had otherwise, but you must regard it as waiting, not as camping. You must keep on praying for light; and of course, even in the hall, you must begin trying to obey the rules which are common to the whole house. And above all you must be asking which door is the true one, not which pleases you best by its paint and paneling. In plain language, the question should never be: "Do I like that kind of service?" but "Are these doctrines true: Is holiness here? Does my conscience move me towards this? Is my reluctance to knock at this door due to my pride, or my mere taste, or my personal dislike of this particular doorkeeper?"[14]

There is a little inconsistency here that even the most fervent of Lewis's admirers must see. Lewis implies that all the rooms off the central hall are of equal value, but he recommends choosing a denomination not according to taste but according to what is true. However, if we must choose according to what is true, then some rooms must be "more true" than others. If this is the case, then the different rooms are not of equal value. On the other hand, if all the rooms are equally true, then the only criterion for choice is taste and preference after all. Of course Lewis is not so relativistic or individualistic as that. He actually says we must choose a church that is true — not a church we like best. If this is the case, then we must keep on searching until we find that church that is "most true." If we find it, according to Lewis, then we must join that church even if we don't necessarily like it.

Notice that this search is for the true church, not the perfect church. In other words, we are looking for a church that holds the truth, not one that has no faults. Many Christians who wish to affirm "mere Christianity" quite rightly conclude that there is no perfect church and they will have to make do with the church they like best. The assumption is that all the side rooms are equally imperfect. In a sense this is true, but the equal imperfection of all the churches does not mean they are all equally untrue. Mormons may be more moral than the Methodists, while the Methodists have more truth than the Mormons. If we are choosing according to perceived perfection or imperfection, we've reduced the whole question once again to personal opinion and we're back to choosing the side room according to which paint and paneling we like best. If Lewis is right that we must choose according to what is most true, then we must look past the human imperfections of any church and try to judge their claim to be most true.

If we are choosing a church that is most true but not necessarily most attractive, then another problem immediately crops up. That is, how do we determine which church is most true? The different churches all seem to have different strengths and weaknesses. Who is to say which is most true? Can we possibly develop some sort of criteria by which to judge? Common sense says a church that is most true will have more truth than the others. In other words, it will be the fullest expression of Christianity. It would make sense therefore to consider questions such as: Which church has thrived and survived in the most places around the world? Which holds the widest expression of different cultures and traditions within it? Which church is both universal and yet identified locally? Which has the largest number of adherents? Which church has stood the test of time? Which has the most impressive historical credentials? Which one has kept the faith despite persecutions from without and problems within? Which church approaches the truth objectively and sticks to it despite personal cost? Which one exhibits the most impressive holiness? Which one is faithful to Scripture and the historic faith? Which one is intellectually, spiritually, and culturally credible?

To say that a particular church is "more true" is not to judge the goodness or holiness of the individuals in either that church or any other church. The goodness of each person is for God to decide. However, just as some Christians know more about the Bible and the faith than others, so some churches simply have better and more trustworthy credentials. You are more likely to find professional doctors and a full range of treatments in an established modern hospital than at the local health food store. Likewise you'll find a wider expression of the truth in a large historic church than in an obscure Christian sect.

In looking for the most true church, one will be tempted to look at the outward appearances, but the things that look best on the outside may not be the best when all the facts are gathered. We might see a wrinkled old crone in a shabby cardigan and dismiss her as an alcoholic tramp when in fact she was Mother Teresa. Likewise the church that is most true might at first glance seem the least likely candidate. Conversely, the church whose "paint and paneling" we admire may turn out, like a beautiful young woman, to be glamorous but shallow and untrue. It might be that the church that seems most attractive may most likely be the one we should *not* join. The religion that attracts us might be pandering to the weakest part of our nature.

More Christianity

Lewis may have claimed that his "mere Christianity" was "the highest common factor." In practice, however, the exercise to define "mere Christianity" is too often an exercise in finding the lowest common denominator. To seek the highest common factor is not to reduce the faith to a little kernel of agreed doctrine. Instead it is to embrace as much of the Christian faith as possible. The highest common factor is for the largest number of Christians to understand and accept the largest amount of truth that has been held by as many Christians in as many places as possible down through history.

F. D. Maurice wrote, "A man is most often right in what he affirms and wrong in what he denies." This little maxim is deceptively powerful, for if we are to affirm as much as possible, then our whole critical mindset will be transformed. To seek the highest common factor in the Christian faith is to affirm as much as possible. Whenever confronted with something new, different, and strange, we will try to see how we can accept it rather than automatically reject it. This positive little saying also forces us to reexamine our own assumed positions. Are the truths we hold actually an affirmation of truth, or are they a denial of some kind?

Too many of our religious positions are assumed more by what we deny rather than what we affirm. So, for example, an ultra-traditionalist Catholic's enthusiasm for the old liturgy may actually be driven more by his dislike of the new liturgy than a genuine love for the old. A Protestant may worship in a bare preaching hall not because he likes bare rooms but because he thinks ornamentation is vain and idolatrous. Time and again our stance is determined by what we are denying rather than what we are affirming.

When faced with the challenge of affirming, not denying, the lifelong conservative Evangelical may well draw back. After all, he's been trained to "be discerning." He's trained to sniff out liberalism and wrong doctrine and pin it to the ropes with a swift right hook. To go about "affirming all things" sounds a bit gooey and "liberal." It's admirable to defend the faith, but too often Protestantism has taught us to protest, and our whole identity is defined by our protest. Protestantism has bred in us the mentality that immediately squints in suspicion and says, "Prove it." No wonder so many religious people and practices come across as sour, negative, and suspicious. Of course our denials are well-meant. We wish to avoid abuses and false teaching of various kinds. Unfortunately the desire to avoid an abuse has too often denied a right use. To make matters worse, in our denials we are almost always denying some misunderstanding that we've inherited rather than the real doctrinal position.

When I was at college, I was invited to join the opera chorus. I had never been to an opera, and as far as I was concerned, opera consisted of fat ladies bellowing in a foreign language. But the director of the opera chorus, who was desperate for more men to join, said I shouldn't reject something I didn't understand, and if so many educated people loved opera who was I to reject it? I decided to give it the benefit of the doubt, joined the opera chorus for Bellini's *Norma*, and turned up for rehearsals twice a week. Eventually I went out on stage dressed like a Druid with fake beard and a wolfskin hat, bellowed out the big tunes, and thoroughly enjoyed myself. When there is something we do not understand, "more Christianity" either leaves it politely on one side, or gives it the benefit of the doubt. If our mindset is determined by skepticism, suspicion, and doubt, we almost always deprive ourselves some great growing point.

In the last Narnia chronicle the children enter the final frontier. They go into the real Narnia and exhort one another to go "further up and further in." As they do, they embark on an adventure of exploration that takes them into more and more truth and beauty while never denying any good thing on the journey previously. This book is an attempt at that kind of journey. In it I hope to encourage others to affirm all things; to explore with abundant joy all that is being offered as a positive gift to the people of God. I hope to exhort my brothers and sisters who have accepted "mere Christianity" to come "further up and further in" and to accept "more and more and more Christianity." More Christianity means leaving behind our preconceptions, prejudices, and pet likes and dislikes. It means leaving behind a suspicious mentality and seeking to affirm as much as possible while denying as little as possible. It means eschewing sects and pressure groups and setting out on an adventure of faith to see what other good things God has to give. It sings with the optimism of St. Paul: "All things are yours, . . . and you are Christ's; and Christ is God's" (1 Corinthians 3:21, 23).

At this point it is natural to draw back. Such an attitude is risky. It means change and requires trust. In the last Narnia story the dwarfs are offered a sumptuous feast, but they cannot see or taste the glorious food for fear of being taken in. Like the dwarfs in Narnia our instinct is to withdraw into our own little group and trust no one. We fear that we may be taken in. We would rather have the half-truths we know than the full truth we do not know. We may end up believing something that is superstitious, strange, and unfamiliar. Does it matter? Which is better, to be guilty of gullibility or lack of belief? At the last day I would rather say, "I'm sorry, Lord, I believed too much," than "Sorry, Lord, I didn't believe enough." Even Aslan can do nothing for the dwarfs. "You see," said Aslan, "they will not let us help them. They have chosen cunning instead of belief. Their prison is only in their own minds, yet they are in that prison; and so afraid of being taken in that they cannot be taken out."[15]

The non-Catholic Christian who considers the Catholic faith may think he has to give up what he already believes; but to accept the "more Christianity" of Catholicism is not to deny the goodness and truth of the Evangelical faith. Catholics affirm all that other Christians affirm; they simply cannot deny what they deny. "Catholic" means universal, so the truly Catholic person affirms all that is good and true in the other forms of Christianity. Indeed the Catholic Church recognizes that her own fullness is depleted because of the divisions in the body of Christ. Catholicism is even more full when the good things from the other Christian traditions are added in.

Because I am a former Evangelical who has become a Catholic, it might be imagined that this book is a simple call for Evangelicals to "come home to Rome." It is more than that. I believe in all the essentials the Catholic Church has reformed herself to such an extent that the reasons for the Reformation no longer apply. But if more Evangelicals are to come into full communion with the apostolic Church, then Catholics need to continue to understand and accept the strengths of Evangelicalism. Evangelical churches are thriving for some good reasons, and many Catholics are joining them because they find in the Evangelical churches something they missed in the Catholic Church. If Evangelicals need "more Christianity," then so do many Catholics. The Catholic Church needs to learn from the

Evangelical experience. She needs to adopt and adapt the strengths of Evangelicalism, and show all the faithful how the strengths of Evangelicalism can be integrated into the Catholic faith. This process will be like the mother who is humble enough to learn from her child; but it will also be like the child returning to the mother's warm embrace.

If the different denominations are rooms off a main hall, then *More Christianity* will introduce you to the Catholic room. However, Catholics wouldn't be totally happy with Lewis's picture. The Catholic Church is not just another room off the hall. It's been around longer, it's bigger, and it's more comprehensive than all the other rooms. Lewis's analogy of a hall with side rooms implies that the hall is part of a larger house. I think Lewis's analogy should be extended. If becoming a Christian is like entering a great hall, then becoming a Catholic is stepping from that entrance hall into an enormous country house. From the vestibule you can go into some side waiting rooms, but if you want to enter the country mansion and live there, go through that door that looks just like the doors into all the other rooms. If you do, you will find that your feet have been planted firmly in a large room (cf. Psalm 31:8). You will have taken a step into a vast and magnificent country mansion that contains not only the hall but all the side rooms as well. In going through the door you may feel full of apprehension and anticipation at the same time. You may feel you have left all to follow Christ (cf. Matthew 19:27), but once inside you will discover that everything has been restored. You will not have left home but arrived home and known the place for the first time. You will not have denied anything of true value; instead you will have discovered the source and fulfillment of all that has gone before. In becoming a Catholic you will have chosen not a hall or a side room but that ancient and glorious mansion that Christ himself has built.

Introduction Endnotes

1. Quoted in R. Green and W. Hooper, *C. S. Lewis, A Biography,* London, Fount, 1974, p. 44.

2. Joseph Pearce, *Literary Converts,* London, HarperCollins, 1999, p. 274.

3. C. S. Lewis, *Surprised by Joy,* Harcourt, Brace and Jovanovich, New York, 1957, p. 216.

4. C. S. Lewis, *The Great Divorce,* London, Fontana, 1988, p. 136.

5. C. S. Lewis, *The Screwtape Letters,* London, Geoffrey Bles, 1942, p. 82.

6. Ibid., pp. 15-16.

7. C. S. Lewis, "Transposition," in *Screwtape Proposes a Toast,* London, Fount, 1986, p. 92.

8. C. S. Lewis, *The Voyage of the Dawn Treader,* London, Fontana, 1985, p. 159.

9. Richard Baxter, *Church History of the Government of Bishops,* quoted in David Mills, *The Pilgrim's Guide: C. S. Lewis and the Art of Witness,* Grand Rapids, Eerdmans, 1998, p. 294.

10. Pearce, p. 271.

11. John Henry Newman, *Essays Critical and Historical,* quoted in Ian Ker, *The Hall and the Side Rooms,* Dwight Longenecker (ed.), *The Path to Rome: Modern Journeys to the Catholic Church,* Leominster, Gracewing, 1999, pp. 54-55.

12. Ibid, p. 54.

13. C. S. Lewis, *Mere Christianity,* London, Fount, 1995, p. 11.

14. Ibid., p. 12.

15. C. S. Lewis, *The Last Battle,* London, Fontana, 1981, p. 141.

chapter ONE

The Bible Church

Pontius Pilate asked Jesus, "What is truth?" (John 18:38). What Pilate didn't know is that truth was standing before him in the form of a human being. Christians answer Pilate's question "What is truth?" with Jesus' own words "I am the way, and the truth, and the life" (John 14:6). Truth is therefore not primarily a doctrine to be believed, or a rule to be obeyed, but a person to be loved. This personal quality is what makes Christianity unique — as St. John says, "The Word became flesh and dwelt among us, full of grace and truth" (John 1:14). The letter to the Hebrews reads: "In many and various ways God spoke of old to our fathers by the prophets; but in these last days he has spoken to us by a Son" (Hebrews 1:1-2). The next question is: "If Jesus is the truth, how do we come to know Jesus?" All Christians agree that a primary way to know Jesus is through the Bible.

I grew up in an independent Bible church. In Sunday school we sang a song with these words: "The B-I-B-L-E, yes, that's the book for me, I stand alone on the Word of God, the B-I-B-L-E." We believe that Jesus reveals God's truth and the God-breathed Scriptures reveal Jesus. But those who sing the children's chorus I've quoted would want to take it further. The Scriptures are a vital source for experiencing God's truth in Christ, but some Christians claim the Scriptures are our only totally reliable source for truth. One of the foundation planks of the Reformation platform was the phrase *sola Scriptura,* which is Latin for "Scripture alone." *Sola Scriptura* is the teaching that the Bible is the only authority for all questions of faith and morals.

The Reformation happened during the time when the printing press had just been invented. Before that time most people were illiterate, and the Bible was only available in precious hand-copied versions. Suddenly with the printing press, everyone could have a Bible in his or her own language. At the same time, the Christian Church was in need of reform. While there were many good and faithful Christians, it is also true that there was complacency and corruption. The clear and beautiful words of Scripture made the corrupt Church look elaborate, decadent, and overcomplicated. No wonder simple, good believers thought the answer was to make the Bible the only rule and authority for Christians. As more people read the Bible, every aspect of the Christian life seemed to be addressed clearly in the Scripture texts.

While it is an understandable ideal, unfortunately, within *sola Scriptura* are the seeds of some serious problems. Any ideology that is defined by the words "merely" or "only" is too limited. Such an ideology often has an ulterior motive. When people use "only," they are often focusing more on what they are excluding than on what they are endorsing. So, for example, when a social worker says a criminal's behavior is "only the result of his deprived childhood," he is not so much focusing on the deprived childhood as he is excusing the criminal's responsibility for his actions. This "only" approach distorts our perception. Truth is rarely expressed with an "only" because truth is always bigger, not smaller than we've imagined. "More Christianity" rightly asks what is being left out or denied. Therefore, when it comes to *sola Scriptura*, "more Christianity" is happy with the *Scriptura* but not the *sola*.

The Jews were given the written word of God, but it was part of the Jewish religion that the law also had to have an interpreter. Along with the law was the tradition of how the law was to be understood and applied. The first Christians in the New Testament were also clear that the Scriptures could not be completely understood on their own. The story of the apostle Philip's conversion of the Ethiopian eunuch is a good example of this (cf. Acts 8:27-39). The Ethiopian eunuch was reading from the book of Isaiah, but he didn't understand what he was reading. "How can I understand," he asked, "unless I have a teacher?" Philip, who was full of the Holy Spirit, interpreted the Scriptures and showed how Jesus was revealed through them. The eunuch's problem illustrates the experience of the whole early Church. It would have been impossible for the first Christians to have been "Bible only" Christians because they didn't have the whole Bible. It hadn't yet been written or compiled. Instead they relied on the Holy Spirit and their apostolic teachers. From the beginning, therefore, the Scriptures did not stand alone. The Holy Spirit and a teacher were needed.

This might sound as if I'm launching an attack on the Bible. I'm not. Catholic Christianity fully affirms the inspiration, the inerrancy, and the utter necessity of the Scriptures. What I am careful to criticize is not Scripture but the idea that we can determine truth by Scripture *alone*. Part of the reasoning behind *sola Scriptura* is the belief that the Scriptures are clear and easy for all to understand. However, if the Scriptures are straightforward and sufficient, one has to ask why there are so many different Christian groups. The *World Christian Encyclopedia* lists over twenty thousand different Christian denominations. Most

Evangelicals would agree with C. S. Lewis that there is such a thing as "mere Christianity" and that while all real Christians agree on the basics, they may disagree on the extras. However, when you examine what the different denominations teach, they not only disagree on little things — such as whether women should wear hats to church or whether you have to be baptized by immersion or sprinkling — they also disagree on important things such as how you can be saved, whether you can lose your salvation or not, whether you need to be baptized or not, what Holy Communion is, who should be in charge of a particular church, and many other things. If Scripture is clear and easy for anyone to understand, shouldn't the whole church be united around one simple, clear teaching from Scripture?

The history of the early Church shows how very vexing the problem of scriptural interpretation actually is. For the first four hundred years Christians debated some of the very central doctrines of the faith, such as the two natures of Christ and the doctrine of the Trinity. They hammered out these doctrines through terrible controversy and divisions. The problem was that all the different factions were sincere believers and all of them supported their various views from Scripture. It was only through the guidance of the Holy Spirit and some very hard-headed theological thinking that the truth was finally puzzled out. The doctrines on which we all now agree are proved from Scripture, but more than Scripture was needed for the truth to finally be understood and defined.

Some of the same problems exist today. The assumption that the truth can be discovered from the Bible alone has actually eroded the core of the faith. We tend to think of conservative Protestants as the supporters of *sola Scriptura,* but the idea that the Bible can be read alone is the underlying assumption of the modernist biblical critics as well. Cutting themselves free from a traditional interpretation, highly qualified Bible scholars now dispute the very fundamentals of the faith. Basic truths like the Virgin Birth, the Incarnation, and the Resurrection have come to be "reinterpreted" in such a way that they mean nothing. Clergy in many denominations may say they believe in the Virgin Birth, for example, but when pressed they admit that by "Virgin" they mean Mary was just a good young woman. They use the word "Incarnation," but what they mean is, "In some way Jesus shows us what it means to be fully human and therefore divine."

Modernist biblical scholars are free to offer their "deconstructed" version of the Christian faith because their underlying assumption is *sola Scriptura*. In other words, they believe there is no authority other than the Bible. If they read the Bible and find that the Incarnation is a myth, the Virgin Birth a fairy tale, and the Resurrection a piece of first-century wishful thinking, then there's no logical reason why their interpretation should be any more invalid than anyone else's. The modernist Bible scholar can show his interpretation to be just as "valid" as the traditionalist, who thinks the Bible teaches the objective historical truth of the Incarnation, the Virgin Birth, and the Resurrection. Is there any authority who can say the modernist's interpretation of the Bible is the wrong one? Those who disagree with the modernist will pile up references, Bible verses, and their own list of scholars who support their view. Unfortunately, the modernist Bible scholar can do the same. Without some larger authority it comes down to a matter of opinion. *Sola Scriptura* leads to private interpretation, and if private interpretation is the right principle, then the radical theologian's conclusions are just as valid as anybody else's. If that is true, then we've ended up like Pontius Pilate, shrugging our shoulders and saying cynically, "Ahhh . . . What is 'truth' anyway?"

Must we end up in such a position? Is it possible that Jesus called himself the way, the truth, and the life and commanded his apostles to go out into all the world to preach the Gospel if — at the end of the day — we can't really know what is true after all? Is it possible that we have a Gospel to proclaim, but God hasn't provided a certain way for us to understand and apply that Gospel? Does truth really rely on "mere Scripture" or must we look for "more" than Scripture on its own?

The First Bible Church

The Evangelical church I was brought up in was called a "Bible church." The founders of the church were keen to use that name to make the point that we were "Bible people," and that the Bible was the only foundation for our teaching. The godly founders of the Bible church probably didn't see that in naming their church they were also making another very fundamental point, and that is that the Bible and the church must always go together. In fact, for all Christians there is more than the Bible. There is the church.

While Bible Christians claim the slogan *sola Scriptura*, they actually do rely on more than the Scriptures. Even the Christians who most fervently believe in *sola Scriptura* don't use only the Bible to discover the truth. They listen to their pastors, who in turn have been to seminary and studied theology. Their teachers have listened to Bible scholars and read commentaries and devotional books. All of this has been done within a particular denominational and doctrinal tradition. In other words, they have read the Bible within the context of their particular church tradition, and it is that church tradition that enables them to read the Bible and come up with an interpretation they think is right. Even the most "Bible only" fundamentalist still reads his Bible with certain denominational assumptions and traditions

— even if he denies that this is so. As I have already mentioned, this has been the case since the Ethiopian eunuch met Philip and since the first Christians relied on the Holy Spirit and their apostolic teachers to interpret God's truth with them.

"More Christianity" recognizes this fact and embraces it. The Bible and the church have always gone hand in hand. The Book and the people of the Book are a unity. The Bible is not just a list of doctrines about God that we must believe. Neither is it simply a set of rules to be obeyed. Instead the Bible is first and foremost the story of God's loving relationship with humanity. The Bible is therefore the chronicle of the people of God. Starting with Adam and Eve, and going through to Noah, Abraham, and Isaac and his sons Esau and Jacob, the Old Testament is the story of God's involvement with his chosen people — the Jews. From the beginning the Spirit of God dwells with God's people. Adam's family is promised God's protection as they leave Eden. God guides Noah; the dove over the floodwaters symbolizes the Holy Spirit's presence. Likewise Abraham is led by the Spirit of God to leave his homeland and search for another country. Isaac is led to his perfect wife, and Jacob knows the presence of God through the ministry of angels.

This presence of the Holy Spirit among the people of God becomes more specific as the story goes on. God speaks to Moses through the burning bush — a symbol of the burning fire of the Holy Spirit; and the people of Israel are led through the desert by a burning pillar of fire — another symbol of the Holy Spirit. With Moses a new revelation takes place. Working through the Hebrew people — and especially through Moses — God reveals his law. The Spirit of God gives a written word for the first time. Then as the story goes on, God reveals more of himself through his relationship with the Jews, and through the preaching of the prophets. The story is written down, the hymns of the people of God are written down, and the preaching of the prophets is written down. Looking at it this way, what is the Old Testament? It is the story of the Spirit-led people of God. The first part is their story, the middle part is their writings and their hymnbook, and the last part is the preaching and teaching of their spiritual leaders — the prophets. The story shows that, strictly speaking, God does not inspire a book. He inspires people.

If the Old Testament is the story and documents of the people of God, then the New Testament is as well. The story of Jesus is written down in the Gospels and one of the things he commanded and prophesied was the foundation of a new people of God — a church against which the gates of hell would never prevail (cf. Matthew 16:18). This church would be his body alive on earth — inspired by his own spirit. At the beginning of the Acts of the Apostles Jesus' prophecy comes true, and a new people of God is born by the outpouring of the Holy Spirit. As the teaching of leaders of the Old People of God were eventually written down, so the teachings of the leaders of the New People of God are written down. As the Old Testament consists of the story of the Old People of God and their worship documents, so the New Testament contains the story of the New People of God, their letters, their teachings, and their documents.

Most people know there were more holy writings of the Jews and the early Christians than were chosen to be included in the Scriptures. Who chose which ones went in, and who decided which ones were inspired and which not? The same people who used the Scriptures, prayed the Scriptures, and learned from the Scriptures selected which writings should go into the Bible. By the end of the first century after Christ the Jews made the final decision about which of their writings were to make up the Old Testament. By the year 130 the early Christians were unanimous in accepting the four Gospels and the thirteen letters of Paul as Scripture. By 170 the Church leaders had put these writings on the same level as the Old Testament, and within another two hundred years — by the year 369 we have the first list of the same New Testament books that we all agree on. Then in 382 at the Council of Rome the whole Church agreed on a list of all the Old and New Testament books. This whole process of living the Scriptures, writing the Scriptures, teaching the Scriptures, and then choosing the Scriptures was done by the power of the Holy Spirit working in and through the whole Church.

From the beginning the Scriptures have been the record of God's work in the world through his people. "More Christianity" is usually "both/and," not "either/or." Therefore, "more Christianity" embraces both the Scriptures and the people of God as being vitally necessary for each other. The people of God cannot exist without the Scriptures, but we would not have the Scriptures without the people of God. This marvelous complementary relationship also helps to explain why we say the Scriptures are inspired by God.

Given by Inspiration of God

One of the first verses I had to memorize in Sunday school was 2 Timothy 3:16, which reads: "All scripture is inspired by God and profitable for teaching, for reproof, for correction, and for training in righteousness." It is a beautiful verse and a foundation for our reverence for Scripture. Catholics affirm this truth fully. The *Catechism of the Catholic Church* teaches that "*God is the author of Sacred Scripture.* 'The divinely revealed realities, which are contained and presented in the text of Sacred Scripture, have been written down under the inspiration of the Holy Spirit.' "[1]

It goes on to say:

God inspired the human authors of the sacred books. To compose the sacred books, God chose certain men who, all the while he employed them in this task, made full use of their own faculties and powers so that, though he acted in them and by them, it was as true authors that they consigned to writing whatever God wanted written and no more.[2]

The Catholic Church also affirms the inerrancy of Scripture, telling us that "we must acknowledge that the books of Scripture firmly, faithfully and without error teach that truth which God, for the sake of our salvation, wished to see confided to the Sacred Scriptures."[3]

In 2 Timothy 3:16 we learn that the Scriptures are inspired, but in my upbringing this verse was often used as a proof text for the doctrine of *sola Scriptura*. There is a problem with this. If the Bible is the only authority, then we can only prove *sola Scriptura* from Scripture itself, and that kind of reasoning makes you dizzy.

To explain what I mean, we can take the question of the inspiration of the Bible. How do we know the Scriptures are inspired? If the Scriptures are the only authority, then they must prove themselves. The circular argument goes like this:

"Chapter 3, verse 16 of 2 Timothy says, 'All Scripture is given by inspiration of God. . . .' "

"But how do we know that 2 Timothy 3:16 is itself inspired?"

"Because we believe the Bible."

"Okay. Why is that?"

"Because it is inspired."

"Why do we believe it is inspired?"

"Because the Bible says it is inspired and we believe the Bible."

"Okay. How do we know the Bible is inspired?"

"Because the Bible says it is inspired and we believe the Bible because it is inspired."

See what I mean? It's like chasing your tail. You mustn't get me wrong; if I challenge this proof for the inspiration of the Bible, it is not because I doubt the inspiration of the Bible — simply that I don't think you can use the Bible to prove its own inspiration. There has to be more to it than that. For logical purposes we need some authority outside the Bible that confirms the scriptural teaching that the Bible is inspired. Catholic Christians don't reject 2 Timothy 3:16, but they do reject the theory of *sola Scriptura*. They don't reject *sola Scriptura* because they reject the inspiration of the Bible but because there has to be a firmer foundation for the inspiration of the Bible than just the Bible itself. In other words, Catholics reject *sola Scriptura* not because it is untrue but because it isn't true enough.

The Bible actually needs another authority to validate and confirm its authenticity. It's not good enough to simply say the Bible is inspired because the Bible says it's inspired. That's why the Church is so important. It is the Church that validates the inspiration and infallibility of the Bible. Instead of a circular argument that tries to prove the inspiration of the Bible from the Bible alone we can see that the inspiration and the infallibility of the Bible are supported by the Church. The Catholic argument for the inspiration of the Bible goes like this:

1. History shows that from the beginning there has been an extraordinary group of people who claim to be God's chosen people.
2. The culmination of God's relationship with his people is the coming of his Son, Jesus Christ.

3. Jesus prophesied that a new people of God would be established. He founded the Church, and promised that his Spirit would empower his new creation.
4. The Spirit came down to inspire the Church at Pentecost.
5. This community is a fact of history. Its amazing growth and survival prove God's inspiration and protection.
6. Because it is filled with the Holy Spirit, the Church's teachings are inspired.
7. Some of those inspired teachings were written down.
8. The inspired Church that writes down the teachings also decides which writings are inspired.
9. God also inspires the people of God to preach the Word and interpret the Scriptures correctly.
10. The whole inspired experience of the people of God down through history thus validates the inspiration of the Bible.

Catholics say the Bible is inspired not just because it says so itself but because it is the product of the Spirit-filled Church that was founded by Jesus, the Word of God made man. The inspiration of the Bible is therefore part of a much bigger work of God's inspiration through his Church. Catholics don't believe we must follow *either* the Church *or* the Bible. We follow both. We recognize that the Bible and the Church have developed together down through history. In other words, the Church needs the Bible, but the Bible also needs the Church.

This actually matches up with St. Paul's view. In Ephesians 3:10 he says it is God's intent "that *through the church* the manifold wisdom of God might now be made known" (emphasis mine). According to St. Paul the foundation of the truth is the inspired people of God. In 1 Timothy 3:15 he writes that "the household of God, which is the church of the living God, [is] the pillar and bulwark of the truth." In other words, it is through the Church that we learn the truth about Jesus — not just the Bible. It is by belonging to the living body of Christ — the Church — that we come to understand and know the mystery of Jesus Christ most fully. Paul says the Church is "the pillar and bulwark of the truth," so it is the Church that is the basis and the foundation for the truth of the Scriptures. It was the Church that chose which books were to go into the Bible, and the Church that establishes and validates the inspiration of the Bible. Historically speaking, without the Church we wouldn't have a Bible at all. Through the power of the Holy Spirit the Scriptures and the Church developed together and rely on one another, but there is even more to it than that. This relationship between Church and Scripture is living and dynamic today.

Two Pillars

The United States is blessed with a written constitution that guides and directs the government of the whole nation. For the Constitution to work, it has to be supported and interpreted by the Supreme Court. Furthermore, the rulings of the judges down through the ages help the present-day Supreme Court judges decide how to understand, interpret, and apply the Constitution of the United States today. The Constitution is necessary, but it is also necessary to have an interpretative authority by which the Constitution can be alive and relevant to the American people.

Similarly, the Bible has always been interpreted, preached, and applied by the people of God. As a result, Catholics conclude that the two pillars of Scripture and Church teaching must stand together. *Sola Scriptura* is good inasmuch as it emphasizes the authority of Scripture, but "more Christianity" reads the Bible within the living experience of the Spirit-filled Church.

This may sound very "Catholic," but as I've pointed out, this is actually the way most Christians read the Bible anyway. We all read the Bible within the context of our Church fellowship. The established viewpoint and theology of our Church enable us to make sense of the Bible. Catholics simply recognize this truth and affirm that this is good and proper.

More Christianity says it is a good thing the Bible is not read alone, and that we turn to the Church to help us interpret the Bible. This is natural, since the Bible is derived from the Church in the first place. As part of this, Catholics recognize that along with our reason, and other books that help us understand the Bible, we rely on the past. We look back to learn from the lessons our Christian ancestors have learned and recorded for us. In denominational terms this means all Christians rely on the traditions from the past. Some Christians rely on Bible interpretations that date back to their pastors a few decades ago or their founders a couple of hundred years ago or even half a century ago. This tradition is passed down from generation to generation as a living body of teaching. More Christianity recognizes our reliance on tradition and embraces it as a dynamic part of what it means to be a Christian.

The word "tradition" is a red flag to some Christians. They rightly want to avoid the kind of traditions that Jesus condemned — human religious traditions that became more important than the Gospel (cf. Mark 7:8-9, 13). Some Christians think "tradition" means the simple Gospel message was encrusted with ornate beliefs and esoteric customs that have no basis in the written word of God, and Paul rightly warned of these empty traditions (cf. Colossians 2:8). It's important, however, to realize that by the word "tradition" Catholics don't mean dead religious customs, ceremonies, rules, and regulations. Instead, when Catholics speak of "tradition" we are referring to a body of teaching that is formed by the experience of the Church — a body of teaching that is at once ancient and yet fresh and alive.

Since tradition is part of the inspired Church's experience, Catholics affirm that tradition is also a vital element in reading the Scriptures. Looking to tradition means looking to the unbroken teaching of the Church to help us determine the true meaning of Scripture. When we look to the New Testament and the witness of the earliest Christians, we can see they valued both tradition and the written word as a source for truth.

Paul certainly rested his teaching on Scripture. He tells Timothy to "attend to the public reading of Scripture, to preaching, to teaching" (1 Timothy 4:13). Elsewhere he tells Timothy to "continue in what you have learned . . . knowing from whom you learned it and how from childhood you have been acquainted with the sacred writings [Scriptures]" (2 Timothy 3:15). But Paul didn't rest his faith *only* in the Scriptures. He speaks of another strand of teaching that was given by God and that was authoritative. This strand of teaching isn't written down. It is the preaching of the apostles. According to the New Testament the apostles believed this oral teaching and preaching also came directly from God.

Jesus tells his apostles that anyone who listens to them listens to him (cf. Luke 10:16) and "he who receives you receives me, and he who receives me receives the one who sent me" (Matthew 10:40). Peter points out that the word of the apostles comes from the Lord himself (cf. 2 Peter 3:2), and Paul proclaims, "I would have you know, brethren, that the gospel which was preached by me is not man's gospel. For I did not receive it from man, nor was I taught it, but it came through a revelation of Jesus Christ" (Galatians 1:11-12). Peter, in 1 Peter 1:23, calls this divinely inspired preaching "the living and abiding word of God" and says that it will stand forever. Thus, along with the written word of God, there was to be an enduring oral tradition — a teaching that would be passed on from generation to generation. Paul uses the word "tradition" for this oral strand of teaching in several places. In 2 Thessalonians 3:6 he says, "Now we command you, brethren, in the name of our Lord Jesus Christ, that you keep away from any brother who is living in idleness and not in accord with the tradition that you received from us." Paul says that these traditions are in both oral and written form: "So then, brethren, stand firm and hold to the traditions which you were taught by us, either by word of mouth or by letter" (2 Thessalonians 2:15).

Some people say the word-of-mouth tradition ceased once the Bible books were written, but Paul acknowledges that both sources of teaching existed when he wrote to the Thessalonians. We also see that Paul not only received this oral tradition from others, but he also passed it on to his hearers. In 1 Corinthians 15:1-3 he says, "Now I would remind you, brethren, in what terms I preached to you the gospel, which you received, in which you stand, by which you are saved, if you hold it fast — unless you believed in vain. For I delivered to you as of first importance what I also received." Paul knows the importance of the oral teaching as well as the written teaching because he tells Timothy to faithfully guard the oral teaching that he had received; so he writes, "Follow the pattern of the sound words which you have heard from me, in the faith and love which are in Christ Jesus; guard the truth that has been entrusted to you by the Holy Spirit" (2 Timothy 1:13-14). Elsewhere he praises the Corinthians for maintaining the traditions he has passed on to them (cf. 1 Corinthians 11:2). Did Paul think this oral teaching was to be passed on? In 2 Timothy 2:2 he says: "What you have heard from me before many witnesses [I want you to] entrust to faithful men who will be able to teach others also." In other words, he commands Timothy to hand on the oral tradition that he had received. It's interesting that in this passage St. Paul is referring to four generations of succession — his own, Timothy's, the people Timothy would teach, and the ones they would teach in turn.

The Apostolic Tradition

To have "more Christianity" means our own Christian experience is endorsed, illuminated, and validated by what the Christians of the past believed. If a non-Catholic's denomination takes him back four hundred or five hundred years into the tradition, that is a good thing, but the Catholic Church claims a line of tradition that goes right back to the apostles themselves. In the New Testament we can see Paul's concern to hand this tradition of teaching on to the next generation of Christians. That next generation has also left us a record of what it thought about the traditions of the apostles. The documents of the early Church show us how important the tradition of the apostles were to the first Christians. Writing about the year 189, Irenaeus, a Church leader in the French city of Lyons, says, "What if the apostles had not left writings to us? Would it not be necessary to follow the order of tradition which was handed down to those to whom they entrusted the churches?" Elsewhere Irenaeus also points out how important this apostolic tradition is for people to know the full truth. "It is possible then for everyone in every church who may wish to know the truth to contemplate the Traditions of the Apostles which have been made known throughout the whole world."[4]

Why does this Church tradition matter? Irenaeus tells us it is important that we have not only the Bible but the most faithful interpretation of the Bible. It is actually quite exciting to think that this ancient teaching of the apostles might be preserved faithfully just as the written word has been. If there is a body of teaching that has been faithfully passed down from the apostles, it would help us interpret the Scriptures the right way today. If an ancient strand of teaching exists that goes back to the apostles themselves, then we have not only the Scripture for a source book, but we have a rich tapestry of teaching that helps us to understand the Scripture.

If we want more Christianity, then it makes sense to turn to the centuries of Christian wisdom to see what we should believe and how we should behave. When we have a difficult question of biblical interpretation, we don't have to rely simply on the rest of the Bible to find the answer. Instead we turn to the tradition to see what the people of God believed before us. Did they face the same question? How did they answer it? Did they face similar circumstances? How did they confront them? Did they face the same doubts, problems, heresies, and attacks? How did they stand up for the truth in their day? How did they interpret the Scriptures then? Can their experience help us determine and defend the truth today?

The Bible contains the written Word of God, but the tradition is a growing and dynamic action of the Spirit in the Church. Through the tradition the whole Church continues to live and breathe today just as a majestic oak tree we see today is the dynamic expression and fulfillment of the acorn, the sapling, and the young tree. Through tradition we not only receive the "faith of our fathers," we actually live and dwell within that living faith. "Through Tradition, 'the Church in her doctrine, life, and worship, perpetuates and transmits to every generation all that she herself is, all that she believes.' . . . 'Its riches are poured out in the practice and life of the Church in her belief and her prayer.' "[5] While tradition is living and growing, it cannot add anything new or different to the original deposit of faith that was given to the apostles. The *Catechism* says, "The Christian economy . . . will never pass away; and no new public revelation is to be expected before the glorious manifestation of our Lord Jesus Christ."[6] Instead of adding anything, the tradition continually grows as the full richness of the Gospel is illuminated by the Holy Spirit.

The doctrine of *sola Scriptura* focuses on the Word of God, and that's good. "More Christianity" embraces the Scriptures, but it places them in the context of the spirit-filled life of God's people. "More Christianity" sees how God revealed himself through the traumas and lessons of the Hebrew people, and finally through his Son, Jesus Christ. That same story continued in the lives of the apostles and flowed into the rich and miraculous history of Christ's Church over the last two thousand years. "More Christianity" rejoices that within the dynamic life of the Church we have a sure foundation for the Scriptures and a reliable authority to interpret the written Word of God. To use an analogy, *sola Scriptura* is like contemplating the beauty of a single diamond, while "more Christianity" expertly uses tradition to cut the diamond, set it in a rich golden ring, put the ring on a beautiful woman called the Church, and then marry her.

Chapter One Endnotes

1. *Catechism of the Catholic Church,* London, Geoffrey Chapman, 1995, para. 105 (hereafter CCC).
2. Ibid., para. 106.
3. Ibid., para. 107.
4. Henry Bettenson, *The Early Christian Fathers,* Oxford, Oxford University Press, 1969, p. 90.
5. CCC, para. 78.
6. Ibid., para. 66.

Who Says So?

Deciding what is true or false can be a bit like peeling an onion. Keep on going and soon nothing is there at all. As soon as someone states the truth, ten clever people come along to pick the statement apart, find loopholes, inconsistencies, and a dozen different interpretations. When the truths in question are religious truths, the disagreement becomes even greater because, being spiritual truths, they are impossible to prove with statistics, facts, and figures. In the end it seems to come down to a matter of opinion.

In the first chapter I recognized that Christians look to the Scriptures as a source of revealed truth, and that all Christians read the Scriptures within the context of their church. The accumulated learning and experience of a particular church helps individual Christians understand the Scriptures. The theological structure of their denomination gives them a grid to analyze and interpret Scripture so they can apply it to their everyday needs. Maybe you agree that all Christians really do read the Scriptures along with their church tradition even if they don't admit it. You might agree that this is actually a good way of going about things. But there's still a problem. If you've read the preceding chapter with a critical eye you may say, "It is all well and good setting the Scriptures in the context of the church, and using tradition to help interpret Scripture, but which church is the best context, and which traditions do we use? Why should the Catholic context be any more true than the Methodist, Baptist, Lutheran, or Anglican contexts? We all have traditions, so why should the Catholic traditions be any more valid than the Orthodox, Pentecostal, Coptic, Armenian, Presbyterian, or Charismatic traditions?" My question in the first chapter was, "Who gives the proper interpretation of the Scriptures?" The answer was: the Church. However, the question then becomes: "Which church? Why should we trust one particular church for a proper interpretation of the Scriptures? Isn't it more likely that all the different denominations have a bit of the truth?"

Of course there are good Christian people in all the denominations, and all the different groupings actually have plenty of truth and goodness to offer. So, for example, the Eastern Orthodox churches have an ancient and venerable tradition. The Baptist emphasis on a personal salvation experience is excellent. The Anglicans have strong traditions of beautiful music and liturgy, while the Pentecostal groups have a great emphasis on healing and the power of the Holy Spirit. The Quakers' interest in listening to the voice of the Spirit is good, while the Lutherans bring a strong reliance on justification by faith and the Presbyterians emphasize a deep trust in God's abiding covenant. Each denomination offers excellent insights on the Christian Gospel. The problem is, choosing one denomination too often excludes the good things from the others.

"More Christianity" wants the best from them all. While it includes the best from the different Christian traditions, "more Christianity" is not merely a patchwork religion that takes remnants from each denomination and stitches them together into a new combination. Neither is it some global confederation of all the different Christian groups. Both of these solutions would be fabricating yet another denomination — one that is the creation of whoever is doing the picking and choosing. Rather than putting them all together, or picking what seems best from the different traditions, "more Christianity" looks for something older and bigger than them all. "More Christianity" looks for the quality that unites them all. It looks for the stem from which all the branches have grown. "More Christianity" transcends the different denominations and includes the best from each one because it returns to the source from which all the good elements in each denomination have come.

Most Christian groups have their particular strength and identity because their founders went to the Scriptures and found there some truth that the rest of the Church seemed to be neglecting. Many of the founders of the different denominations believed they had rediscovered the true faith of the early Church. They believed they had uncovered the faith that the apostles had received from Jesus Christ and handed on to their followers. This attempt to get back to the roots of Christianity is good, because if we discover the basic faith that was taught by the apostles we will naturally include all the strengths of the different denominations because we've accepted the essential kernel from which all of them have grown.

Looking for the apostolic faith also answers the question "Why should we trust one church for the correct interpretation of Scripture more than any other church?" By being in touch with the faith of the apostles we will base our interpretation on their teachings rather than our own, or those of our particular denomination. The more we are in touch with the apostolic faith, the more deeply rooted our Christianity will be. The apostolic faith takes us past history, past the religious quarrels of our own time, back to the faith of our fathers. Most importantly, getting in touch with the apostolic faith gives us a foundation authority for interpreting the Scriptures properly. Because we are going back to the original sources to interpret the Bible, we are not so reliant on our own opinions, the pressures of our particular circumstances, the bias of our time period, or the slant of our own denomination. Being in touch with the faith of the apostles is a risky business because we have to be prepared to test our own opinions and the views of our denomination against the teachings of the apostolic faith.

Finding the Foundations

It sounds like I am calling for everyone to return to the pure and unadulterated Church of the first century. Various Christian groups down through the ages have tried to re-create the New Testament Church by forming communes and practicing the form of Church government they discovered in the New Testament. While such an ideal is understandable, in reality it is impossible for anyone to get back to the pure apostolic Church because none of us have figured out how to travel in time. It is fascinating to read about the Church of the first century, but this is the twenty-first century. Things have moved on. Those who simply wish to return to the early Church miss this point: The early Church was a mustard seed that has fallen into the ground, and from it a great tree has grown in which all the birds of the air can find a nest (cf. Matthew 13:31-32). Even if it were possible, it would be a misguided thing to cut down the tree to find the kernel again.

Others who wish to follow the faith of the apostles do not wish to re-create the early Church in the twenty-first century. They understand that times have changed and the demands on the Church are very different now than they were in the first century. Instead of re-creating the first-century Church they wish to preserve and follow the apostolic faith. In other words, the apostolic faith is the teaching of the apostles as recorded in the New Testament. By reading the Bible they believe all Christians will be able to understand and follow the simple teachings of the apostles today.

But if it is impossible to reestablish the Church of the first century, it is also impossible to re-create the apostolic beliefs exactly as they were two thousand years ago. We certainly do hold to "the faith which was once for all delivered to the saints" (Jude 3), but that faith has grown and developed. In every age the faith that Jesus planted has faced new challenges and fresh opportunities. As the Church faced these challenges, our understanding of the depth and beauty of the faith has grown. Furthermore, it was the needs of the Church that helped the faith to develop. The Church and the faith have always been interrelated. The demands of one have challenged and illuminated the other. So the faith has demanded the Church to follow the Gospel, but the needs of the Church have helped the faith to develop in its depth, power, and beauty.

This is why in the creed we do not say, "I believe in the apostolic faith," but "I believe in the apostolic *Church*" (emphasis mine). The apostolic faith cannot be isolated from the apostolic Church that defines and defends that faith. Trying to isolate the apostolic faith from the apostolic Church is like trying to separate out what it means to be an American from the daily reality of *being* an American. A constitutional expert or an academic historian may provide a useful study explaining what it means to be an American, but this will only be a tiny fragment of the whole picture. Similarly, a return to the roots of colonial America will help us understand how to be a modern American, but it would be foolish to think that you could only be an American if you wore a powdered wig, knee breeches, and carried a flintlock musket. Being a modern American might mean dressing up as a Revolutionary War soldier for a parade or a historical pageant, but being an American is much more than a costume. Being an American is a total experience, not a theory.

This is why Catholics say the apostolic faith is not the same thing as the first-century Church, nor is it simply what the first apostles taught. Certainly the apostolic faith includes all that the apostles taught, but it also includes that which has grown from their teaching. The apostolic faith is not a static statement of beliefs. Instead the apostolic faith is living and dynamic. More Christianity therefore challenges us not only to believe the apostolic faith but to be living members of the apostolic Church. When looked at from this perspective, being an apostolic Christian involves both believing and belonging. Belonging to the apostolic Church means belonging to a living organism that grows, changes, and develops in time. After all, the apostolic Church is the Body of Christ, not the corpse of Christ.

In the Beginning . . .

Jesus commanded his apostles to go into all the world and teach the Gospel (cf. Matthew 28:19-20). The teaching of the apostles has spread through the whole world just as Jesus promised and prophesied. But to continue that work in every age, the deposit of faith needs to be interpreted according to the needs of different cultures around the world and different sets of personal circumstances. In other words, the faith of the apostles has to be adapted without being changed. Christian pastors and teachers struggle with this activity all the time in their day-to-day pastoral work. Catholics believe that for this to be done reliably, God has seen fit to not only leave the apostolic teaching but also the apostolic authority to teach, interpret, and apply the truth.

Catholics believe the fullness of the apostolic faith is alive today because the authority Jesus gave his apostles is alive today. The foundations for this belief are there in the Gospels. Jesus makes an amazing claim to universal authority. He says, "All authority in heaven and on earth has been given to me" (Matthew 28:18). The Father has placed everything into his hands (cf. John 3:35). He has authority over all people (cf. John 17:2), and his authority has been given to him by his Father in heaven (cf. Luke 10:22). In his epistles St. Paul also affirms the divine authority that Jesus commanded (cf. 1 Corinthians 15:27, Ephesians 1:20-22, and Philippians 2:9-10).

Jesus knew he couldn't stay on the earth forever, and the Gospels show how Jesus intended his ministry to be continued on earth. He called twelve men to lead his followers. So they could lead the Church with power and authority, Jesus gave the apostles a share in his own divine authority. So Jesus says the apostles are sent just as the Father sent him (cf. John 20:21). Jesus had the authority to cast out demons and teach the truth. In Luke 9:1-2 he gives his apostles the authority to do the same. They are to speak the truth with the same kind of authority Jesus had because Jesus says whoever listens to them listens to him (cf. Luke 10:16). At the end of all four Gospels Jesus gives the apostles special authority to continue his work. In Matthew 28:18-20 and Mark 16:15-16 he tells them to preach the truth and baptize. In Luke 24:45-48 he commands them to understand the Scriptures and preach repentance for the forgiveness of sins, and in John 20:23 he specifically gives them his authority to forgive sins. Jesus must have intended this ministry to continue because in Matthew 28:20 he promises to be with the apostles until the end of time. Then in John's Gospel he promises the Holy Spirit to help with the work of understanding the truth (cf. John 16:13), and says the Spirit will remain with the apostles forever (cf. John 14:16).

The Acts of the Apostles tells how the apostles followed the Lord's command and went into the whole world to preach the truth, admonish evildoers, and forgive sins. As the foremost apostles, Peter and Paul take the responsibility for proclaiming the truth of God. As we've seen in the last chapter, both of them claim their message comes directly from God. The authority to preach God's truth is given to the apostles, but the apostles also claim the authority to interpret the Word of God. Paul, for example, assumes the authority to forge a new interpretation of the Old Testament that unlocks Jesus' true identity as eternal Son of God. Peter also claims the authority to interpret Scripture the correct way. In his second epistle he says, "No prophecy of scripture is a matter of one's own interpretation" (2 Peter 1:20). If we are not to interpret the Scripture on our own, who is to interpret it for us? Jesus says the Holy Spirit will guide us into all truth, so the Holy Spirit plays a part. But Peter himself answers the question in the same epistle. In verses 16 through 18 of chapter 1, Peter claims teaching authority because he was an eyewitness of Jesus' life and glory. Peter has the authority to interpret Scripture because he received the truth directly from Jesus. He then says in verse 2 of chapter 3 that the truth was spoken in the past by the holy prophets but that the commands are now given by Jesus Christ through the apostles.

What is interesting here is that Peter compares the role of the New Testament apostles to the Old Testament prophets. As a practicing Jew, Peter understood that the prophets were directly inspired by God. Their preaching was considered to be a direct word from God to the people of God. We have already seen that Peter considered his preaching to be "the word of the Lord [that] abides for ever" (1 Peter 1:25). As such, the apostles are the prophets — the God-inspired teachers of the New Testament people of God. When Peter says, "No prophecy of scripturc is a matter of one's own interpretation" (2 Peter 1:20), he also means that only the prophet — that is, the apostle — is entitled and empowered by the Holy Spirit to give the right interpretation.

Paul agrees with Peter. In Ephesians 3:5 he says the mystery of God has now been revealed by the Spirit to God's holy apostles and prophets. It is the same Spirit-led group of men who are the foundation of the Church. Paul says that his hearers are members of the Church, "the household of God, built upon the foundation of the apostles and prophets, Christ Jesus himself being the cornerstone" (Ephesians 2:19-20). Jesus is the cornerstone of this Church, but it is the apostles and the prophets — inspired by God's Holy Spirit — who provide the foundation. When St. Paul says the Church "is built upon the foundation of the prophets and apostles" (Ephesians 2:20), what is interesting is that he does not say the Church is built on the foundation of the *teachings* of the prophets and apostles. He says the Church is built on *them*. In other words, the person and his teaching are a united entity. In both the prophets and the apostles, their teaching cannot be separated from the authority by which they teach.

From the beginning God's truth has been revealed through the lives of ordinary people. The Incarnation is the climax and summary of this truth. Therefore, in the New Testament, God continues his chosen way of working, and it is through twelve men that he decides to spread his good news to the whole world. A crucial part of the apostolic faith, therefore, is the apostles themselves. "More Christianity" embraces not only the teaching of the apostles but also their God-given authority to know the truth and teach it in the first place. Some people believe the authority Christ gave his apostles died with them. They say the truth that the apostles taught is authority enough. But why would

God leave the teaching but not the authority to maintain and interpret that teaching? That would be similar to a kingdom having a law code but not having lawyers and judges to interpret it and apply it to everyday life.

The Apostolic Church

In the New Testament we see the apostles dealing with the question of authority in the Church. As the Church grew, the apostles were faced with the problem of leadership. They couldn't be everywhere at once, and it was important to ensure the fledgling Christian groups remained both faithful to the Gospel and united in that faith. From the very earliest times the apostles appointed leaders in the Church. The early Christians believed these leaders inherited both the teaching and the authority to teach that Jesus first gave to the apostles themselves. One of the first of the epistles to be written was 1 Thessalonians, and in it St. Paul says, "We beseech you, brethren, to respect those who labor among you and are over you in the Lord and admonish you, and to esteem them very highly in love because of their work" (1 Thessalonians 5:12-13).

In the last chapter we've seen that Paul explicitly handed on his teaching authority to Timothy, and commanded him to hand on that authority to others who would in turn hand it on to their successors (cf. 2 Timothy 2:2). Timothy wasn't the only one. Paul also sent Titus to Crete to organize the Church there. He calls Titus his son in the faith and says, "This is why I left you in Crete, that you might amend what was defective, and appoint elders in every town as I directed you" (Titus 1:5). Paul then explains what kind of a man this elder must be. Just as Paul told Timothy that the elder must be a good teacher (cf. 1 Timothy 3:2), he says to Titus that the elder "must hold firm to the sure word as taught, so that he may be able to give instruction in sound doctrine and also to confute those who contradict it" (Titus 1:9). The Church leader is expected to be a master of the tradition. He is to be faithful to the apostolic teaching, but he is also given the authority to rebuke those who oppose the truth.

Peter also received authority from Christ and handed it on. After his Resurrection, Jesus, the Good Shepherd, had entrusted the flock of God to Peter when he said, "Feed my lambs" (John 21:15), then, "Tend my sheep" (John 21:16), and finally, "Feed my sheep" (John 21:17). Just as Paul entrusts his authority and leadership to Timothy and Titus, so Peter entrusts his role of shepherd of the flock to the next generation of elders. He addresses the elders of the Church: "I exhort the elders among you, as a fellow elder and a witness of the sufferings of Christ as well as a partaker in the glory that is to be revealed. Tend the flock of God that is your charge. . . . And when the chief Shepherd is manifested you will obtain the unfading crown of glory" (1 Peter 5:1-2, 4).

Jesus handed his authority on to the apostles, and the New Testament shows the first signs of the apostles handing on that authority to their successors. This was the authority, not only to teach the truth faithfully, but to define the truth and rebuke false teachers. If this was the teaching of the apostles, then the first Christians would have been faithful to it. If they were faithful to this idea, then we would expect to find evidence of this belief in their writings. This is precisely what we find in the documents of the early Church. From the very earliest letters and theological writings of the Church we can see that the first generation of Christians believed their Church leaders had inherited the same teaching authority that Jesus had given his apostles. One of the earliest leaders of the Church in Rome was a man called Clement. He was probably instructed by Peter and Paul and may even have been that Clement that Paul calls a fellow worker (cf. Philippians 4:3). Bishop Irenaeus, a leader of the following generation, writes about Clement, "He not only had seen the blessed Apostles, but had also conferred with them, and had their preaching still ringing in his ears, and their tradition still before his eyes."[1]

Around the year 95 Clement wrote a letter to the Church at Corinth pleading with them to maintain unity with the properly appointed leaders. In his letter he explains clearly from what source those leaders had received their authority. He writes, "The Apostles received the gospel for us from the Lord Jesus Christ . . . and they went out full of confidence in the Holy Spirit . . . and appointed their first fruits . . . to be bishops and deacons. Our apostles knew there would be strife on the question of the bishop's office. Therefore, they appointed these people already mentioned and later made further provision that if they should fall asleep other tested men should succeed to their ministry."[2]

Ignatius of Antioch was martyred in the year 115. He was probably instructed by Peter and Paul during their time in Antioch. In writing to the Trallian Church, he equates the Church elders with apostles, "When you obey the bishop as if he were Christ Jesus, you are living not in a merely human fashion, but in Jesus Christ's way. . . . It is essential, therefore, to act in no way without the bishop, just as you are doing. Rather submit even to the presbytery [the body of elders] as to the apostles of Jesus Christ."[3] To the Christians at Smyrna Ignatius writes, "You should follow the bishops as Jesus Christ did the Father. Follow too the presbytery as you would the apostles. . . . You should regard that Eucharist as valid which is celebrated either by the bishop or by someone he authorizes."[4]

By the middle of the second century — less than a hundred years after the death of the last apostle — the whole Church had recognized the apostolic authority of properly recognized and appointed bishops. The evidence comes from Christians in North Africa, Syria, France, and Italy, and they all recognize that the proper authority in the Church must be descended historically from the apostles. Irenaeus was a theologian and bishop who wrote around the year 160. Irenaeus actually knew Polycarp, who was a disciple of the apostle John, so in Irenaeus we are just one generation removed from the apostles themselves. According to Irenaeus it is because the Church leaders have inherited the apostolic authority that they can interpret Scripture properly. So he writes, "By knowledge of the truth we mean the teaching of the Apostles; the order of the Church as established from earliest times throughout the world . . . preserved through the episcopal succession: for to the bishops the apostles committed the care of the Church in each place which has come down to our own time safeguarded by . . . the most complete exposition . . . the reading of the Scriptures without falsification and careful and consistent exposition of them — avoiding both rashness and blasphemy."[5] Elsewhere Irenaeus says that the bishops of the Church not only received the apostolic teaching but also the apostolic authority to define and defend that teaching. "We can enumerate those who were appointed bishops in the churches by the apostles and their successors down to our own day. . . . They [the apostles] were handing over to them their own office of doctrinal authority."[6]

For the first generation of Christians "more Christianity" meant being part of a church that not only taught the apostolic faith but had leaders whose authority descended historically from the apostles. According to the early evidence, the Church was organized with a chief elder (bishop) in each city, and with elders (priests) to oversee the local congregations. The priests and bishops were assisted by deacons who also exercised a teaching and ministry role. Even in those early days there were some groups who broke off from the established apostolic authority to do their own thing. Ignatius called them to return to the unified Church led by the apostolically appointed leaders. Irenaeus insisted that the fullest expression of Christianity was to be found in the churches that traced their authority right back to the apostles themselves. He says of those who broke away from the apostolic Church, "We challenge them by an appeal to that tradition which derives from the Apostles, and which is preserved in the churches by the succession of presbyters. . . . Those who wish to see the truth can observe in every church the tradition of the Apostles. . . . It is our duty to obey those bishops who are in the church, who have their succession from the Apostles, as we have shown, who with their succession in the episcopate have received the sure spiritual gift of truth according to the pleasure of the Father."[7]

If the historical record is true, then part of the apostles' teaching is actually that their authority would be handed down in a historically recognized system. To have the fullest version of the apostolic teaching, therefore, we must accept what is called apostolic succession. If we accept apostolic succession and want "more Christianity," then we should look seriously at the churches that claim, even today, to have preserved the line of apostolic authority down through the ages from Christ himself.

Apostolicity Today

Many Christians use the creed in their worship, and if they use the ancient creeds, they profess to believe in one, holy, catholic, and apostolic Church. If this is so, what do non-Catholic Christians mean when they say they believe in an apostolic Church? For some Christians the idea of apostolic authority is a completely new concept. Others know of it but reject the idea of apostolic succession altogether. Still others think the main thing is that those in a particular church today remain faithful to the apostolic deposit of faith. They say those who remain faithful to the apostolic faith as found in the Scriptures are maintaining the essential fullness of the apostolic faith. Still other non-Catholic Christians respect the idea that the apostles handed on both their teaching and their authority, and they claim apostolic succession for their leaders, even though they are not Catholics.

While Catholics glory in the unbroken line of succession back to the apostles, we don't claim that the apostolic faith exists only within the Catholic Church. The Eastern Orthodox churches are just as ancient as the Catholic Church, and Catholics recognize that they too have maintained the apostolic faith as well as the apostolic succession. Catholics also recognize that other Christians may share in a part of the apostolic faith even though they reject the idea that the apostolic authority continues to live today through apostolic succession.

These quarrels can become both petty and fairly nasty, but to give everybody the benefit of the doubt, I think it is possible to recognize four levels of apostolicity. I believe non-Catholic Christians do share in a kind of apostolicity if they hold to the basics of the Christian faith. The first and most basic level of apostolicity is faithfulness to essentials of the apostolic teaching. In other words, if a non-Catholic Christian believes the simple Gospel, and accepts the "old-time religion," it can be said that he shares to a certain degree in the apostolic faith. This is where "mere Christianity" comes in. Inasmuch as any Christian repents of his sin and trusts Jesus Christ as his Savior, it can be said that he participates to some extent in the apostolic faith.

This is good, but "more Christianity" wants more apostolicity than that. The individual who repents of his sins and trusts Jesus Christ as his Savior is taking part in the apostolic faith; however, if there is nothing but personal experience, that individual is cut off from a large part of the apostolic faith. It is a bit like a person looking through a keyhole into a ballroom. He or she certainly sees part of the ballroom, but there is not only far more to be seen, there is a dance to be joined. According to the New Testament, individual believers have to be baptized into the body of Christ, and the body of Christ has recognized leaders. In other words, the person looking through the keyhole has to come into the ballroom and join the party. A second level of the apostolic faith means an individual joins a church and so shares in some sort of recognized ordained ministry. If an individual joins a church with an ordained ministry, or if he or she is ordained, then by virtue of that fact that person is sharing in another degree of apostolicity. Almost all Christians belong to a church with some sort of ordained ministry, and that ministry is usually patterned on the guidelines in the New Testament. Because they belong to a church with an ordained ministry, most Christians also share in this second informal degree of apostolicity.

Two levels are better than one, but "more Christianity" wants a greater identification with the apostolic faith. The New Testament and the documents of the early Church show that the apostles established a recognized historical succession for the Church leadership. The historical succession is important because through it a particular church claims a living link with the apostles, and therefore claims that its teaching and authority structure is part of that Church founded two thousand years ago. The third level of the apostolic faith means a denomination or individual shares in some way in apostolic succession. In other words, those churches that have bishops who claim historical succession from the apostles may share in this third level of apostolicity. The Orthodox, the different Anglican groups, and some other Catholic-minded Christian denominations would all claim to share in this third level of apostolic authority. Even if their claims to apostolic succession are spurious, their desire to be a part of this higher level of apostolicity shows an awareness and a sharing in something greater.

Christians can share in one level of apostolicity by believing the simple Gospel message. They go "further up and further in" when they join a church with an ordained ministry. They penetrate further into the mystery of the apostolic Church once they have entered a denomination that claims to share the historic connection with the apostles through the ministry of bishops. But I suggested that there are four levels of apostolicity. The fourth level is being a part of the historic Catholic Church. The Eastern Orthodox churches enjoy a high degree of apostolicity, but only the Catholic Church expresses historic apostolic authority in a universal way. I will talk more about this universal ministry later on, but for now it is enough to say that in the Catholic Church there is a fullness of the apostolic faith that is not present elsewhere. A person who enters into full communion with the Catholic Church enters into a fullness of the faith that is very difficult to describe to those outside. In the Catholic Church the link with the apostles is vivid, dynamic, and real. In saying this we do not deny the goodness of other Christian groups or the holiness of individual non-Catholic Christians. We are simply stating the historic fact that the fullness of the apostolic faith is found in Catholicism. In this largest and most historic Church we find the roots of all the other churches, and it is this fullness of apostolicity that calls all who wish to find "more Christianity."

How Do the Apostles Speak?

The evidence from the New Testament and from the documents of the early Church shows that the first Christian leaders held a responsibility for the whole Church. Like the apostles they succeeded, the bishops were busy spreading the Gospel. They also realized that there could only be "one Lord, one faith, one baptism" (Ephesians 4:5) and only one church of Jesus Christ (cf. Ephesians 1:22-23 and 4:4, 13; also John 17:20-21). As the Church grew, the bishops of the various local churches corresponded with one another, discussed questions and problems in the churches, and sought unity under the guidance of the Holy Spirit. When the Church leaders met together in council, they were assured of the continued guidance of the Holy Spirit. The first council to decide an important question is recorded in Acts 15. In the letter the apostles sent out, they stated clearly that their decision at Jerusalem was that of the Holy Spirit (cf. Acts 15:28).

Through the centuries, various councils of the bishops have led the Church. In these councils the bishops have met together, discussed, and prayed over difficult matters of doctrine and discipline in the Church. Catholics believe that just as the Holy Spirit guided the apostles in the Council of Jerusalem, so that same Spirit has continued to guide the bishops of the Church "into all the truth" (John 16:13). Because Jesus handed his authority to teach the truth to his apostles, and because he promised to be with them for all time, we believe his promises are fulfilled technically through the teaching ministry of successive generations of Catholic bishops. In other words, in the gathering of the Catholic bishops the teaching authority Christ gave to his apostles lives on in a powerful and real way.

This is not so different from the way most non-Catholic churches govern themselves. Synods, groups of elders, councils, and committees of Christians meet together, pray for the guidance of the Holy Spirit, and make decisions about the Church government, finance, and discipline. Invariably their pastors lead

these groups, and those who have the best theological education and spiritual experience influence decisions. Within these
groups there is a certain assumption that is rarely considered,
and that is where the group actually came from in the first place.
As soon as we consider the facts of history, it becomes clear that
all the different denominational synods, councils, and committees have come from the first experience of the apostles meeting
in council being led by the Holy Spirit. My final point is simply
this: Most churches already practice a simple form of leadership
and decision-making that echoes the apostolic way. If one is
seeking "more Christianity," then it is a joy to be part of a decision-making process that is not only local but global. In the
Catholic Church the decisions are made not by one man with
his Bible, nor by the local pastor with his board of deacons, nor
by the council of the particular denomination or the elected
synod of a national church. Instead the pastors of the whole
Church around the world make the decisions. This means the
truth is determined not by the political pressures of a particular
area or the needs of a local congregation but by a universal
authority.

Anyone who wants the fullness of the apostolic faith can
find it. The Christian who believes the simple Gospel message,
has tasted the apostolic faith; but the Master of the banquet is
always beckoning us with the welcome, "Friend, go up higher"
(Luke 14:10). There is a freedom and joy when our individual
interpretations of the faith are gathered up in the ancient beauty
of the apostolic faith. Suddenly it is not up to us or our pastor
to decide the complicated questions of the faith; instead we im-
merse ourselves in a living faith that is ever ancient and ever
new. In the words of the psalmist, it is as if we have been lifted
up and our feet placed on solid rock (cf. Psalm 40:2) in a large
room (cf. Psalm 31:8).

When the simple believer immerses his own life of faith in the fullness of the apostolic faith, it is as if he has entered a great river. It may be alarming at first because the river is full and deep and wide. His own small faith is gathered up by the faith of the whole Church, for he swims there with the saints and sinners of the past. He has entered a river that can safely bear him down to the eternal sea. It is the faith of the ages, the faith of his brothers and sisters all over the globe. It is the faith of the apostles, a faith that is far more profound and beautiful than he ever could have imagined.

Chapter Two Endnotes

1. Henry Bettenson, *The Early Christian Fathers*, Oxford, Oxford University Press, 1969, p. 91.

2. Ibid., p. 33.

3. Ibid., p. 44.

4. Ibid., p. 49.

5. Ibid., p. 89.

6. Ibid., p. 90.

7. Ibid., pp. 90, 94.

The Keeper of the Keys

A couple of years after moving to England I happened to be in London one day and noticed that a crowd was gathering. Streets were blocked off and the police were out in force. When I asked what was going on, I was told it was the annual ceremony of the trooping of the colors. Within the hour the queen and members of the royal family would ride on horseback to review the troops on parade. I joined the crowds and couldn't help but be impressed and moved as the royal family rode past, followed by the various regiments in their ceremonial colors, who were marching or riding to the parade ground with their banners and flags fluttering in the summer breeze.

The most memorable part of the ceremony was our waiting near Buckingham Palace for the return of the monarch. First we heard the distant drumbeats and the sound of hooves on pavement. Then the sound of the military bands prepared the way, and at last at the far end of the mall, which leads up to the palace, we saw the first lines of soldiers marching back to the palace in front of the royal party. There was something powerfully moving about the return of the monarch and the majestic silence as the crowd listened, then the bursts of cheering as the head of state rode by.

I came away impressed with the English ability to mount a spectacle. As a fellow American tourist at my elbow said, "These limeys sure know how to do a parade." But there was more to it than that. Beneath all the pageantry and ceremonial was a deep instinct that a country needs a head of state. A good head of state helps provide a stable society, which makes for a prosperous and noble people. When the head of state is bad, the whole nation feels dispirited. The monarch or the president carries in himself or herself the values, hopes, and aspirations of the people. A head of state is a symbol of the whole nation. A head of state is not only a symbol of the whole nation living today, but he or she sums up and stands for the entire history of that country. Like the head of a body, the head of state summarizes and expresses the entire body. As a body needs a head to live and move and have unity, a nation or a church also needs a head. Without a leader the people are in chaos. Without a shepherd the sheep are scattered.

If you have been following my line of argument so far, you may have agreed with me that for us to know the fullness of the truth we need not only the revelation of Jesus Christ as found in the Scriptures; but we also need a venerable, universal, and trustworthy authority to interpret the Scriptures. I have tried to show why it is the apostolic Church that offers us the fullest, most historical, and most universal interpretation of the truth. Like any organization, that apostolic Church needs a leader. St. Paul calls the Church the body of Christ. The head of the body is Christ himself, but Catholics believe Jesus has also created a voice for his headship here on earth.

Jesus gave a measure of his God-given authority to his twelve chosen apostles, but the authority Jesus gave all his apostles is seen even more clearly in his gift to Peter. Jesus gave Peter a special responsibility to carry on Jesus' own leadership role on earth. There are three different images that Jesus uses to show that he is handing a special measure of his authority to Peter as the leader of the apostles. The first is the image of the rock; the second is the keys of the kingdom that Jesus hands to Peter; the third image of authority is the Good Shepherd. According to Catholic belief, when Jesus said Peter was the rock on which he would found the Church, he was establishing a foundation authority for the Church on earth. Since Peter was the first leader of the Church in Rome, Catholics believe the Bishop of Rome (the pope) is his successor. I first want to explore the three biblical images that are the foundation for Catholic beliefs about Peter; then in the second half of this chapter I want to explain how Catholics face the reality of wicked popes, and the thorny question of papal infallibility.

Peter the Rock

One of my favorite stories from the Gospels is the one Jesus tells about two men who went out to build a house. The wise man built his house upon the rock but the foolish man built his house upon the sand. When the storms came, the house on the sand collapsed, but the house on the rock stood firm. In the context, the person who obeys the Lord's teachings builds on the rock. I don't think it is a coincidence that in the same Gospel Jesus gives his leading apostle a new name that means "rock."

As I heard the Bible stories in Sunday school, Peter was a heroic character. He was the one who walked on the water, witnessed the Transfiguration, and first recognized Jesus for who he really was. In a moment of cowardice Peter betrayed Jesus three times, but he was also the one who ran with John to find the empty tomb, received a special commission from Jesus, spoke courageously at Pentecost, and went on to be one of the first great missionaries. My Sunday school understanding of Peter

— that he was a courageous but flawed disciple — was certainly based on the Gospel account; yet there is more about Peter in the Gospels than I was told. This is not because anyone was dishonest but because all of us read the Gospels in our own religious context, and my Bible-Christian context understood a courageous missionary Peter but had no context for a Peter who was more than that. If you like, I had "mere Peter," but as I moved toward Catholicism I discovered "more Peter."

In the Gospels Jesus chose twelve men to bear his authority on earth, but Peter was chosen as the leader of the apostles. In the Gospels whenever the twelve are listed Peter comes first — and Judas last. Peter is the one who declares that Jesus is the Christ, the Son of God, and Jesus says it was by special divine revelation that Peter was able to say this (cf. Matthew 16:17). With John, Peter is the one to set up the Last Supper, and at that supper, in Luke 22:31-32, Jesus affirms Peter's importance by telling him to hold the faith. He then gives Peter a special commission to strengthen his brothers in their belief.

Peter must have been a natural leader, but he was chosen to be leader of the twelve apostles for another reason as well. When Peter says Jesus is truly the Son of God — as recorded in Matthew 16:13-20 — Jesus says that it was not flesh and blood that revealed this truth but God himself. Jesus then says that this truth that Peter confesses is the rock on which the Church will be founded. Then Jesus makes a pun on the name Peter — which means "rock." Because he was able to receive this fundamental revelation from God, Peter himself will be the rock on which the Church is founded. In other words, Peter's leadership is based on divine inspiration. Next Jesus gives Peter's leadership role a future dimension: Peter is the rock on which the Church will be built. Jesus' prophecy that Peter would be the rock on which the Church is built fits perfectly with Paul's understanding of the Church. In

Ephesians 2:20 Paul says the Church is built on the foundation stone of the prophets and apostles.

It's easy to read the conversation between Jesus and Peter in Matthew 16 and treat it like just another Gospel story. All the Gospel stories are full of meaning and interesting details, but this passage in Matthew is especially revealing. For example, we're told that this conversation took place near Caesarea Philippi. At that place was a huge natural rock formation on top of which the Romans had built a temple to the pagan shepherd god Pan. So when Jesus said, "You are Peter, and on this rock I will build my church" (Matthew 16:18), he was looking at this great rocky foundation on top of which stood a temple to a shepherd god. Jesus' meaning was clear: Peter, whose name means "rock," was to be a great foundation for Christ's Church — the Church of the real Good Shepherd. But there is another significance to this location as well. Because of language details, some Christians think when Jesus called Peter "the rock," he was using a term that really meant "the pebble" or "the little stone." This is not true for linguistic reasons (Jesus spoke in Aramaic and there is no difference between the words for "rock" and the name "Peter" in Aramaic), but it is also not true because of the visual aid Jesus was using. The rock with the temple on top at Caesarea Philippi was a huge rocky outcrop — not a little pebble.

Other interpreters of this passage say the "rock" is the truth about Jesus that Peter confessed. Some non-Catholics claim the "rock" is only Peter's confession and not Peter himself. This is an either/or position. More Christianity says the truth is both/and. The *Catechism of the Catholic Church* agrees: "Moved by the grace of the Holy Spirit and drawn by the Father, we believe in Jesus and confess: 'You are the Christ, the Son of the living God.' On the rock of this faith confessed by St. Peter, Christ built his Church."[1] This is not a recent teaching of the Catholic Church. The quotation from the *Catechism* is actually a reference to a sermon by a fifth-century pope, Leo the Great. In another passage the *Catechism* reaffirms that the rock is both Peter and the faith he confessed. "Because of the faith he confessed, Peter will remain the unshakeable rock of the Church."[2]

The passage in Matthew's Gospel reveals other truths about Peter's special relationship with Jesus. It reminds us that it was Jesus who gave Simon the name "Peter" in the first place. In the Bible when God gives someone a new name it means that person is given a new calling and a new identity. So when God called Abram to be the father of his people, his name was changed from Abram to Abraham. Matthew's Gospel was addressed to a Jewish audience, so when Simon is given a new name an interesting parallel between Peter and Abraham is produced. Both Matthew's audience and Jesus' hearers would have understood that a comparison was being drawn between Peter and Abraham. In Isaiah 51:1-2 the prophet says to the Jewish people, "Look to the rock from which you were hewn, / and to the quarry from which you were digged. / Look to Abraham your father." The Jewish teachers said about this passage, "When God looked upon Abraham, he said, 'Behold I have found a rock on which I can build and found the world.'" Of course Jesus — as a faithful rabbi and teacher — knew this passage from Isaiah, but he also knew the rabbinic comment on the passage. In calling Peter the "rock" he is saying Peter — who was also given a name change — is like the new Abraham, the one who will be the foundation stone of the Church and the spiritual father of his people.

Prime Minister Peter

When I saw the trooping of the colors in London, the spectacle revealed the historic claims of the English monarch. The power and the glory were expressed through the pageantry and pomp. In England the queen is the head of state, but she rules from a distance. In fact, she has a prime minister — one who bears her authority and governs the nation on behalf of the people. England is a kingdom with a monarch and a prime minister, and the illustration of present-day England provides a good picture of the situation Jesus establishes for his Church.

In Matthew 16:19, Jesus equates the Church with the kingdom of heaven. In other words, the Church is like a kingdom, and Jesus is the king. But a good king delegates power to ministers beneath him. As in England the prime minister runs the country on behalf of the monarch, it was the same thing in the Old Testament. The Israelite king had a "prime minister," and in Isaiah 22:22 we get a fascinating glimpse into the royal court of Israel. In this passage, the prophet Isaiah recognizes the prime minister of the king, and describes his royal appointment. Isaiah addresses the former prime minister and says, "In that day I will call my servant [and prime minister] Eliakim the son of Hilkiah, and I will clothe him with your robe, and will bind your girdle on him, and will commit your authority to his hand; . . . I will place on his shoulder the key of the house of David; he shall open, and none shall shut; and he shall shut, and none shall open" (Isaiah 22:20-22).

This passage sheds light on Matthew 16:19, in which Jesus says to Peter, "I will give you the keys of the kingdom of heaven, and whatever you bind on earth shall be bound in heaven, and whatever you loose on earth shall be loosed in heaven." The apostles would have been completely familiar with the Old Testament. Matthew's first-century Hebrew Christians would have been also. The apostles and the early Christians understood the keys to symbolize royal authority. They knew Jesus was referring to the passage in Isaiah, and they understood clearly in a moment what we have to struggle to grasp: that Jesus — in granting Peter the keys to the kingdom — is appointing him as the prime minister of his kingdom. As God gave "Prime Minister" Eliakim in Isaiah the authority of the king — symbolized by the keys — so Peter was being specially appointed and chosen by Christ himself to exercise Christ's own authority on earth. Furthermore, the office of prime minister was, by its very nature, a successive office. In other words, it was an office that was handed on from one prime minister to another in succession by handing over the symbols of office. The keys were the abiding symbol of the permanence of an office that was greater than any one holder of the office.

It is interesting to see that non-Catholic scholars also understand the background for this important verse. F. F. Bruce says, "What about the keys of the kingdom? The keys of a royal or noble establishment were entrusted to the chief steward. . . . They were a badge of the authority entrusted to him." Bruce then refers to the passage in Isaiah 22 and says, "So in the new community which Jesus was about to build, Peter would be, so to speak, chief steward."[3] This link between Isaiah 22 and Matthew 16 is also attested to by Anglican scholar R. T. France, who writes about Matthew 16, "Isaiah 22:22 is generally regarded as the Old Testament background to the metaphor of the keys here."[4] Finally J. Jeremias says, "The keys of the kingdom are not different from the keys of David. . . . Handing over the keys does not imply appointing a porter. . . . Handing over the keys implies appointment of full authority."[5]

The Good Shepherd's Shepherd

When taken together with Isaiah 22, the passage in Matthew provides rather strong evidence that Jesus intended Peter to bear his authority in a special way. However, we should be careful not to build too much on one passage of Scripture only. There is another important passage of Scripture that backs up Peter's special relationship with Jesus. We know that Jesus called himself the Good Shepherd (cf. John 10:14). All through the Gospels he talks about sheep, goats, and shepherds, and likens the people of God to the flock of God. This was nothing new. The Old Testament prophets had also seen God as the shepherd and his people as the flock. In the image of Jesus as the Good Shepherd he is fulfilling the prophecy from Ezekiel 34:23, where God himself promises to become the Good Shepherd who will judge his people with justice. Jesus fulfills this prophecy when he declares himself the Good Shepherd.

Who would be the shepherd after Jesus returned to heaven? Jesus said there would be only one flock and one shepherd (cf. John 10:16). After his Resurrection, in a moving and tender conversation with Peter, Jesus delegates his job as shepherd of the sheep to Peter himself. In John 21:15-17 Jesus solemnly commands Peter three times to feed his sheep and take care of his lambs. So in three powerful images Jesus hands over his own authority in a special way to Peter, and in a general way to the other apostles. Peter is — like Abraham — the spiritual father and foundation stone of the People of God. He is to be the prime minister of the kingdom in Jesus' absence, and Peter is to take charge as the chief shepherd of the flock for Jesus. It makes complete sense that Jesus — knowing he would return to his Father in heaven — would take care to set up a system to continue his presence and power on earth.

So far, we've seen that Jesus is sent by God the Father, and given God's own power and authority over all things. He shared that authority with his twelve apostles, and they in turn passed the authority to forgive sins, overcome evil, and teach the truth to their successors — the leaders of the early Church. We've also seen that Peter was not only the natural leader among the apostles, but Jesus chose him specially to be the rock on which the Church would be built. Jesus chose Peter to be spiritual equivalent of Abraham — the founding father of the people of God. He chose him to be the prime minister of his kingdom, and the earthly shepherd of the flock of God. But what happened to Peter afterward? The New Testament doesn't tell us much about his missionary journeys and we don't have much Bible evidence about his leadership role in the city of Rome. Did Peter really end up as the leader of the Roman Church? Catholics believe he was not only the leader of the Roman Church but that the leaders who followed him were the successors of his special commission from Jesus to lead the flock of God.

Peter's Destiny

The first chapters of the Acts of the Apostles show Peter's natural leadership being exercised. After the ascension of Jesus, Peter takes the leadership role just as Jesus had predicted and commanded. The first thing he does is help choose a successor for Judas. Peter is the leader of the Church in those days before Pentecost, and he is the main preacher on the day of Pentecost. He is the first of the apostles to perform a miracle in Jesus' name, and he is a spokesman for the disciples before the Jewish leaders. When he stands up to preach, Peter exercises the authority to teach the inspired truth of God's good news. When he leads the Church to accept non-Jewish believers, he exercises his authority to teach the truth — even when that truth seems new and controversial (cf. Acts 15:7-8). We know Peter set out from Jerusalem on missionary journeys. But then the book of Acts shifts its attention from Peter to Paul. This was because Luke, who was a companion of Paul, wrote Acts. So where else can we get information about what happened to Peter?

First of all, there is the rest of the New Testament itself. Most scholars agree that Peter wrote the first letter of Peter. In 1 Peter 5:13 we find that Peter is writing from a place he calls "Babylon." From the book of Revelation we know that "Babylon" is an early Christian code word for the city of Rome. The first letter of Peter tells us quite a lot about the situation at that time — about thirty years after Jesus' death and Resurrection. By then the Church was established in Rome, and the apostle Paul was also ministering there. From Rome Peter writes to churches throughout Asia Minor — what is now Turkey. The fact that he addresses these churches suggests that is where Peter went on his missionary journeys. The historians of the early Church back up the scriptural evidence that Peter went on missionary journeys and ended up in Rome. Clement of Alexandria lived about one hundred years after Peter's death. Looking back to much older accounts, he records how the Gospel of Mark came to be written down. He says, "As Peter had preached the Word publicly at Rome and declared the Gospel by the Spirit, many who were present requested that Mark, who had followed him for a long time and remembered his sayings, should write them out."[6] Other earlier writers named Papias and Irenaeus also record the fact that Peter and Mark — his "son in the faith" — ended up in Rome and that the Gospel of Mark was written there, and was based on Peter's preaching and eyewitness accounts.[7]

What else can we reconstruct to get a picture of the early Church in the city of Rome during Peter's lifetime? The Church was an underground movement. We assume from 2 Timothy 4:13 that Paul himself was in chains in a damp prison, since he asks for his cloak. Peter probably kept on the move, visiting outlying churches, and meeting in the homes of the Christians for secret worship. In fact, in 1915, an ancient house in Rome called the House of Hermes was excavated and many inscriptions on the walls indicate that Peter used that very house as a center of his ministry. While there are scraps of evidence that tell us what the Church was like, in reality we have very little written evidence about the Church from those early days. The reason so little exists is that part of the systematic persecution of the Church over the next two hundred years was the widespread destruction of all the Christian holy writings. When the Christians weren't actually being thrown to the wild beasts, their property was confiscated, their books burned, and their worship disrupted.

Nevertheless, the historians and writers of the Church who lived just following the time of the apostles did record that Peter and Paul resided in Rome. They recorded that both met their deaths in the terrible persecutions of Nero around the year 65; that Paul was beheaded and Peter crucified upside down. They also record that both Peter and Paul were buried in Rome. In fact, when Christianity became legal in 315, the Roman emperor Constantine built the first basilica of Peter on the traditional site of Peter's tomb. About fifty years ago, excavations under the great church of St. Peter in Rome uncovered a first-century tomb. On the wall was an inscription from the first century that read, "Here is Peter." Inside, the workers found the bones of a stocky man in his mid-sixties. The skeleton had no feet, which would be consistent with the ancient tradition that Peter was crucified upside down. The absence of feet can be explained by the fact that the weight of a body crucified upside down would finally make the ankles so weak that the feet would tear off when the body was removed from the cross. Because of the ancient writings and the archaeological evidence, many scholars believe the basilica of St. Peter really is built over the actual tomb of Peter himself.

All the evidence points to the fact that Peter ended his earthly life in the city of Rome. As such, along with Paul, he must have been the leader of the infant Roman Church. But what happened next? What about those who came after him? We've already seen how the apostles passed on their authority to the Church leaders they appointed in various places. So in the New Testament Paul appoints Titus as the Church leader for Cyprus and tells him to select and appoint other Church elders. Likewise, in his first epistle, Peter addresses the elders in the various churches he founded as "his fellow shepherds" — in other words, those with whom he shared his Christ-given role of earthly shepherd of the flock of God.

But what did the Christians in Rome think about their leaders during the years just after the apostles died? We've already seen from the epistle of Clement to the Corinthians that the Roman Christians considered their leaders to be the successors of the apostles. Because the question of leadership was important, the Christians in Rome were careful to record who their own leaders were after Peter and Paul were killed. So we have a list of the first leaders of the Roman Church after Peter. The list says that a man called Linus was the next leader after Peter, and a person with this name appears in 2 Timothy 4:21. This epistle was written from Paul's prison in Rome, and Paul says to Timothy that Linus sends greetings. The second leader after Peter was Cletus, about whom we know very little. The third man was Clement — the one who wrote the famous letter to the Church at Corinth.

Why go into all this detail? First of all, I think it's fascinating to discover what really did happen to Peter and Paul, and to uncover what the Church was like just after their deaths. For a long time I didn't know we had any writings of the Christians from just after the apostles' time. These writings aren't the same as Scripture of course, but they were written just after the last New Testament books were written. They are interwoven with the New Testament events, and they tell us more of what that first generation of Christians believed and did. In this particular context they confirm that Peter — the one Jesus appointed as leader of the apostles — did end up in Rome, and that he was the leader of the Church there. These early writings also tell us that the apostles appointed successors in the different churches, and that the successors were considered the rightful inheritors of the apostolic authority — an authority given to them directly by Jesus.

The Petrine Office

Peter may have been the leader of the apostles, and he may have ended up as the leader of the Church of Rome, but does that mean he was considered the actual leader of the whole Church? Did his successor as the leader of the Roman Church continue to be seen as the leader of the whole Church? If so, then we can see how the idea that the Bishop of Rome continues to be the prime minister of Christ's kingdom on earth might have developed. Jesus commanded Peter to be in charge of his flock as the head pastor in his place, but did that job of overall leadership pass on to those who stepped into Peter's shoes?

Did Peter exercise an authority over the whole Church? Certainly in the Acts of the Apostles he emerges as the key spokesman and authoritative teacher. When the whole Church leadership met in Jerusalem as recorded in Acts 15, it was Peter — under the guidance of the Holy Spirit — who decided that they should accept non-Jewish Christians. Even Paul tells us in Galatians 1:18 that he went to see Peter, probably to validate his own teaching and authority. We know that Peter took on missionary travels, and we know from his epistles — written from Rome — that he felt confident to write authoritatively to Christians throughout the known world. His epistles are actually called "catholic" (that is, "universal") epistles because they were addressed to all Christians everywhere. In other words, even in his lifetime, Peter — based in Rome — was the spokesman and leader of the whole Church.

This authority of the Roman Church over other churches continued after Peter's death. I have already mentioned the letter of Clement written from Rome to the Church at Corinth. Clement, writing just thirty years after Peter's death, calls the Corinthian Church into order and exercises authority over them. Writing just sixty years later, Irenaeus — a French bishop who had studied in Rome — says, "We will point to the tradition of the greatest and oldest church, a church known by all men, which was founded and established at Rome by the most renowned apostles Peter and Paul. . . . For this church has a position of leadership and authority and therefore every church, that is, the faithful everywhere, must needs agree with the church at Rome, for in her the apostolic tradition has ever been preserved by the faithful."[8]

Irenaeus and the rest of the Christians in those first hundred years after the death of Peter and Paul all agreed that the Church of Rome had a special teaching ministry and leadership role over the whole Church. Most Christians don't object to the idea that Church leaders should exercise a teaching ministry, a ministry that overcomes evil and a ministry that forgives sins in Jesus' name. Many Christians wouldn't even mind that one Church — a church that is most ancient and wise — ought to exercise some sort of leadership. But a problem arises when Catholics claim that the Bishop of Rome exercises a teaching ministry that actually claims to be infallible. This is a difficulty, and the idea that the pope is infallible is not only a problem for non-Catholics but for many Catholics, who also have trouble understanding and accepting it.

To understand what we mean by the pope being infallible, we should set the whole idea in the larger context. It is important to understand that while we believe the pope may exercise infallible authority, the power of infallibility is not his but Christ's. First and foremost it is Jesus Christ who is infallible. It is Jesus who is "the way, and the truth, and the life" (John 14:6). It is Jesus who gives us the only way to the Father that is reliable and without fail. The infallibility of Jesus is based on the authority that he was given by his Father. But where is this infallible Christ alive in the world today? Paul says the body of Christ is the Church. In Ephesians, in the same passage where he expresses Christ's universal power, he says that power finds its fullest expression in the Church (cf. Ephesians 1:17-23). Later, in Ephesians 5:27, Paul says that Christ has washed the Church and presented her "without spot or wrinkle or any such thing, that she might be holy and without blemish." In 1 Timothy 3:15 Paul says the Church is "the pillar and bulwark of the truth." Again, in Ephesians 3:10, Paul says it is God's design that through the Church all the wisdom of God should be made known. So first and foremost it is the Church — the body of Christ — that holds and teaches the truth infallibly.

Paul also says in Ephesians that the Church is built on the foundation of the apostles and prophets. Christ gave his authority to his apostles in the Gospels specifically to teach the truth. But surely he had to give his apostles the grace to teach the truth without fail — reliably and in a trustworthy manner so we could be assured of the truth. This must be so, for our very salvation depends on it. Therefore, what we are saying is that Christ — who is infallible — shares a measure of that complete reliability with his body the Church. That infallible teaching has to be expressed by someone, and so it was through the preaching and writings of the apostles that we are given the

Word of God. All Christians regard the Scripture as completely reliable — a source that can bring us to the saving knowledge of God's love without fail. All Christians agree that in the Scriptures we have a sure, reliable, and infallible source of truth that comes to us from the apostles. Catholics, however, believe the same infallible Spirit of Christ — the Paraclete who filled the apostles, fired the Church into birth at Pentecost, and went on to inspire the Scriptures — still dwells in the apostolic Church today. We believe this because Jesus promised to be with us to the end of time. Catholics believe that the Church, led by the successors of the apostles, continues to proclaim and teach the Gospel without fail.

So "infallibility" means that the teaching of the Church — in matters vital for salvation — is without error. This doesn't mean every detail of Catholic history or Church discipline is automatically perfect. It also doesn't mean that the Church is without human sin. From the beginning the Church was made up of sinful people, and when people bowed down to Peter, he always told them to get up, since he too, as he readily admitted, was just an ordinary sinful man (cf. Acts 10:26). What infallibility does mean is that the Church is preserved from teaching error despite being led by sinful men. This seems like a contradiction, but in fact this is something all Christians take for granted. We believe the Bible is without error even though it was written by sinful men. When we say the creed, we believe it is without error even though it was devised and written by sinful men. We all believe that God can express his eternal truth infallibly through the channel of sinful people. Catholics simply believe that this is still the case.

The pope's role in all this is simply as the spokesman for this infallible truth. As the leader of the apostles, as the head shepherd of the Church on earth, he speaks the truth that the whole Church affirms. But he only does so infallibly when he speaks *ex cathedra* — that is, "from the chair" of Peter. When we say the pope is infallible, we do not mean that he never sins. Like Peter, the pope is an ordinary sinful man. Also when we say he is infallible we don't believe that whatever he says is always infallibly true. He usually speaks as an ordinary man, or as an ordinary Christian teacher. However, on the specially designated times when the pope states that he is making an infallible statement, we believe that, through the power of the Holy Spirit, he is speaking the truth reliably and without error. An example of this is given in the Gospel itself. Jesus asked his apostles who he was, and Peter spoke up, "You are the Christ, the Son of the living God" (Matthew 16:16). At that point Peter was the spokesman not only for all the apostles but for all of us. Despite being a sinful man, Peter spoke the truth infallibly by the power of the Holy Spirit. When Jesus goes on to say that Peter is the rock on which he will build the Church, he is also implying that this God-given ability to speak the truth without error is part of the foundation authority of the Church.

Saints and Sinners

Down through the ages many men have stood in the shoes of Peter as Bishop of Rome. Some have been saints, some have been sinners. The popes haven't all been angels; some have been very wicked indeed. Because of their human failings they have caused scandal and division in the Church. Sometimes they have not only been guilty of immorality and greed, but they have also condoned the persecution of minority groups and other Christians. Some popes have been lazy, inept, or poorly qualified. Some were put in office by political powers. Others bought their high office, schemed to gain power, or even committed murder to gain the throne. Despite this, in reading the history of the Church it soon becomes clear that most of the popes have been hardworking, prayerful, and dedicated leaders of Christ's Church. Many of them have been truly great and spiritual men. Others have been persecuted and some have even been martyrs for the faith.

It's true that some of the popes were bad men, but there are three points to consider about this fact. First of all, there have been bad men and women in leadership roles of all churches. This is not to throw stones at other Christian groups but to make the point that it is obvious that along with power goes the tendency to become corrupt. In other words, bad popes shouldn't surprise us. What would be unusual, on the other hand, would be for every single leader to be a saint. Second, the fact that there are some shameful episodes in the history of the papacy makes the whole thing seem real. Third, the fact of terrible corruption within the papacy suggests that there really is a divine hand of protection over this institution. After all, what other organization that was started in Roman times is still going strong? What other power structure has been rocked with the most appalling wickedness and yet survived and gone on to prosper? The gates of hell really have not prevailed against the papacy despite the best efforts to erode it from within by corruption and destroy it from without by persecution.

Of course it is best when a pope is a truly great and spiritual leader of the Church, but when considering the problem of bad men who have been popes we have to consider the basic claims made for the papacy. The Catholic Church doesn't claim that all popes will be saints. It doesn't claim that they will all be great spiritual leaders. It simply claims that they will not formally teach error in Christian doctrine or morality. We do not want to dismiss the wrongdoing of popes, but the point is, while they may have stolen and murdered, none of them taught that stealing and murder were good. They may not have lived like Jesus, but they never taught that Jesus was not God.

One of the amazing things that scholars tell us about the popes is that despite their moral, political, and spiritual failings, not once has any Bishop of Rome formally taught heresy. David Currie records a list taken from Warren Carroll's *History of Christendom* series that shows how, down through the ages, the bishops from every other ancient city had fallen into error at one time or another, but the Bishops of Rome never did.[9] Every Bishop of Rome has held firm despite persecution, deprivation of his rights, and being sent into exile. Despite their human failings the popes have held fast to the unfailing Gospel of Jesus Christ. They did so in the footsteps of Peter — that amazing man Jesus called to continue his work on earth. Peter's name means "rock," and it is his life as well as his example that remains the foundation of Christ's Church just as Jesus promised.

For Catholics the pope is the earthly head of the Church. He is the prime minister in Jesus' kingdom, but he is also the good shepherd who bears the rod and staff of Jesus' authority until the Chief Shepherd appears. Some Christians do not have time for an earthly institution of the Church, and they especially don't have time for someone who claims to speak the truth of Christ infallibly. But when we come to consider it, most Christians actually behave as if their leaders were infallible even though they say they do not believe in such a theory. Infallibility in this context simply means "without error in matters pertaining to salvation and morals." In practice, all Christians take their leaders' word for it. When their preacher or minister proclaims the way of salvation and the rules for Christian living, they do their best to believe it and live by it. They assume without question that the preacher is interpreting the Bible without error in these matters. They have to do this for their religion to make any sense. They know their preacher is an ordinary sinful man. They know he is not always right about every single thing he says, but in matters pertaining to salvation and the Christian life they trust him to speak the truth. This is, if you prefer, "mere Christian leadership," and Catholics offer "more Christian leadership." In the Bishop of Rome we believe God has given us a leader who speaks the Gospel truth without fail. He is a figurehead and leader for the whole Church throughout the world. He is a focus of unity for all Catholics. With an unbroken historical link back to Peter himself, the pope is a focus of our common faith with all the Christians who have gone before us as well. To become a Catholic means entering into a full and dynamic unity with him and with his teaching. By doing this we enter into a full and dynamic relationship not only with the apostolic teaching but with the whole Church, living and departed, in all times and in all places.

The power and the glory of being in communion with the successor of Peter is illustrated by the magnificent church built over Peter's tomb. Visitors to Rome can take the tour down to the archaeological site beneath the great basilica. As you go down the narrow staircase you enter the *scavi* (excavations) of an ancient Roman cemetery. Gradually your guide takes you past the mausoleums of Christians from the third and second centuries. Finally the tour comes to a point where you can see a simple, broken-down brick wall topped by the remains of the second-century memorial, which is referred to in writings from the third century. At that point you can look up and see the floor level of the church built by Emperor Constantine in the fourth century. Above that is the floor level of the present church, then above that is the altar table at which the pope celebrates the Eucharist. Soaring high above the whole site is the great dome built by Michelangelo, and around the dome, in letters seven feet tall the inscription reads, "You are Peter, and on this Rock I will build my church." The whole experience is an amazing and moving visual aid that shows the power of the Gospel. From the humble grave of a murdered fisherman-turned-missionary the great Church of Christ has literally been founded. At that point Peter has become the foundation of the Church in a more literal way than anyone could have imagined. Seeing that site is a powerful illustration of the continuity that the ministry of the pope represents.

To enter into full communion with the successor of Peter is to be part of that great Church that God has preserved down through the ages. The word "communion" means "union with," and to be in full communion with the Catholic Church means being in union with the fullest expression of apostolic Christianity possible. That communion is a daily living experience. It means my own individual faith is submerged into the universal Church. It means my faith is as simple as that broken missionary's grave and as glorious as the dome above it. It means that I have not only the apostolic faith, but I am part of the apostolic Church. It means my house is not built on the sand of my own opinions but on Peter — the "rock" that was chosen by Jesus himself — a rock that he promised would never fail.

Chapter Three Endnotes

1. *Catechism of the Catholic Church,* London, Geoffrey Chapman, 1995, para. 424.

2. Ibid., para. 552.

3. F. F. Bruce, *The Hard Sayings of Jesus,* Downers Grove, Ill., InterVarsity Press, 1983, pp. 143-144.

4. R. T. France, *Matthew: Evangelist and Teacher*, Grand Rapids, Mich., Zondervan, 1989, p. 274.

5. Gerhard Kittel and Gerhard Friedrich, eds., *Theological Dictionary of the New Testament*, 10 vols., Grand Rapids, Mich., Eerdmans, 1968, vol. 3, pp. 749-750.

6. Eusebius, *Church History,* 6, 14. Cited in Stephen Ray, *Upon This Rock,* San Francisco, Ignatius Press, 1999, p. 81.

7. Ibid., pp. 69, 70, 76.

8. Henry Bettenson, *The Early Christian Fathers,* Oxford, Oxford University Press, 1969, p. 90.

9. David B. Currie, *Born Fundamentalist, Born Again Catholic,* San Francisco, Ignatius Press, 1996, pp. 92-94.

One Saving Action

I married my wife, Alison, about ten years ago. On that day we made a vow to remain married — for better, for worse, for richer, for poorer, until death should part us. That vow was a once-and-for-all mutual promise. It was a step of faith. I accepted Alison and she accepted me. We loved each other but realized that our love would have to grow over the years. Our marriage vow took place in one moment in time, but you could say it is present in every moment of our married life. We took a step of faith to marry each other, but we have to live within that faith day by day and moment by moment for our vows to be real.

If we do not perform the faithful actions of love within our marriage and family life, then that promise of love eventually dies. However, if we lived together without having made the vows, our life would not be the same as if we had married. A legal analyst might wish to study the purely formal aspect of our marriage, but that wouldn't be the marriage. Likewise a psychologist or sociologist might like to study the day-to-day life of our relationship, but that wouldn't be the marriage either. The vows and the daily life go together. The vows we made help us live in love day by day, and our daily life of love is the fulfillment of the vows. Separating our marriage vows from our marriage is impossible. Separating the two would be like trying to separate the light from the sun, the scent from the flower, or the music from the violin from which it comes.

One of the biggest areas of confusion and misunderstanding between Catholics and other Christians is in the area of salvation. How is a person saved? How do people get to heaven? Is it by their works or by their faith? One of the classic Protestant doctrines is that we are saved by faith alone. In the sixteenth century Martin Luther and others felt their Catholic faith was legalistic and meaningless. It was just a set of rules and routine, formal prayers that meant nothing and could never save a person. When Martin Luther read St. Paul's letter to the Romans, he discovered for himself the wonderful biblical doctrine that a person is saved by grace through faith — and not by any works they have done.

This was exciting and liberating news. No longer did the followers of Jesus have to be good enough to please God by reciting endless liturgies, enduring grueling asceticism, and achieving an impossible standard of goodness. God had saved them through the work of Jesus Christ and all they had to do was trust in him through faith to be saved. Because they had discovered salvation by grace through faith some of them took the extreme position that a person is saved through faith alone. In their enthusiasm to embrace salvation by faith alone, and remembering how they felt helpless to do all the good works they thought were expected of them as Catholics, they couldn't help drawing the conclusion that the Catholic Church taught that a person was saved by good works.

It must have seemed like that was the teaching of the Catholic Church at the time, and perhaps for a lot of ordinary people it felt as if their salvation was won by endless prayer and good works. In fact, the Catholic Church has never taught that salvation is through good works. The idea that we can work our way into heaven is a heresy called Pelagianism after a fourth-century teacher named Pelagius. From that time, and down through the ages, the Catholic Church has repudiated such teaching. That doesn't mean the Catholic Church believes in salvation by faith alone, though. We believe salvation is through faith, but we believe faith consists of more than an individual's personal belief. For faith to be real it has to include the person's whole life. Catholics agree that we are saved by grace alone but not by faith alone. An exciting new document was signed in 1999 by high-ranking Lutherans and Catholics. The Joint Declaration on the Doctrine of Justification included this statement: "By grace alone, in faith in Christ's saving work and not because of any merit on our part, we are accepted by God and receive the Holy Spirit, who renews our hearts while equipping and calling us to good works."[1] The zeal of Catholics for salvation by God's grace alone is summed up in the words of one of the greatest saints of modern times. Thérèse of Lisieux wrote, "In the evening of this life I shall appear before you empty-handed, for I do not ask you, Lord, to count my works. All our justices have stains in your sight. So I want to be clad in your own justice and receive from your love the possession of yourself."[2]

One of the problems in this debate between the need for faith or works is that both sides have tended to pull out certain verses from the New Testament to use as proof texts. The Evangelicals use some verses from St. Paul's teaching that "by grace you have been saved through faith; . . . not because of works, lest any man should boast" (Ephesians 2:8-9). Catholics respond with verses from the epistle of James that say clearly that "faith apart from works is barren" (James 2:20). But this is a bit like two cowboys in a shoot-out — both of them pull out their six-guns and shoot from the hip. The problem is, they're arguing away, but nobody's actually listening to anyone else, and the only people they convince are themselves.

Common sense tells us that faith and works are both important, and in practice most Catholics and Protestants actually agree that both are necessary to some extent. I think the best way to confront this whole issue is to avoid simple proof texts on their own, and to steer around the strong language and emotional experiences of the Reformation times by turning back to the Bible as a whole. The Bible shows that faith and works are one. The first part of this chapter is going to be an exploration of what the Bible says about faith and works. The second part will explain in more detail how Catholics see the two operating together. This is a huge issue to which shelves of theological libraries devote yards of space. I should say that I'm neither a Bible scholar nor a theologian. I write this as a layman in hopes that what I say might help others to think through this issue.

Faith of Our Fathers

The place to begin is the Old Testament, but in the Old Testament we don't actually hear too much about faith as such. When the word "faith" is used, it usually means keeping one's word — keeping a solemn agreement between two parties. Where it is used in a religious context, faith for the Jewish person means keeping his part of the solemn covenant between God and his people. The way the Jewish person kept his side of the covenant was by obeying the law. It almost sounds like the Old Testament definition for faith is actually good works because the basic meaning of "keeping faith" in the Old Testament means keeping the law, or obeying God's commandments.

However, there are one or two other hints in the Old Testament that "having faith" could mean something more. In

2 Chronicles 20:20 the good king Jehoshaphat calls on the people to "believe in the LORD your God, and you will be established; believe his prophets, and you will succeed." Then the prophet Habakkuk looks forward to the day when the Lord's messenger will come and bring the revelation of God. In that day, says the prophet, "the righteous shall live by his faith" (Habakkuk 2:4). But in the context the word "faith" also means "faithfulness," so Habakkuk is saying that the one who is loyal, or faithful, or who keeps his part of the bargain will be considered righteous.

All through the Old Testament the person who has faith is also faithful, or loyal. The person who has faith obeys the covenant and keeps his side of the bargain. But what does this mean in action? Are there any illustrations of faith in the Old Testament? What does the person of faith look like? What does he believe and what does he do to keep his side of the bargain with God? The New Testament book of Hebrews helps us see the Old Testament through Christian eyes, and in chapter 11 it speaks at great length about the faith of the Old Testament characters. Hebrews sees that they were faithful because they had faith in God. In other words, they were able to be loyal and obedient because they trusted in God's faithfulness. They were able to keep their end of the bargain because they had faith that God would keep his.

Hebrews 11 goes through a list of the Old Testament characters showing their faithfulness. It reads like an Old Testament Hall of Fame. First is Adam and Eve's son Abel. He makes a better sacrifice than Cain because he has faith in God. By faith Noah believed God and built an ark to save himself and his family from destruction. By faith Abram (later renamed Abraham by God) left the city of his fathers and set out to a country that God promised to him. By faith Abraham was able to become a father even though he was past the age because he considered God to be faithful. By faith Abraham offered his son Isaac as a sacrifice — believing that God could even raise the dead.

The interesting thing to note in this list from Hebrews is that each one of the Old Testament characters is considered to have faith, but as a result of this faith they all perform faith-full actions — that is, actions that are full of faith. Abel offers a sacrifice; Noah builds an ark; Abraham sets out on pilgrimage, fathers a son, and then offers him as a sacrifice. Hebrews says by faith they performed these obedient and faith-full actions. The list from the Old Testament goes on, and in each case the Old Testament hero is able to perform acts of faith because he believes in God. So Hebrews 11 continues — Isaac blessed Jacob because he had faith. By faith Jacob blessed his sons; by faith Joseph prophesied the Exodus from Egypt. By faith Moses' parents hid him in the river. By faith Moses led the people of Israel and instituted the Passover meal. By faith he led them through the Red Sea, conquered Jericho, and entered the Promised Land. The writer to the Hebrews goes on to list the heroes from the book of Judges and beyond. By faith they conquered kingdoms, administered justice, shut the mouths of lions, quenched the fury of the flames, became powerful in battle, and survived terrible persecutions.

The list recounting the Old Testament heroes is dynamic, full of action and excitement. Faith enabled all these heroes to perform actions that were courageous and faithful to God's commands. Those actions were not mindless and arbitrary acts of obedience. The actions themselves were meaningful. They taught the faithful ones lessons about themselves and God. They performed God's will in the world and they helped bring the faithful ones to a higher perfection. The great chapter on faith in Hebrews shows that personal faith and faith-full actions together helped bring the believer into a deeper relationship with God. Their faith was not simply belief in God's promises or a personal belief in certain truths about God. Instead their faith was inner belief lived out through their decisions and actions.

Faith in the Faithful One

In the Old Testament the righteous person lives by faith, and his faith or trust in God is always shown through his obedient faith-full actions. The Old Testament therefore doesn't say too much about faith as such, but when Jesus comes on the scene the Scriptures suddenly explode with references to faith. Time and again Jesus scolds his disciples because they do not have enough faith. He says if they had only a little faith they could move mountains. It is by faith that people are healed, and it is through faith that his disciples will do great signs and wonders. In the Old Testament, faith was linked with faithful obedience to God's law, but now faith becomes a dynamic power source in the person's life. Suddenly Jesus' disciples will be able to do great things through faith.

Jesus doesn't say whom or what they are to have faith in. As Jews, his disciples would have put their faith in God alone — the ultimate faithful one; and for them having faith meant obeying God's commands. But in John 2:11 we read that the disciples put their faith in Jesus, and throughout the Gospel we're told that people put their faith in Jesus himself. In other words, they transferred their faith in the law-giving God to the person of Jesus Christ. This is an astounding transition, because in putting their faith in Jesus they were recognizing him to be the faithful one. In other words, they were recognizing that their solemn agreement to be in a covenant relationship with God was fulfilled by being in a relationship with Jesus.

Then in the Gospel of John Jesus says something even more stupendous. Just before he promises the Holy Spirit he says, "Truly, truly, I say to you, he who believes in me will also do the works that I do; and greater works than these will he do, because I go to the Father" (John 14:12). All through the Gospels Jesus fulfills the Old Testament and here he fulfills the incomplete Old Testament idea of faith. In the Old Testament, faith was the obedient response to believing in a God who was trustworthy and good. Now faith is linked to a real person in place and time — Jesus. Furthermore, faith now includes a personal relationship and it empowers the disciples to do what Jesus does.

In the next passage in John 14 Jesus speaks further about the person who has faith in him. He will receive the Holy Spirit, and he will also have a certain new responsibility. In verse 15 he says, "If you love me you, you will keep my commandments. And I will pray the Father, and he will give you another Counselor, to be with you for ever, even the Spirit of truth." Jesus promises that he will live in them and they will live in him. The evidence of this is that they will obey his teachings and do what he has done. In verse 20 he says, "In that day you will know that I am in my Father, and you in me, and I in you. He who has my commandments and keeps them, he it is who loves me." This is the final and most profound dimension to faith. In John's Gospel it becomes clear that having faith in Jesus means entering into a supernatural union with him. If you like, faith makes the person a part of Jesus — a member of his body. Through this faith the followers of Jesus think his thoughts and do his actions in the world. Faith here is not simply belief that Jesus is the Son of God — it is a personal union with him.

The fact that this passage is intertwined with his promise of the Holy Spirit shows us that the faith and the good works that flow from faith both have their ultimate origin from God the

Holy Spirit. In other words, both faith in Jesus and the actions of Jesus that we do are initiated and carried out by the working of God within us. God gives us a little bit of his power in order to become unified with Jesus Christ and then do his works in the world. This gift of God's goodness, power, and light is called "grace." Both Catholics and Evangelicals agree on this point — that we neither can have faith nor can we do faith-full good works without the gift of God's grace, which empowers us.

A person may have faith, but what does this person of faith have to do? Must he or she still obey the Old Testament law? Well, in one passage Jesus tells the disciples that they must actually be more righteous than the scribes and Pharisees — those respectable religious people who obeyed every detail of the law. What he meant by this was not so much that they had to obey the Old Testament law but that their new kind of righteousness was to outstrip the Old Testament obedience. It was to be a fresh kind of goodness — as different from the old legalistic way as a color photo is from a black-and-white picture. Obeying Christ's commands actually is not just an action of pure obedience, as it was in the Old Testament. Instead, obeying Christ's commands is the way to enter more fully into unity with him. As the apostle John says, "Whoever keeps his word, in him truly love for God is perfected. By this we may be sure that we are in him: he who says he abides in him ought to walk in the same way in which he walked" (1 John 2:5-6). Therefore, obeying his commands in faith is the method by which Jesus' disciples will dwell in him, become like him, and be made perfect.

The book of Hebrews always shows that the Old Testament heroes of faith did certain actions by faith. Likewise in the Gospels, Jesus, the man of faith, is always acting out that faith with his life, his teachings, his death, and his Resurrection. So faith that is not acted out in the world is not faith at all — it is only an idea. Faith that is just a personal inner religious experience is incomplete. So in Matthew 7:21 Jesus says, "Not every one who says to me, 'Lord, Lord,' shall enter the kingdom of heaven, but he who does the will of my Father who is in heaven." Jesus tells the parable of the sheep and the goats, in which those who acted out their faith through charitable works are welcomed into heaven while those who only gave lip service to their faith are rejected (cf. Matthew 25:31-46). In the story of the wise and foolish builders, the story of the Good Samaritan, and that of the different talents, the faithful ones always perform positive faith-full actions while the unfaithful do nothing — even though with their lips they say they believe (cf. Matthew 25:1-30).

Oh My Goodness

We should also stop for a moment and ask what happens when we do a good work. Let's say we pay a visit to a person in prison. The visit helps that person, but it also helps us. It is not a meaningless act of obedience to God; the action itself is worth something — it has done some good in the world. As such it has changed us for the better, and therefore been a small step toward our becoming more Christ-like. In Hebrews we read that faith is the substance of things we are hoping for, the evidence of things we cannot see (cf. Hebrews 11:1); and when we do a faith-full good action we do just that — we give substance to the thing hoped for and that action becomes evidence for our unseen belief. The actions of faith that we complete through God's grace are a vital dimension to faith itself, and without them there is no faith at all.

How does this keep from becoming a religion in which we rely on good works to get us to heaven? The early Church struggled with the relationship between faith and the Old Testament law. The early Christians were Jews and many of them thought they had to continue obeying all the Old Testament rules and regulations. But St. Paul tried to make it clear that it was not by obeying the rules of the Old Testament law that we are saved. In a famous passage from Ephesians St. Paul says, "For by grace you have been saved through faith; . . . it is the gift of God — not because of works, lest any man should boast" (Ephesians 2:8-9). Paul reminds the early Church that they are saved not by obeying the Jewish law but through faith. So he says in Romans 4:9-15, and he summarizes it in Romans 3:28 when he says, "For we hold that a man is justified by faith apart from works of law."

In these passages St. Paul is not saying that faithful good works are unnecessary. Rather, he is saying that salvation does not come by obeying the Jewish law. In fact, Paul, like the rest of the New Testament writers, says clearly that we are destined to accomplish good works if we are people of faith. Right after the famous passage in Ephesians where he says that we have been saved by grace through faith, and not of works, he goes on to say, "For we are his workmanship, created in Christ Jesus for good works" (Ephesians 2:10). In other words — just as the Gospel taught — through faith we become one with Christ in order that we may speak his words and do his works in the world.

It is the epistle of James that ties together all the strands from the Gospels, from St. Paul's letters, and from the Old Testament. St. James writes, "What does it profit a man, my brethren, if a man says he has faith but has not works? . . . Faith by itself, if it has no works, is dead. . . . Do you want to be shown, you foolish fellow, that faith apart from works is barren? Was not Abraham our father justified by works, when he offered his son Isaac upon the altar? You see that faith was active along with his works, and faith was completed by works. . . . You see that a man is justified by works and not by faith alone" (James 2:14, 17, 20-22, 24).

In fact, there are not many Evangelicals who say that faith completely on its own is good enough. Most non-Catholics also recognize the need for good works to be present. They usually take the view that if the person is really united with Christ, then good works will be the fruit of that faith. The famous reformer John Calvin put it this way: "Salvation is by faith alone, but true faith is never alone." Much progress has been made in recent years in the attempt to find agreement between Protestants and Catholics on this issue. The biggest milestone has been the signing of the Joint Declaration on Justification between Catholics and Lutherans. Officials on the highest levels of the Catholic and Lutheran churches signed a statement on October 31, 1999. On the basis of this detailed theological statement the Lutheran World Federation and the Catholic Church declared together, "The understanding of the doctrine of justification set forth in the declaration shows that a consensus in basic truths of the doctrine of justification exists between Lutherans and Catholics."[3] In the sixteenth century, leaders of the Lutherans and the Catholics had condemned each other for their mutual doctrinal positions. Now both sides say, "The teaching of the Lutheran Churches presented in the Declaration does not fall under condemnations from the Council of Trent. The condemnations in the Lutheran Confessions do not apply to the teaching of the Roman Catholic Church presented in this document."[4] The signing of this statement is a historic moment in the Church's life. Now we can say there is no formal reason why Protestants and Catholics should disagree over the doctrine of justification.

In the light of this formal agreement both sides still need to continue explaining what they really do believe about salvation, and the relationship between our faith and our good works. Evangelicals admit that people who claim to have faith in God will have to show their faith through the fruit of their lives, but they will still say that the good works themselves are not worth anything, and that they have nothing to do with a person's entrance into heaven. This is not quite what Catholics believe, and it is important to emphasize the differences — not to cause division and controversy, but because until the differences are brought out into the light and understood, they can never be resolved.

In the Joint Declaration on Justification, Catholics and Lutherans both affirm that our faith and our good works are initiated and empowered by God's grace alone. But Catholics disagree with the extreme Protestant view that our good works are still worth nothing. That doesn't fit with common sense. Neither does it fit with the many passages of Scripture that show us being judged according to our works. Catholics admit that our good works can only be done through the power of God, but we also say the good works that we do in this way help to contribute to our final destiny. This is a little bit complicated, but it is vital to think it through. Catholics fully accept that our salvation was won for us by Christ's work on the cross and by his mighty Resurrection. We accept his saving work through faith in him, and we can only take the step of faith through God's grace, which empowers us. But our good works are worth something. Our good works are important for several vital reasons.

First, our good or evil works are important for a very basic reason. How we choose to act is eternally important because our decisions and actions change things. This power to change things by our decision and action is called free will. Free will is actually God sharing some of his power with us to change the universe eternally. Now if our good decisions and actions arc

not worth anything, that means they cannot change things. If
they do not change things, our decisions and actions are indeed
meaningless. If this is true, then the feeling we get that things
are changed is simply a huge illusion. If that is so, then everything in the world that seems to occur by human decision and
action is also an illusion, and we are all simply robots in a vast
computer game that is preprogrammed. If it is true that our
decisions and actions are meaningless, then we actually do not
have free will at all. This way of looking at things may protect
faith from getting cluttered up with good works, but the problem is that if we do not have freedom to choose, then it is impossible for us to make any real choices at all. If we are not able
to decide anything, then it is impossible for us to step out in
faith in the first place. Logic insists that if we have the free will
to make the step of faith, then we also have the free will to make
other decisions and take other actions that affect our eternal
destiny. On the other hand, if our decisions and actions have no
power, then neither does our initial decision to follow Christ.
Once we separate faith from works, both faith and works become impossible. It is only by keeping the two together that
both become a reality.

The second reason good works are vitally important is the
fact that we have bodies. It is through our bodies that we can
actually work out what we believe, and if we don't do this, then
our faith remains a head-and-heart game. The Christian religion is not simply a good idea or an inspiring feeling. As the
saying goes, "Love is a verb." So is Christianity. It is with our
bodies that we live out the faith of our head and heart. The
Docetists were early heretics who believed Christ only "seemed"
to be human. Ignatius of Antioch noticed that this wrong belief
about Jesus affected how they behaved. He wrote, "They have
no concern for love, none for the widow, the orphan, the af-

flicted, the prisoner, the hungry, the thirsty. They stay away from the Eucharist and prayer."[5] The physical world is the stage on which we play out the drama of our salvation. This is vitally important because at the core of our faith is the belief that God himself took a human body and worked out our salvation through shedding his blood. Good works are physical, and God works through the physical. We can pray for the housebound widower next door, but only through our bodies can we get up out of a chair, bake a pie, and take it around to his house.

The third reason good works matter is that it is through good works that our faith is perfected. Good works add charity to faith, and that charity is actually the faith in action and made real in the world. Through discovery and learning, our faith matures into a deeper understanding. Through our living the faith, the faith grows and matures. Through our attempts at good works we learn just how difficult faith really is. Through our failures we learn again and again how much we need to rely on God's grace, and how much more we have yet to learn. Through our successful attempts we understand what faith is really about at the very depths of our whole person. It is through our struggle to live out our faith that our faith comes to fullness and perfection. Finally, through our good works the seedling of our faith grows strong and tall. Without those good works it remains a frail and tender shoot.

Practice Makes Perfect

Let's say a child is extremely gifted musically. She has perfect pitch, she has an instinctive ear for melody, and she understands music with an amazing God-given talent. Her gift is extraordinary and wonderful, and it will take her to the very top of her profession as a world-class musician. Despite all this, the little girl still needs to practice. The practice isn't the talent;

the practice cannot take the place of the talent, but without the practice the talent lies dormant. It is the practice that makes the talent live. It is the practice that gets rid of the imperfections, the mistakes, and the human failures. It is the practice that makes perfect, as the old saying goes. The good works of worship, prayer, and Christian action are the means by which Christ comes alive in us and by which we become fit for heaven. Through good works, practice makes the perfect Christian.

Because of this, Catholics believe that good works are necessary. They are not necessary to earn our way into heaven; they are necessary to equip us for heaven. They are not necessary to please God but to make us more like God. When we do something good, it actually accomplishes a real benefit in ourselves, in the world, and in eternity. It is through our good works that we work with God to become more like his Son, whose Spirit dwells within us. The good works are necessary because this process cannot be done in any other way. The good works are also necessary because by doing the good works we engage our will. We get involved. God has given us free will, and through our good works we use it to keep our side of the bargain.

All through the Scripture, the heroes of faith are refined and purified by their actions of obedience. Through their obedience, pain, and sacrifice they are brought to the perfection that God wills for them. The Gospel says it is the pure in heart who see God, and Jesus says in Matthew 5:48 that we are to be perfect as our Father in heaven is perfect. It is the life of faith that brings us to this purity and perfection. Somewhere along the line, that life of faith includes discipline, self-sacrifice, and suffering. Unless we take up our cross, Jesus says, we cannot be his disciple (cf. Luke 14:27). God plans not only to save us but to make us like his Son. This purification can only be done through God's power at work in us, but we have to cooperate with his power. Through our choices, through our good works, and especially through our suffering we work with God to grow toward wholeness.

If our good works and the difficult circumstances of life toughen and purify us, then these same disciplines help to weed out the sin in our lives. In other words, it is through our good works, discipline, and sufferings that we can counter the effects of sin. What do I mean by this? Let's say we have stolen a thousand dollars from a neighbor. If we go to the neighbor and confess what we've done, he may very well forgive us, but he will quite rightly still expect us to pay back the thousand bucks. Paying back the money will be a good deed, but it may cause us some pain. It takes a good deed and some suffering to counter the effects of the sin of stealing. It is the same in our relationship to God. God forgives the fact of our sin through Jesus Christ, but we are still responsible for the effects of our actions. We still have to deal with the fallout from sin. You might be forgiven for breaking a vase, but you still have to pick up the pieces.

Suffering is another way this process of purification can take place. Through suffering we identify with the painful consequences of sin and by accepting suffering we can counterbalance its deadly effect in our life. According to Hebrews, Jesus did this perfectly: "Although he was a Son, he learned obedience through what he suffered; and being made perfect he became the source of eternal salvation to all who obey him" (Hebrews 5:8-9). The same truth applies to us. In a wonderful passage at the beginning of Romans, Paul says how he is justified by faith, but he rejoices in suffering because it is suffering that brings him a deeper hope and identification with Christ (cf. Romans 5:1-5). Suffering helps to purify us, but in a mysterious and exciting way the Scripture says our suffering may also help other people spiritually. So St. Paul writes to the Colossians,

"Now I rejoice in my sufferings for your sake, and in my flesh I complete what is lacking in Christ's afflictions for the sake of his body, that is, the church" (Colossians 1:24). In some mysterious way our human good works, self-denial, and suffering help to complete the work of Christ in the world. Good works and suffering are not just the empty fruit of our faith. As Hebrews 11:1 points out, they are the substance of our faith. Furthermore, good works and suffering have value in themselves. They actually have a spiritually beneficial effect on others. They change the world and they change us. They don't save us, but they make our faith real and through God's grace they can help to transform and purify us.

Getting Saved

When I was five years old, I came home from church one Sunday night and told my mother I wanted to get saved. I must have heard something in the sermon that prompted my young heart to realize its need. I can remember kneeling down with my mother, telling Jesus I was sorry for my sins and asking him to come into my heart. This simple act of repentance and faith was the basis for my Christian life. I was told that I was now "born again" and that I was bound for heaven, and nothing could take away my salvation. Being "born again" or "receiving Jesus Christ as your personal Lord and Savior" is the bedrock of the Evangelical experience. This personal relationship with Jesus Christ is a valuable and important contribution to the whole Church — both Catholic and Evangelical. My acceptance of Jesus when I was five years old was a good thing, and part of our Evangelical teaching stressed that while my salvation was certain I still had to grow in the faith. I needed to learn more about the Bible. I needed to pray, go to church, and strive to obey the Lord's will for the rest of my life. In this way the whole Evangelical system properly encouraged a life in which faith was worked out in the person's life.

I was told that because of my simple profession of faith I was saved for all eternity. The Protestant view of justification gives the true impression that because of Jesus' work on the cross our salvation is accomplished for us. Different images are used for this. One of them is the judicial model, which says God the Almighty Judge sees that justice is accomplished on the cross and so does not hold us guilty any longer. This is a valuable and good insight, and from the eternal perspective it is true. In one sense our salvation and perfection *are* already accomplished in Christ, but it is also true that our salvation still needs to be "worked out in fear and trembling." Some forms of non-Catholic theology suggest that since our salvation is accomplished, there is nothing further we can do, and our status as children of God is written forever in the heavenly register.

Extreme views in this direction wind up taking away our free will and are contrary to the New Testament teaching. Grace may be at work in our life. We may have faith and choose to follow Christ. But if it is true that our free will may be used to choose Christ, it must also be true that the same free will may be used to deny Christ and turn away from him forever. The book of Hebrews, which tells us so much about the life of faith, also tells us that our salvation is not signed, sealed, and delivered for all eternity (cf. Hebrews 10:26, 36). Perseverance is needed if we are to finally enter the kingdom of God. Matthew 7:19 says trees that bear bad fruit will be thrown on the fire. Hebrews warns, "If we sin deliberately after receiving the knowledge of the truth, there no longer remains a sacrifice for sins, . . . For you have need of endurance, so that you may do the will of God and receive what is promised" (Hebrews 10:26, 36). Hebrews says not only that one may fall away from faith, but it may be impossible for such an individual to return: "It is impossible to restore again to repentance those who have once been enlightened, who have tasted the heavenly gift, and have become partakers of the Holy Spirit, . . . if they then commit apostasy, since they crucify the Son of God on their own account and hold him up to contempt" (Hebrews 6:4, 6). In verses 10 and 11 the writer of Hebrews stresses that the believer's faithful work is necessary for him to retain his salvation: "God is not so unjust as to overlook your work and the love which you showed for his sake in serving the saints, as you still do. And we desire each one of you to show the same earnestness in realizing the full assurance of hope until the end." St. Peter teaches the same thing: "Make every effort to supplement your faith with virtue. . . . Therefore, brethren, be the more zealous to confirm your call and election, for if you do this you will never fall; so there will be richly provided for you an entrance into the eternal kingdom of our Lord and Savior Jesus Christ" (2 Peter 1:5, 10).

God created us in his image. Part of this truth means that when he gave us the power to choose, he also gave each of us a tiny bit of his own power. We may choose to follow him to glory or we may choose to be separated from him forever. If we choose to open our lives to his grace, then we have a sure and certain hope of heaven. Furthermore, if we cooperate with God's grace, it gives us the power to be completely transformed. St. Paul sums up this confidence in 2 Corinthians 5:17-18 where he says, "Therefore, if any one is in Christ, he is a new creation; the old has passed away, behold, the new has come. All this is from God, who through Christ reconciled us to himself."

Some non-Catholic thinking says the new creation is a kind of legal fiction. It is said that God looks on our sinful condition and sees Jesus instead. Luther said our condition was like "a dunghill covered with snow." Catholics don't accept this view. We believe Jesus' death and Resurrection make the new creation a real possibility — not just a legal fiction. Not only are we justified, but we are actually given the power to become the sons of God (cf. Galatians 3:26, 4:6). The early Church Fathers put it in a striking way — they said in Jesus God became man so that man could become like God.[6] In other words, the real physical and historical event of the Incarnation enables real physical and historical people like you and me to become like God.

Through faith we are made just in God's eyes, but based on this fact Catholics believe we have the potential to actually become like Christ. This is not just something that will happen in heaven. We believe it can happen here and now. In St. John's first epistle he says the Christian is one who no longer sins. Is this really possible? The saints show us that it is. A saint is an ordinary person who has been totally transformed by grace. The saint has become all he was made to be through God's goodness. While Catholics recognize that this is hard work, we have also insisted from the earliest times that this is not something we can do on our own. St. Augustine said:

> Indeed we also work, but we are only collaborating with God who works, for his mercy has gone before us. It has gone before us so that we may be healed, and follows us so that once healed, we may be given life; it goes before us so that we may be called, and follows us so that we may be glorified; it goes before us so that we may live devoutly, and follows us so that we may always live with God: for without him we can do nothing.[7]

More Christianity fully affirms that we are saved through grace by faith, but it affirms more than that. The same grace

that saves us through faith also enables us to live a victorious
faith-full life. Furthermore, that grace which calls and saves us
is available for our day-to-day walk with God in floods of
blessing we can hardly imagine. This amazing grace is present
in the world to bring us into the abundant life that Christ
promised.

More Christianity affirms fully that we are saved by faith
in Jesus Christ, but "faith in Jesus Christ" also means a daily
life that is lived in his presence and power. By faith Christ
lives in me and through my life. Through faith in Christ I can
become a new Incarnation of Christ in the world. Because of
this amazing reality, what I say and do really matters. Because
of this kind of faith, real people matter. Real choices matter.
Real actions matter. If our decisions and actions matter, then
there is everything to play for. We may lose our soul to gain
the world, or we may lose the world and gain our soul. We
may forfeit everything through our sinful choices or we may
inherit all things through faith in God's promises. If we work
alongside God's grace, then we really can be healed. We really
can become whole. We really can make an eternal difference.
In Christ, our potential is enormous and the challenge is exciting. More Christianity accepts the challenge. It works daily
to move further up and further into God's amazing new life.
It builds on the foundation of our justification and cooperates
with God's grace to become more and more like Christ himself. The possibility of perfection spurs us on to greater and
greater devotion to the Lord who calls us to himself until, as
St. Benedict says, "We run on the path of God's commandments with an inexpressible delight of love."[8] This is a cause
for great enthusiasm and supernatural joy. Knowing the possibilities of healing and transformation that grace provides,
Thérèse of Lisieux encourages us to move forward with great

zeal, saying, "You cannot be half a saint. You must be a whole saint or no saint at all!"[9]

Furthermore, this possibility of total transformation is not only for us. It is for the Church and for the whole world. Jesus died to save not just my soul but to redeem the whole fallen creation. If the possibility really exists that I can be transformed into his likeness, then the possibility also exists that, through his power, the whole Church can continue to be transformed into his likeness. If I can be changed, that means the whole world can be changed. This is not simply a future reality in heaven. It means we can change ourselves and change the world right here and right now. As Christ's agents in the world we have the real power and responsibility to effect that transformation. This is why Christians are called to get involved in ministering to the sick, the poor, the uneducated, the downtrodden, and others who need the help of Jesus' followers. The good news is that through faith real change is possible. It only depends how much we respond to God's grace in our lives.

That real change, *that* required change, happens through the nitty-gritty of our real ordinary lives. More Christianity is glorious, complex, and majestic, but it is also humble, simple, and plain. It is the religion of the Incarnation where kings and shepherds meet, and where angels sing the praises of the One born in a stable. Our justification by grace through faith enables us to gaze up at the stars with hope while keeping our feet firmly on the ground. Our good works are the physical outworking of our faith, and our faith is the elevation and glory of our good works. Through the two together we get a glimpse of a God who reaches down to work within this physical realm. As he modeled the first man out of a lump of clay, so he is still getting his hands dirty granting us the gift of himself through our ordinary physical lives.

Chapter Four Endnotes

1. *L'Osservatore Romano*, November 24, 1999, p. v.
2. John Clarke, O.C.D. (tr.), *The Story of a Soul: The Autobiography of St. Thérèse of Lisieux*, Washington, D.C., ICS Publications, 1976, p. 277.
3. *L'Osservatore Romano*, November 24, 1999, p. v.
4. Ibid.
5. Henry Bettenson, *The Early Christian Fathers*, Oxford, Oxford University Press, 1969, p. 49.
6. Athanasius, *Oratio Il contra Arianos*, 70, *Patrologia graeca*, 26, 425 B-426 G.
7. Augustine, *De natura et gratia*, 31, *Patrologia latina*, 44, 264.
8. Abbot Parry (tr.), *The Rule of St. Benedict*, Leominster, Gracewing, 1990, p. 4.
9. John Clarke, O.C.D. (tr.), *General Correspondence, Vol. II*, Washington, D.C., ICS Publications, 1988, p. 1133.

Channels of Communication

I confess. What am I confessing to? I confess that I believe in miracles. I really do. I believe there is a supernatural realm and a physical realm and that the two realms are not such watertight compartments as some people think. Here's an example of a miracle that happened in our family. When my parents were a young married couple they were the leaders of a Christian youth club that met in a nearby town. One night they were driving home from the youth club down a country lane. I was asleep in the back of the station wagon along with my older brother and sister. My parents describe their horror as they came over the crest of a hill and saw a car coming in the opposite direction at a very high rate of speed.

Ahead, the road went through a deep cut with steep banks on both sides. There was no place for them to pull over and no room for the other car to get by. They knew when they went down into the next dip that the other car would hit them head-on. Sure enough, the car came over the next hill. They saw the shocked and terrified expression on the other driver's face as he saw them for the first time. They braced themselves for impact. Then suddenly they were going down the road safely as if nothing had happened. They turned to look behind them and saw the receding taillights of the speeding car. There was no explanation except that the physical laws that govern speeding cars had somehow been suspended. Who knows what the other driver made of the experience, but my parents were convinced that God had intervened in the usual physical world for their deliverance.

I wanted to begin this chapter with this true story of a miracle because it draws together two very different sorts of Christians who, despite their historic disagreements, actually have the same underlying religious perspective. Put simply, Catholics and Evangelicals may disagree about many things, but both believe in miracles. A belief in the supernatural element of religion is vital for both Evangelicals and Catholics. Both sides believe prayer changes things. Both sides believe their faith is grounded in the supernatural actions of God. Both groups believe miracles are possible today. In our age the big differences are not between Catholics and Protestants but between supernaturalists and naturalists, between those who believe in a revealed religion and those who believe in a relative religion. The gap is between those who believe mankind is a creation of God and those who believe God is a creation of mankind.

This underlying affinity between Evangelicals and Catholics was assessed by a famous Evangelical scholar, J. Gresham Machen. In the 1920s he had fought long, hard battles against the "progressive" element within his own church. In his book *Christianity and Liberalism* he admitted that a wide gulf existed between Evangelicals and Catholics, "but profound as it is, it seems almost trifling compared to the abyss which stands between us and many ministers of our own church."[1] A Catholic writer, the former Anglican bishop of London, Graham Leonard, sums it up:

There is a realignment between those on the one hand
who believe that the Christian gospel is revealed by God,
is to be heard and received and that its purpose is to enable men and women to obey God in love. On the other
hand are those who believe that it can and should be
modified and adapted to the cultural and intellectual at-
titudes and demands of successive generations and indeed originates in them.[2]

Both Evangelicals and Catholics believe God is at work in
the ordinary world through a personal interaction with real
people. Evangelicals believe in the power of prayer. Evangelicals
believe a person who is converted can really be transformed by
God's grace. They believe the Bible is supernaturally inspired
and that the Holy Spirit enables us, through the supernatural
gift of grace, to understand and preach the Gospel faithfully.
Catholics believe all these truths as well; it's just that Catholics
believe this supernatural working presence of God in the world
is even more pervasive and thoroughgoing.

In the first four chapters I tried to show how Catholics understand this indwelling, dynamic power of God to be working
not only invisibly through individuals but also visibly through
the actual historic Church. Just as God supernaturally inspired
people to write the Scriptures, then provided for the word's continued preservation and proclamation, so Catholics believe that
Jesus supernaturally founded a church built on the authority he
gave to Peter. We really believe that he has upheld, guided, and
guarded that Church down through the ages. The fact that the
Catholic Church is still going strong despite persecution from
without and corruption within is a sign of God's supernatural
support. We believe the whole Church "subsists" within the
Catholic Church, and that while God's hand of guidance and

protection is over all Christian people, if you want to identify the historic, universal Church in one particular place you can do so in the Catholic Church. The Church is more than an organization or a human institution. It is the physical, historical presence of Christ in the world today and for all time. Because the Church is God's physical way of working in the world, it is a pointer to the way God is constantly at work in our day-to-day lives.

Near the end of the last chapter I said that for Christians real people and real decisions matter. In the same way, by virtue of the Incarnation, we believe physical things matter. When Jesus was born of the Virgin Mary, we believe something stupendous happened. The Divine infiltrated the created order in a new and powerful way, and this event has altered the relationship between the invisible and the visible realms forever. When Jesus died on the cross, the great curtain in the temple, which divided the Holy of Holies from the Inner Court, was torn in two from top to bottom. From then on the curtain between the physical realm and the spiritual realm was also torn in two, and now because of Christ the tissue between the physical and the eternal is very thin indeed.

God entered the physical world through Jesus Christ, and we believe through the resurrected Christ that God is still active in and through the physical world. This physical way of working in the world we call "sacramental." The word "sacrament" is the Latin translation of the Greek word for "mystery." God's sacramental way of working in the world is a mystery. It's the subject of miracles, and like the birth of Jesus, this whole topic is surrounded with mystery, wonder, and love. In pondering how God works in the world we shall see how God continues to "get his hands dirty" by coming to us through the physical realm. In the sacraments God comes to us in working clothes. He is humble enough to stoop down and mingle with the physical. That he does so is a strange and awesome paradox. It is summed up in the words of a poet who says with wonder: "Here in dust and dirt — O here, the lilies of His love appear."[3]

As I discuss sacraments in this chapter I hope you will remember that I am not a theologian or Bible scholar. If you want to read theological treatises or Bible studies on the sacraments, there are plenty available. I am, however, an Evangelical whose faith has been fulfilled by becoming a Catholic. In my approach to the sacraments I will follow my theme of "more Christianity" and try to show that the Catholic sacraments do not contradict Evangelical experience. They are not something different but something more. In each of the sacraments God's grace is flowing to his people. Saving grace can flow within non-Catholic worship and practice, but within Catholicism this miraculous work of God in the world is recognized in all its fullness without the denials by which some Christians unwittingly limit their experience of the love of God. The other reason why I will be steering clear of theology and Bible study is that sacraments are extremely practical, and I think a practical consideration of what we actually *do* in our two different traditions is more enlightening than theorizing and yet more abstract thinking. My consideration of the sacraments will be more about experience than theory. Like miracles, I hope this discussion of the sacraments will reflect what a sacrament is: the meeting place of the supernatural and the natural, a ladder of grace from this world to the next.

Getting Started

As a former Evangelical teenager, I can remember the evangelists who used to preach at our summer camp. In the heat of August when our minds were more on the beach and our girl-

friends, we crammed into the preaching hall to hear long sermons exhorting us to repent of our sins and get saved. At the end
of the sermon the preacher would ask for the hymn "Just As I
Am" to be sung. He would ask us to bow our heads and close our
eyes, then he would begin the "altar call." We were asked to put
up our hands to invite Jesus into our hearts. Then, after a time of
getting people to raise their hands, we were asked to come forward to the front of the church. To step out and walk forward in
front of a group of teenagers required an awful lot of courage. It's
easy for some people to be cynical about some of the emotional
tactics the evangelists used. Nevertheless, there was something
simple, powerful, and elemental about that form of Christian
evangelization. To raise your hand and go forward was a kind of
initiation ceremony. Once it was done, you never forgot it.

To become a Christian in the early Church was an even
greater ordeal. In order to join the Church you had to profess
your faith and be baptized. The preparations for baptism could
sometimes take two or three years. Justin Martyr, who gave his
life for his faith in the year 165, describes the process in his day:
"I shall now explain our method of dedicating ourselves to God
after we have been created anew through Christ. . . . All who
accept and believe as true the things taught and said by us, and
who undertake to have the power to live accordingly are taught
to pray and entreat God, fasting, for the forgiveness of their
former sins, while we join in their prayer and fasting. Then we
bring them to a place where there is water, where they are regenerated in the same way as we were, for they then make their
ablution in the water in the name of God the Father and Lord
of all and of our Savior Jesus Christ and of the Holy Spirit."[4]
During that time those who wanted to be baptized had to go
through rigorous instruction, and their sponsors had to oversee
their progress not only in learning the faith but also in their

behavior. Finally, the night before Easter, the new converts would be received into the Church through the great ceremony of baptism. As they went down into the waters of baptism they identified with Christ's death. The new believers would be baptized naked to symbolize their being "born again." Then as they came out of the water they would be dressed in white robes and take their place with the rest of the Church members. Only then, as the sun was rising on Easter morning, would they receive communion for the first time.

The practice of the early Church was very strict. It wasn't enough to simply want to be a Christian. It wasn't enough to have had an emotional experience in which the person turned from his sin and accepted Christ. For the early Christians it wasn't enough to have spent three years under watchful discipline learning the truths of the Christian faith. There was more to it than that. Their mental experience of learning and their spiritual experience of conversion had to be combined with the physical experience of baptism. Baptism was not only the sign and seal of their inner faith. The physical action was actually the means by which God planted the seed of saving grace in their lives for the first time. Baptism was understood to be not just a physical action or a religious ritual. Instead it was an action that was at once physical, mental, and spiritual.

This is why, when Jesus said that we must be born again by water and the spirit (cf. John 3:5), the early Church understood him to be referring to baptism. The New Testament makes it clear that baptism is not only a sign of a person's new birth but is the action by which that person's faith is made real. When Peter is preaching at Pentecost, he says, "Repent, and be baptized every one of you in the name of Jesus Christ for the forgiveness of your sins; and you shall receive the gift of the Holy Spirit" (Acts 2:38). Similarly, St. Paul says to Titus that "he saved us, not because of deeds done by us in righteousness, but in virtue of his own mercy, by the washing of regeneration and renewal in the Holy Spirit, which he poured out upon us richly through Jesus Christ our Savior" (Titus 3:5-6). In the New Testament, baptism is always linked with faith, so St. Paul says to the Philippian jailer, "Believe in the Lord Jesus, and you will be saved, you and your household" (Acts 16:31), and immediately they were baptized.

I understood as an Evangelical that the vital thing was to repent and believe in the Lord Jesus Christ. This was the act of faith that was required to become a Christian. I can see that this is a vital component, but we were also taught that while baptism was good, it was not necessary for our salvation. In a sincere attempt to stress personal salvation and avoid the idea that salvation was automatic just by going through a ritual, we denied an important part of the Christian faith. This denial that baptism was necessary also implied that the body was unimportant and unnecessary. Irenaeus, writing around the year 160, states the necessity of baptism like this:

> As dry earth does not produce fruit unless it receives moisture; so we, who are at first "a dry tree" (Isa. 61:3) would never have yielded the fruit of life without the "willing rain" (Ps. 67.10) from above. For our bodies have received the unity which brings us to immortality, by means of the washing [of baptism]; our souls receive it by means of the Spirit. Thus both of these are needed, for together they advance man's progress towards the life of God.[5]

"More Christianity" says personal faith and baptism are *both* necessary. That's why within Catholicism every effort is made for a person to be baptized, but every effort is also made for that person to be instructed fully and eventually come to his or her own personal decision to follow Jesus Christ. The personal relationship with Jesus is important to Catholics too. The whole system of Catholic worship, doctrine, and devotional life is an attempt to nurture that relationship and bring it to fullness.

Evangelical Christians are wary of granting too much power to the sacrament of baptism because they fear the individual's responsibility to personally repent and turn to Christ might be compromised. It's important to remember that linked with baptism is Catholicism's understanding of salvation. When we say a person is regenerated by baptism or "saved" by baptism, we don't mean he is "saved" in quite the same sense that an Evangelical uses the term. A typical Evangelical means that when a person is saved, that person is totally redeemed and headed for heaven no matter what happens. A Catholic, on the other hand, always believes in the possibility that the person might reject the religion he was given. By his own failure or the failure of his family or Church he might never take up the gift that was given to him in baptism. Because there is always the possibility that a person may not persevere in the faith, baptism is seen as the supernatural start of the person's faith journey rather than a sign that the journey is already completed.

Because baptism is the start of the faith journey, Catholics and Christians of many other denominations baptize infants. We do this because the child of believing parents is considered to share in God's blessing. Peter proclaimed this truth on the day of Pentecost (cf. Acts 2:38-39), and it is a truth that Evangelicals recognize as well. In my Evangelical church we had a ceremony of infant dedication. In the service the Christian parents asked God to bless their child and offered the child to his service. This is a good and beautiful thing, and all of this is part of infant baptism too. However, baptizing the infant takes it further and admits that God wants to bless that child fully by giving him the gift of regeneration right from the beginning. As infant Jewish boys were ceremonially initiated through circumcision as infants (cf. Colossians 2:11), so the early Christians welcomed their children into the family of God by baptizing them from the earliest age. The family baptisms in the New Testament (cf. Acts 16:33) certainly included children. There is explicit reference to the baptism of infants from the second century in the Church, and it has been the custom of Christians since then.[6]

The gift of new life that is given at baptism is like a seed of grace. It has to grow and it has to be confirmed in the individual's life. Each Christian has to come to the point where he personally repents of his sins and turns to Christ. Evangelicals, of course, are strong on the personal element of faith. The story of my experience at Christian summer camp — along with many other experiences of personal evangelization — affirms the strength of the Evangelical movement in this area. Often the decision a teenager made at camp was the confirmation of the Christian teaching and grace he had already received at home and at his church. Because Catholics stress the sacraments it is sometimes thought that they do not stress personal conversion. However, the sacrament of confirmation is the Catholic's answer to such criticism. When Catholics are of a mature enough age, they are expected to go through a course of instruction that teaches them more about the faith. This instruction is also designed to bring them to a point of personal repentance and faith if they have never come to that point before. Usually this takes place at adolescence when a person has enough knowledge and self-consciousness to make a mature choice. That choice is sealed through the sacrament of confirmation when the bishop comes to the local church to hear each person affirm his or her faith in Christ publicly. Then the bishop lays hands on each person's head to complete and seal the individual's baptism.

Catholics believe their bishop is a successor of the apostles, and the idea that an apostle should lay his hands on the head of the already baptized so that the person might receive the fullness of the Holy Spirit is clear from the New Testament. In the Acts of the Apostles we are reminded: "Now when the apostles at Jerusalem heard that Samaria had received the word of God, they sent to them Peter and John, who came down and prayed for them that they might receive the Holy Spirit; for it had not yet fallen on any of them, but they had only been baptized in the name of the Lord Jesus. Then they laid their hands on them and they received the Holy Spirit" (Acts 8:14-17). The same thing happens when Paul visits some new Christians (cf. Acts 19:1-6). Catholics and some other denominations still maintain this biblical practice in the sacrament of confirmation. Here, I'm afraid, there is no question of "more Christianity." Most Evangelicals don't have confirmation at all, and yet it is one of the sacraments most easily shown in the New Testament.

Nevertheless, when the teenager goes forward in the Catholic Church to be confirmed, the public nature of his witness is very similar to the evangelist expecting us to walk forward at the evangelistic rally at summer camp. There is more to it in the Catholic experience, though. The person going forward for confirmation will have been through an extensive course of Christian instruction. Furthermore, the presence of the bishop indicates the fact that the individual's faith is intimately linked with belonging to the Church. The bishop is the head of the local Church and the link with the universal Church. He conducts this ceremony because confirmation is also the sacrament that seals the individual's full membership in the Church.

Within both the Evangelical system and the Catholic system things may go wrong. We try as hard as we can to bring up our children to know and love the Lord, and to come to their own personal trust in him. For me it was through weekly worship in church, Sunday school, vacation Bible school, summer camps, and youth weekends. For Catholics the same process of learning in the faith takes place through their own children's liturgy in church, Catholic schools, the first communion program, and confirmation preparation. If things sometimes go wrong and the faith doesn't "stick," that is a problem both traditions have to keep working on.

The third sacrament of initiation is the greatest sacrament of all — the Eucharist, or Lord's Supper. As this is an area of disagreement between Catholics and Evangelicals I will leave it until the next chapter. It is enough to say at this point that the Eucharist is not separate from baptism. In the Eucharist we "proclaim the Lord's death until he comes" (1 Corinthians 11:26) and in baptism we are "baptized into his death" (Romans 6:3). Both the Eucharist and baptism are part of our physical, mental, and spiritual participation in the death of Christ. This unity between baptism and the Eucharist has been seen from the earliest days in the Church. So St. Ambrose in the fourth century writes, "See where you are baptized, see where Baptism comes from, if not from the cross of Christ, from his death. There is the whole mystery: he died for you. In him you are redeemed, in him you are saved."[7]

Ransomed, Healed, Restored, Forgiven

We were certainly never told to go to our pastor for confession in our Evangelical church. There was plenty of teaching on sin and forgiveness, but we were assured that all we needed to do was confess our sins to God in our own prayers and we would be forgiven. As Christians we have direct access to the Father of all forgiveness. Like the father in the story of the Prodigal Son, God is waiting for our return and will always welcome us home with open arms. We were suspicious of the Catholic idea that to be forgiven one had to go to a priest. Wasn't it clear that only God could forgive sins and not another ordinary person?

Catholics also believe it is possible to go straight to God for forgiveness. However, there are certain verses in the New Testament that indicate that God's forgiveness comes to us more powerfully through those he appointed. Jesus was confronted with this same question. When he forgave sins, the Pharisees accused him of blasphemy, saying, "Who can forgive sins but God alone?" (Mark 2:7). By healing the sick Jesus claimed the power he was given by God to forgive sins on earth. In the Gospel of Matthew, just after Jesus heals someone and forgives the person's sins the crowds marvel that God had given "such authority to men" (Matthew 9:8). This implies that they thought forgiveness of sins and healing, through Jesus, might be delegated to other men as well. Catholics believe Jesus delegated that power to his apostles, and that even today Jesus Christ forgives sins and heals us in a powerful way through the ministry of the apostles' successors. In Matthew's Gospel he gives the apostles power to bind and loose until the end of the age (cf. Matthew 16:19, 18:18, 28:16-20). In John's Gospel he says to the apostles, "If you forgive the sins of any, they are forgiven; if you retain the sins of any, they are retained" (John 20:23).

Because he gave his apostles power to forgive sins until the end of the age we believe that same supernatural gift of healing and forgiveness exists within the ministry of the apostolic Church today. At first, Christians made public confession of their sins. This practice is mentioned in James 5:16. In the seventh century the practice of "confessing our sins to one another" was done by confessing in private to a priest, and that is still our practice today. I want to emphasize that we do not believe the priest forgives sins. It is always Christ himself who forgives us through the ministry of his Church. The priest listens to our sins and by God's grace he speaks for the whole Church and announces Christ's forgiveness to us. Catholics are concerned about Christ's call to personal conversion and one of the most moving, intimate, and powerful ways to embrace conversion is to go through the humbling experience of confessing our sins to a priest. Like confirmation, this is a biblical practice that Evangelicals don't maintain at all.

Nevertheless, when my father was very ill a couple of years ago, the family called the elders of his Evangelical Presbyterian Church. They gathered around his sickbed and asked if he had any sins to confess. After his confession the elders laid hands on him, prayed for his healing, and anointed him with oil. The service followed the simple, ancient pattern laid down in the letter of James. There it says, "Is any among you sick? Let him call for the elders of the church, and let them pray over him, anointing him with oil in the name of the Lord; and the prayer of faith will save the sick man, and the Lord will raise him up; and if he has committed sins, he will be forgiven. Therefore confess your sins to one another, and pray for one another, that you may be healed. The prayer of a righteous man has great power in its effects" (James 5:14-16). Within their Evangelical practice there was an echo of the full Catholic belief in the power of confession, and certainly within the Evangelical's stress on asking forgiveness for sin there is a realization that renewed forgiveness and restoration are necessary.

In the New Testament, healing is always linked with the forgiveness of sins. So in the Catholic Church the two sacraments of confession and anointing are linked together as the sacraments of healing. There are various names for these two sacraments. Sometimes confession is called "reconciliation" or "penance." Anointing of the sick is sometimes called "Extreme Unction" or "The Last Rites," since it used to be reserved until the person was actually dying. Many Evangelical churches practice anointing of the sick, and the Catholic Church does as well. In anointing, the priest comes to visit the person who is sick. He asks the individual to confess his sins and then lays hands on him, prays for healing, and anoints him with oil that is specially blessed for the purpose by the bishop of the diocese.

The fact that many Evangelical congregations practice anointing shows that there is a "sacramental mentality" in this one sacrament that is lacking in the others. When a non-Catholic Christian follows the New Testament command to anoint with oil and pray for healing, he may not actually say he believes in a sacrament, but his actions show that he does. He believes that through the combination of faith, prayer, and a physical action, God's grace will flow to the sick person and that, even if he is not physically healed, he will receive some great benefit. The fact that many Evangelicals practice anointing shows that they do have room for a wider "sacramental mentality."

If God can work through faith, prayer, and oil, does it make sense to deny that he also works through faith, prayer, and water in the case of baptism or through faith, prayer, bread, and wine in the case of the Eucharist? If God can work sacramentally through faith, prayer, and oil in anointing, can he not also work through faith, prayer, and our physical bodies when a bishop lays hands on a child to be confirmed or a man to be ordained, or when husband and wife love each other? Catholics believe God is working sacramentally in all these ways. We believe he chooses to pour his grace into our lives through these physical channels. Through prayer and faith we believe water is empowered to wash us inwardly. Bread and wine are transformed into Christ's body and blood to feed us. Oil is granted the power to be a vehicle of God's healing in our lives, and the hands of our elders become the transmitters of God's blessing, confirming our faith and empowering some of us for ministry.

Holy Orders

A friend of mine once said that I couldn't really understand his life because I wasn't in "holy orders." I said I didn't know much about "holy orders" but that being married couldn't be too different because married life was a matter of taking orders every day.

There are two other formal ways Catholics see God's grace flowing to us through physical channels. These sacraments are called the sacraments of service because they give us special grace to serve others with our lives. When a man is ordained as a priest, he is given special power by God to serve the Church and the world in a unique way. Similarly, when a man and woman marry, they are given special grace by God to serve each other and the whole community with their shared life and love.

Once again, almost all Christian denominations recognize the sacredness of both marriage and the Christian ministry. Most Christians wish to be married in church, and when a man is called to a specific ministry in the Church almost all denominations recognize that calling with some special service of commissioning or ordination. Although non-Catholics do not call them sacraments, still they consecrate their marriages and their chosen ministers through a ritual of recognition. Catholics understand marriage and ordination in the same way, but we take things further.

When a man and woman marry, the Catholic Church understands that it is more than a civil ceremony. When they come to church to be married, Catholics believe more is taking place than simply asking God to bless the bridegroom and bride. From the time of Adam and Eve onward, the Jews and then the Christians have had a complex and beautiful theology of marriage. A man was to leave his mother and father and cleave to his wife and they are to be one flesh (cf. Genesis 2:24, Matthew 19:5-6, and Ephesians 5:31). This physical action is a sign of the deep union that exists between Christ and his Church (cf. Ephesians 5:32). Like many other Christians, Catholics understand marriage as an especially sacred and beautiful covenant. However, while many Christians see that marriage reflects the union between Christ and his Church, Catholics believe a sacred Christian marriage actually helps to make us more unified not only with one another but also with Christ himself. This is what we mean when we say a sacrament "effects what it signifies."

In the sacraments we find that faith, prayer, and the physical dimension come together to open a window of grace into our lives. For the sake of understanding, it could be broken down into three elements. Through faith our souls are transformed. Through prayer our minds are transformed. Through the physical matter of the sacrament our bodies are transformed. For a sacrament to be effective, all three need to be present and interact together. In fact, the sacrament works as a unity. The physical, mental, and spiritual dimensions cannot be separated out any more than harmony, melody, and rhythm can be separated out from the performance of a piece of music. In the sacrament of marriage, this belief is most vivid because the action involved is the most physical of all actions.

The physical aspect of the sacrament of marriage is not the exchange of rings or the signing of a marriage certificate. The physical part of marriage takes place in the marriage bed, after the religious ceremony. It is in the act of making love that a couple experience the fullness of the sacrament of marriage. This most physical of sacraments actually sheds light on the physicalness of all the sacraments. What we believe is an astounding and beautiful doctrine. We believe that through the ordinary human and basely physical act of a man and woman coming together, God is pouring his own love, forgiveness, and grace into their lives. As they experience the depth and tenderness of love together, they also have the opportunity to know the depth and tenderness of God's love. If this is true, it becomes clear why any sexual sin is so twisted — it is because one of the most precious, intimate, and spiritually powerful opportunities has been trampled in the mud.

When a man is called to minister in the Church, a similar kind of self-giving is required. The Catholic Church is often blamed for insisting on celibacy for priests, but the ideal of a priest giving his entire life to his ministry and his people runs parallel to the self-giving required in marriage. It is an ideal upheld by St. Paul himself (cf. 1 Corinthians 7:32). There is also a long tradition of priests being married, and for priests to remain unmarried is only a discipline of the Church — not a doctrine that cannot be changed. Nevertheless, the special ideals that the Catholic Church has set out for ministers helps to lift their calling to the high realm of a sacrament.

In his life of ministry, the priest finds that the channels of grace are open to him, just as they are for a married couple within marriage. Of course priests and married people often fail to live up to the ideal, but one doesn't get rid of the ideal because no one reaches it. If we did that, there would be no law nor a need for mercy. When the Church ordains a man to be a priest, she opens those channels of grace, and through faith, prayer, and the physical laying on of hands, the priest is given the power to consecrate the bread and wine at communion, pronounce God's blessing and absolution for his people, and give himself totally to the service of Christ. Through this consecration the priest is given his own way to be drawn into that intimate union with Christ to which each one of us is called. The sacraments are a beautiful wedding gift that Christ has given his bride, the Church. The sacraments are meant to bring us spiritual pleasure because through the physical world we experience the most ordinary of pleasures. In *The Screwtape Letters*, C. S. Lewis expresses the devil's rage at the fact that God has granted us ordinary and physical pleasure. "He's vulgar, Wormwood. He has a bourgeois mind. He has filled his world full of pleasures. There are things for humans to do all day long without His minding in the least — sleeping, washing, eating, drinking, making love, playing, praying, working. Everything has to be twisted before it's any use to us."[8] Through the sacraments this ordinary pleasure is lifted up and transformed so that through the most physical materials of bread, oil, wine, and water, as well as physical touch, God actually enters our lives and changes us.

The fact of this transformation through the physical should come as no surprise to us. We take it for granted every day that we are transformed inwardly by what we do outwardly. The exercise we take affects us mentally and spiritually. Our posture and facial expression affect the way we feel and think. The things we watch on television or read change us. Our actions change us. The food we eat changes us. Throughout life in a multitude of ways the physical things we do transform us both outwardly and inwardly. The sacraments are simply God's ways of infusing his grace through these already natural happenings. That he comes to us through ordinary pleasures both humbles and exalts us. It humbles us because the small pleasures and pains are reminders of our earthiness, our creatureliness, our dependence on our Creator. His coming through the ordinary exalts us because his presence lifts the ordinary to heaven. The one who is born in a stable transforms not only that stable but every stable. The one who lay in a manger full of hay makes every blade of hay in every manger surge with uncreated light. From that moment every ox, every ass, and every other creature is touched by that same light. Because God himself chose to put on our mortal flesh, every man is as humble as a peasant and as royal as a prince. As humble as a peasant because Christ is a prince; as royal as a prince because he makes us like himself.

It is therefore a sad waste of a great and beautiful gift when some Christians deny the grace that God wishes to pour into their lives through ordinary physical things. Some Christians insist on saying that the sacraments do nothing, that they are mere signs or symbols — no more than reminders of what God does for us. Despite the denials, the wonderful thing is that the vast majority of Christians do still practice most of the sacraments. Almost all Christians baptize and have some form of communion service. Almost all have ordination, Christian marriage ceremonies, and have provision for anointing. Many practice confession and many have the rite of confirmation. I believe God wishes to pour his grace through all these forms of Christian worship if we will let him. The *Catechism of the Catholic Church* (quoting Vatican II) also recognizes that grace flows through the non-Catholic denominations.

"Furthermore, many elements of sanctification and of truth" are found outside the visible confines of the Catholic Church: "the written Word of God; the life of grace; faith, hope, and charity, with the other interior gifts of the Holy Spirit, as well as visible elements." Christ's Spirit uses these Churches . . . as means of salvation, whose power derives from the fullness of grace and truth that Christ has entrusted to the Catholic Church. All these blessings come from Christ and lead to him, and are in themselves calls to "Catholic unity."[9]

Once again, the question is not one of denying all the good things within the non-Catholic traditions but of being open to receive more. Non-Catholics denied the efficacy of the sacraments because they wished to avoid superstition and salvation by ritualism. But in denying the truth that God works through the physical sacraments, they were in danger of closing off the most effective channel of grace that God could give — one that ministered to the whole person, body, mind, and spirit. It is this narrowing of vision that only hurts the one who is doing the denying. Like the dwarfs in Narnia, they might have had a sumptuous feast but because of their suspicion they were left tasting exactly what they thought they were eating — straw.[10]

In this area more than any other, the fire of God's love burns within the heart of ordinary life. Here in the sacraments Christ works with us to redeem our whole selves. The waters of baptism cleanse, revive, and quench the thirst of our wilderness hearts. The bread and wine of his love permeate deep into every cell of our bodies. The oil of his anointing penetrates to each crevice and corner of our mind and heart. The blessing of his hands on our heads shatters the darkness and embraces us in his eternal acceptance and love. Through the mighty sacraments of the Church we are caught up in the physical glory of his work in the world. Through the humble sacraments of the Church we are brought down to our own dust and simplicity. It is through this means that we are called to work with him to redeem and embrace the whole world. Through the sacraments the physical world is transformed. The sacraments help us affirm with God that everything he made was very good (cf. Genesis 1:31). As St. Paul claims: "All things are yours, . . . and you are Christ's; and Christ is God's" (1 Corinthians 3:21, 23).

The World Is Charged with the Grandeur of God

Because God took flesh in Jesus Christ we believe the whole physical world is good. It is twisted by selfishness and false desire, but it is part of the work of Christ to straighten out the twists and restore the physical realm to its original role of declaring the glory of God (cf. Psalm 19:1). The sacraments of the Church are the formal ways we identify with this action and recognize God's grace coming to us through the physical. However, there are other aspects to Catholic faith and practice that are also very physical. We decorate our altars and churches with flowers. We like stained-glass windows as well as Christian art, architecture, and music. In our worship we kneel to pray, we cross ourselves, sprinkle holy water on the people, and use incense as a symbol of our prayers rising to heaven. I will have more to say about our use of images in worship in a later chapter, but it is enough to say here that the reason we use images in worship is our feeling that if Christ himself took physical form, we are pleased to use physical images of his goodness in our worship of him.

The Catholic faith is not only physical in these ways. There is something whole and complete about Catholicism that is lacking in some other expressions of the Christian faith. Catholicism has a way of sanctifying time. We not only believe physical things are holy and good, but we also believe time is given to us by God. While we believe physical things and time are holy and good, we recognize that they, like all of creation, have suffered from the fall and need to be redeemed. So it is through our worship and our sacraments that we extend God's saving love to the physical realm and seek to redeem all things and bring all things into the saving embrace of Christ. This applies to time as well. St. Paul said that Christ came into the world "when the time had fully come" (Galatians 4:4). We believe that through time we are saved, and that through our faith, our prayer, and our sacramental life we are able to redeem the time.

The way we redeem the time is through the discipline of our worship. Seeing that God created the world in six days and rested on the seventh, we — like most other Christians — observe the commandment to keep holy the Sabbath day. The best way to keep the Sabbath holy is to worship God on that day. It is the Sabbath principle that consecrates our time and makes every day of the week special. Furthermore, through the regular, rhythmic observation of the cycle of time and worship, all time through the week becomes holy. Each week is set in a season of the year, so Catholics also observe an ancient annual cycle of redemption. The cycle begins in the autumn each year with the season of Advent — four weeks that look forward to the annual celebration of Christ's birth at Christmas. After the Christmas celebrations comes the Epiphany, which is the commemoration of the arrival of the Wise Men to worship the Lord. The Epiphany season is followed by Lent — forty days of fasting that lead to the great spring celebration of Holy Week and Easter. The summer months commemorate the ascension of the Lord, the coming of the Holy Spirit at Pentecost, and the life of the Church through time until we come full cycle back to Advent. Punctuated in this annual cycle are celebration days of a whole range of saints who have served the Church down through the ages.

This physical sense of our Christian life is repeated through an annual cycle that, like the natural cycle, has both repetition and variety. If time is sanctified through this annual cycle, it is also sanctified by the whole sacramental program. At each stage of life there is a sacrament through which God's grace flows into our lives, strengthening us for the passage of time and the difficult transition of that stage of life. So in infancy we are baptized into the body of Christ, and enter our pilgrim journey. At the age of seven most Catholic children receive instruction for their first confession. They then begin to receive Holy Communion. Around the age of fourteen, children are encouraged to learn more about their faith and renew their commitment to Christ. As we enter adulthood the sacrament of marriage or of holy orders can seal our calling and help us to pursue a consecrated life dedicated to our faith within our ordinary world. As we journey on through life we come back time and again to confession to ask God for new forgiveness and renewed strength to walk in his way. We also come to communion on a daily basis to receive him into our life, and in times of illness we receive anointing for healing and God's blessing. At death the priest brings us our final communion and anoints us for our journey.

Through the sacraments Catholics see God blessing the whole of the created order. Through a sacramental mentality we should also see our own responsibility in the work of redemption. God has granted the human race the honor and duty to look after the physical realm — to use it and not to abuse it. With a sacramental mentality each person becomes sacred, each moment becomes sacred, and each physical object becomes sacred. No one is to be abused because he or she is a window to heaven and channel for grace. Nothing in all creation is to be denied or abused or discarded, for all things have their place and each thing has the honor for which it was created. In the sacramental vision, each and every person, place, and time has its own unique voice with which it praises God in its own way.

It is the sacramental life that brings each of us to participate in that fullness that Christ, by his mighty Incarnation, has destined for the whole world.

Chapter Five Endnotes

1. Cited in Thomas Rausch, *Catholics and Evangelicals: Do They Share a Common Future?*, Downers Grove, Ill., InterVarsity Press, 2000, p. 3.

2. Dwight Longenecker (ed.), *The Path to Rome: Modern Journeys to the Catholic Church*, Leominster, Gracewing, 1999, pp. 19-20.

3. Henry Vaughn, "The Revival," in *Faber Book of Religious Verse*, Helen Gardiner (ed.), London, Faber and Faber, 1972, p. 182.

4. Henry Bettenson, *The Early Christian Fathers*, Oxford, Oxford University Press, 1969, p. 61.

5. Ibid., p. 94.

6. Cf. *Catechism of the Catholic Church*, London, Geoffrey Chapman, 1995, para. 1252 (hereafter CCC).

7. Ibid., para. 1225.

8. C. S. Lewis, *The Screwtape Letters*, London, Geoffrey Bles, 1942, p. 112.

9. CCC, para. 819.

10. C. S. Lewis, *The Last Battle*, London, Fontana, 1985, p. 141.

The Real Presence

In our Bible church, on the first Sunday of the month, after the main worship service was over, the pastor and about a dozen deacons would go to the front of the church. The table in front of the pulpit was covered with a crisp white tablecloth. Two piles of round interlocking trays were placed on the table. The trays contained broken pieces of unleavened bread that resembled the sort of biscuits you might eat with cheese. The other trays held tiny glasses filled with grape juice. The pastor and deacons sat with their backs to us; the pastor read various passages of Scripture to help us meditate on the death of Jesus. Then the deacons would distribute the bread and grape juice and we would all hold the bread and grape juice until everyone had received. Then after a pause for silence we would eat together at the same moment. The service was treated with solemnity and dignity. Furthermore, the formality of it along with the repeated words and actions turned the worship into a simple form of liturgy.

As I moved through the Anglican Church to become a Catholic, I have often remembered that simple Bible-based communion service. I was impressed with the fact that even in the most nonliturgical church communities, there seems to be an instinct to turn the Eucharist into a ritual. With set roles for each person to play, with a set form, traditional words, and significant actions, the pastor and twelve deacons reenacted the Last Supper. By participating, we felt as if we were there in the Upper Room with Jesus and his apostles. This is the way liturgy works. The word "liturgy" means "work of the people," and I think it is a beautiful thing that even there in an independent Bible church God's people were working out their worship by "doing liturgy." By reenacting the Last Supper, we were doing more than simply remembering it together. In a way, we were reliving it together. We were entering into the saving events of Jesus' last week on earth. As a result, what we experienced there was a simple and faithful memorial of the death and Resurrection of Jesus.

While I can see all of this significance and meaning within that simple communion service, I can never remember anyone teaching us that this is what we were doing. In fact, I doubt if the pastor and deacons themselves saw that they were reenacting the Last Supper. If we were taught anything at all about the communion service, it was that the communion service was an optional extra. It took place after the main worship only once a month. Somewhere along the line I was also told what the communion service meant and did not mean, and the emphasis was always on what it did *not* mean. Our communion service was a "commemoration of our Lord's death until he comes again." Despite the solemnity of the service, we were clear that the bread was still bread, and the grape juice was still grape juice. Now that I'm a Catholic, I can recognize that this memorial service was good as far as it went; but the New Testament and the tradition of the early Church actually go further than that.

I believe in this area, perhaps more than any other, the profound gap between Evangelical and Catholic thinking appears. There is also a disturbing inconsistency within Evangelical thought itself. On the one hand Evangelicals, like Catholics, believe in the supernatural. God is at work in the world in a powerful way, but when it comes to Holy Communion that miraculous power is ruled out. The denial of God's miraculous work through communion is not even consistent with the founders of the Reformation. Martin Luther insisted that Christ is really present in the Eucharist. In fact, he execrated the Zwinglians, who taught that Christ is only spiritually present. "Yours is a different Spirit," Luther said to Zwingli at their famous Marburg colloquy. An Evangelical friend of mine laments, "There now prevails in Evangelicalism a 'mere symbolic' view that goes even beyond Zwingli's view in its denial of the supernatural. Today's Evangelicals are taught that communion is just an object lesson, a picture. I know of well-respected Evangelical missionaries who de-emphasize communion, and even defer giving it to new converts for fear that they'll be misled into some magical view of the ritual." My friend goes on, "The Evangelical version of *Mere Christianity* has deconstructed and minimized the Eucharist, denied its supernatural quality, to a 'mere' status well below the Reformation era's lowest common denominator. Is this all God wants us to have? It is 'mere' indeed."

The way through this impasse is not for Catholics to bang Evangelicals over the head with what they perceive as their errors. I believe most Evangelicals deny the supernatural dimension of the Eucharist through an inherited misunderstanding of the Catholic position combined with a concession to the spirit of the age that is skeptical of anything supernatural. The way forward is to remind Evangelicals that they do actually believe in the supernatural; they do believe God is at work in the world in wonderful ways. The other way forward is to express what Catholics really believe in this matter. Evangelicals may still disagree, but at least they will disagree with what Catholics really

believe rather than what they think Catholics believe. Therefore, in this chapter I want to discuss the biblical background
for the Eucharist, but I will also try to show how "more Christianity" opens the door to a rich and full understanding of the
Eucharist, an understanding of the Eucharist that is profound
and awesome — that takes each one of us to the very threshold
of heaven where we can be lost in wonder, love, and praise.

Transposition

Throughout his writings C. S. Lewis meditates on the experience of beauty and how it produces a sensation of joy within
us. What Lewis calls "joy" is a transcendent experience that
rumbles through the physical world hinting of some greater reality. Lewis says, "The books or the music in which we thought
the beauty was located will betray us if we trust to them; it was
not *in* them, it only came *through* them. . . . They are not the
thing itself. They are only the scent of a flower we have not
found, the echo of a tune we have not heard, news from a country we have never yet visited."[1] Because we are locked in time
and space, it is easy to think our physical world is more real
than that other country that is glimpsed for a moment within
our experience of joy. Because we know this physical world with
our five senses, we conclude that the other world is vague, insubstantial, and unreal.

Lewis stands our perception on its head. He tells us that the
spiritual realm is more real, not less real, than this realm. We
think of the spiritual realm as insubstantial, ethereal, and vague.
In fact, "it is the present life which is the diminution, the symbol, the etiolated, the substitute. If flesh and blood cannot inherit the kingdom, that is not because they are too solid, too
gross, too 'illustrious with being,' but because they are too 'flimsy,
too transitory, too phantasmal.' "[2] And yet, as a candle flame

hints of the sun, it is through this physical realm that we creatures can best sense that solid, real, and eternal world beyond. Through art, through love, through physical pleasure and pain, through the beauty of nature and the exquisite moments of music we get glimpses of a distant country and echoes of a deeper music.

Physical things may be hints and guesses of a deeper reality, but Lewis takes it further than that. In his essay "Transposition" he suggests that the physical things are more than snapshots from a land we've never visited. He says that through our experience of "joy" the physical objects that point to the eternal can actually carry a quality of eternity within them. In other words, the physical realities are profoundly linked with the spiritual realities. A painting of a landscape with a brilliant morning sun is itself a part of that landscape because it exists in the same world where such a landscape exists. The sun in the picture has a measure of true reality because it can only be seen and understood by the light of the real sun. There is therefore a real and vital connection between the painting and the physical world. In the same way, Lewis says the things that cause that mysterious joy to spring up in our heart have a vital connection with the real but unseen world. Our participation in the beauty of that physical object or experience therefore connects us with the eternal. At that point what was merely a symbol becomes something more. "It is a sign, but also something more than a sign: and only a sign because it is also more than a sign, because in it the thing signified is really in a certain mode present. If I had to name the relation I should call it not symbolical but sacramental."[3]

Because the physical world itself is taken up and suffused with a new reality, when we experience that transcendent joy in the face of overwhelming beauty, pain, or pleasure, we are actually touching the hem of eternity's garment through the physical world. Because the physical object is transformed, as we listen to the concerto, look at the picture, or kiss the girl, we partake in the eternal reality as well. However, we desire more than simply good feelings about beautiful things. We also desire more than beautiful thoughts about the meaning of beautiful things. Lewis says, "We do not want merely to *see* beauty, though God knows, even that is bounty enough. We want something else that can hardly be put into words — to be united with the beauty we see, to pass into it, to receive it into ourselves, to bathe in it, to become part of it."[4] What if there could be even more than that? What if there is an objective, reliable, and true way for us to contact the eternal through the physical world each day?

Lewis's ideas about the transposition of the physical by the spiritual points to a good description of the Eucharist. If Lewis was right that physical things can be our connecting points with the spiritual realm, then the sacraments are the specific and powerful ways for this transposition to happen within our Christian life. Through the sacraments, but especially through the Eucharist, Jesus steps through the veil between the spiritual realm and the physical. The veil that he steps through is the veil of material things. For the Christian, matter matters. Modern physics has given us a new vocabulary for the material world. These days when we think of "matter," we think in terms of molecules, atoms, and scientific definitions. An older term for matter is the matter of our own bodies: that is, flesh and blood. Flesh and blood is as physical as it gets, and it is through flesh and blood that God has seen fit to come to us. It is the sheer ordinary physicalness of flesh and blood that both hides Christ from us and reveals him to us. Within the Scriptures, flesh and blood are the mysterious contact points between earth and heaven.

God coming to us through flesh and blood was not a sudden new idea at the Incarnation. From the beginning it is through flesh and blood — through the physical — that God came down to establish peace with mankind.

Animal Sacrifices

For a modern person one of the most confusing and dismaying aspects to primitive religion is the virtually universal practice of sacrifice. From Africans to Aztecs and from India to Ireland, the primitive peoples killed children, maidens, warriors, enemies, and animals in ritual sacrifice. In an agrarian culture it's easy to understand that to sacrifice a sheep or goat is to give the god something valuable. But there was more to it than that. People were also sacrificed. What kind of a mindset could put up with such bloodshed? Were ancient people simply bloodthirsty barbarians who liked the squeals of death and the spurting of blood? Was their religion really just some kind of cruel and mindless sport?

Many of the cultures that practiced blood sacrifice were also very sophisticated. They had extravagant mythologies, fantastic architecture, refined arts and crafts, literature, music, and a high level of political, economic, and cultural sophistication. What did they think was happening when they slaughtered thousands of their fellow humans, their own children, or herds of animals as part of their religion? The ancient peoples believed "the life of the flesh is in the blood" (Leviticus 17:11), so to shed blood was to release the life force. I think the ancient pagans also believed something else about their sacrifices. If the life or spirit of the flesh was in the blood, then to kill a person was to tear apart their flesh and blood and break the bond between the lifeblood (the spiritual part of them) and their flesh (the material part of them).

Therefore what the ancients were doing in their blood sacrifices had a metaphysical motive. They were separating the spirit from the flesh, the unseen from the seen, the spiritual from the material. If you prefer, they were tearing apart the veil of matter, and by this action the impenetrable veil between the worlds was opened. As the veil between the worlds was opened, the sacrificial victim could go to the gods; but the way was also open for the blessing of the gods to flow into the physical world. When the worshipers ate the meat of the sacrifice, they were taking into themselves the blessing from the other world that came through the torn veil.

This gruesomely logical mindset is very much the context of the Old Testament. The terrible story in Genesis 22, in which God asks Abraham to sacrifice his son Isaac, shows a development in religious understanding. Abraham must have thought the sacrifice of his son was nothing unusual, but God was making it clear that human sacrifices were abhorrent. Abraham didn't have to indulge in such horrible magic. God himself would provide the sacrifice. A ram caught in a thicket was substituted for the boy Isaac and a new principle was established that for the ritualistic opening of heaven, God would take the initiative, and an animal could take the place of a condemned human. With the shedding of an animal's blood, the same effect of the material world being torn open could be effected. Divine blessings could still flow, and the humans could make contact with the spiritual world.

Abraham lived in a world where a blood sacrifice was expected, but there is a mysterious hint in Genesis, where Melchizedek, the "king of Salem . . . [and] priest of God Most High" (Genesis 14:18), honors Abraham with an offering not of flesh and blood but of bread and wine. The first Christians saw Melchizedek's gift as a prophecy of the final step away from an offering of flesh and blood to a sacrifice of praise using bread and wine.

The shedding of blood had a fresh significance at the Passover. On the night of their delivery from slavery, God told the Hebrews to kill a young lamb. The blood of this lamb was to be put on their doorposts and lintels. The conflation of the two symbols (blood and a door) was a reminder that the shedding of blood opened a door into the unseen realm. That night the angel of death from the "other side" came into their world and destroyed the firstborn, but the way was also open for the Israelites to be saved and delivered from slavery by the supernatural intervention of their God.

As part of their salvation, the Jews were instructed to eat the meat of the slaughtered lamb with unleavened bread and prepare for their journey to the Promised Land. The Passover lamb was also known as the "Lamb of God." Like the ram that took the place of Isaac when Abraham went to sacrifice him, the lamb took the punishment of sin on itself for the people. The lamb — like Abraham's ram — died so that the angel of death would spare the oldest son in the family. When the people ate the lamb and bread, they were accepting the lamb's sacrifice. In their eating the meat from the lamb, the lamb's life and death became a part of them. Because the lamb died, they could live, and in a way this became literally true as they ate the meat — the flesh of the lamb.

When they were in the desert and Moses went up Mount Sinai, he received the law from God, but he also received detailed instructions for the worship system of the Hebrew people. The priests were instructed to make several different types of offerings. They offered grain or animals to God in thanksgiving and for the forgiveness of sins. After a sacrificial animal was killed, part of it was burned on an altar. When the smoke went up, the Bible says God was pleased, and sent down his blessing (cf. Leviticus 9:22-24). What was hinted at with Abraham and at the Passover now became specific. The sacrifices opened the way to heaven, but now the sacrificed animal was more than a practical substitute for human victims. The sacrifice now had a deeper meaning. The animal's death was an atonement for the sins of the people. The final part of the sacrifice was that the priests were required to eat the bread made from the grain and the meat from the sacrificed animal. As they ate the flesh and bread they accepted the life of the sacrifice and claimed the forgiveness that was won for them. In addition, when they ate the bread they themselves were made holy (cf. Leviticus 6:16-18, 10:12-17).

During the time of Jesus, the Jewish sacrificial system had been restored in the new temple that King Herod had built. There priests offered daily sacrifices for the forgiveness of sins, and the climax of this sacrificial system was the solemn celebration of the Passover feast each spring. Every year the Passover lamb would be sacrificed according to the proper rituals, and the people would share the sacred meal — eating the lamb and the bread and drinking the wine. As they did they relived the first Passover, bringing it alive in the present moment. By eating the sacred meal they expressed their unity with one another and with the God who had bound them in a sacred covenant by the shedding of blood.

We should remember that the first Christians were Jews. The Jewish sacrificial system provided the rich background for them to understand who Jesus was and what his death accomplished. This same Jewish sacrificial system provides the background for the early Church's understanding of the Eucharist, and it is from this early New Testament Church that the Catholic understanding of the Eucharist originated. To see how this developed we need to know how the sacrificial system fits in with Jesus. What did Jesus say and do with this ancient Jewish system of worship, and what did he pass on to his apostles? Did he establish a system of worship for the early Church? Did he give his flesh and blood for us to eat? If so, what did he mean by that, and how does the Church celebrate his teaching and his commands?

'This Is My Body'

There is a marvelous hymn by W. Chatterton Dix that sings to Jesus: "Thou within the veil has entered, robed in flesh the Great High Priest."[5] With this poetry the hymnist is alluding to the great curtain in the temple that was torn from top to bottom at the death of Jesus (cf. Mark 15:38). Christ's death tore the curtain between God and mankind, but it also broke through the permanent barrier between heaven and earth, between the physical and the spiritual realms. Given the Old Testament emphasis on blood sacrifice, it is very important to see what Jesus says about flesh and blood.

Jesus said he came to fulfill the law and the prophets (cf. Matthew 5:17). In other words, everything in the Old Testament was a pointer to him. The most powerful and moving way Jesus fulfilled all the law and the prophets was simply by being born. At that point the law and the prophets "became flesh and dwelt among us" (John 1:14). In other words, by taking flesh God gathered the whole world of matter to himself. When C. S. Lewis talks of the eternal penetrating the physical world and transforming it from the inside out, he is also describing what happened in a mighty way in the Incarnation: "In the Incarnation, God the Son takes the body and human soul of Jesus, and, through that, the whole environment of nature ... into his own being so that 'He came down from heaven' can almost be transposed into 'Heaven drew earth up into it.' "[6] Because of the Incarnation, the physical is taken up into the spiritual and actually given a new dimension of being. In this process the physical is not destroyed but fulfilled. The lesser thing becomes all that it can be. The black-and-white landscape drawing is subsumed by the real landscape of mountains, forests, and lakes. So the early Church Fathers spoke of mankind being "taken up into the Godhead" through the Incarnation, death, and Resurrection of Christ.

Incarnation literally means "enfleshment." It's no mistake and no coincidence that from the very beginning with Abel — the son of Adam and Eve — God demanded a sacrifice of flesh and blood. Through the sacrificial system God met his people through the tearing apart of flesh and blood. All of the old pagan meanings about sacrifice being a release of the lifeblood and tearing down the barrier between the physical and spiritual worlds were true in a crude way, but in the history of the Jews God was drawing mankind to an even more profound and beautiful truth. God meeting his people through the mystery of flesh and blood was a prophetic pointer to the amazing fact of the Incarnation. Every time the blood and flesh of a lamb was offered it was a pointer to the God who would one day offer himself to us in flesh and blood. When Jesus was born in Bethlehem, taking on flesh and blood, the whole sacrificial system was fulfilled in a way no one could have imagined. When Abraham had prophesied so long ago that God himself would provide the sacrifice (cf. Genesis 22:8), the prophecy was fulfilled at Bethlehem.

Now here's another curious point: In the Old Testament the sacrifice of flesh was always linked with a sacrifice of bread. Melchizedek made an offering of bread and wine. In the Passover meal the flesh of the lamb was eaten along with unleavened bread. In the wilderness the Israelites were given both miraculous flesh and bread to eat called manna; and in the sacrificial system the grain offerings were just as important in their way as the flesh offerings. If all the flesh offerings were fulfilled when Jesus took human flesh at Bethlehem, it is also true that all the bread offerings were fulfilled. It is no coincidence that the name "Bethlehem" actually means "house of bread," and that Jesus calls himself the "bread of life" (John 6:35).

Jesus' flesh-and-blood human life becomes the fulfillment of all the sacrifices the world had seen. In their own dark and limited way, even the horrific pagan sacrifices pointed to him. Most of all, the refined and complex system of sacrifice in the Old Testament was fulfilled in him. The most striking first witness to this comes from John the Baptist. As soon as he sees Jesus, John the Baptist cries out: "Behold, the Lamb of God, who takes away the sin of the world!" (John 1:29). John's Jewish hearers would have known exactly what he was talking about. The Lamb of God was the Passover Lamb. But not only was he the Passover Lamb; every Jewish man knew his Old Testament Scriptures, so he would have also thought of Isaiah 53:7 and Jeremiah 11:19 where the specially anointed suffering servant of the Lord is said to be like a lamb led out to the sacrificial slaughter. The Passover Lamb of God was a sacrifice that had to be eaten, and from his first appearance in John's Gospel Jesus is that Lamb. To hammer the point home, when John tells us the story of Jesus' death he reminds us that Jesus dies precisely on the day that the Passover lambs would have been slain in the temple (cf. John 19:14).

This link between Jesus (the Passover Lamb) and the sacrificial system is a very important element in John's Gospel. John is very careful to tell us when Jesus is about to celebrate a Passover feast, and each time he does so, the events are packed with meaning. So in John 2:13-16 it is at Passover time that Jesus clears the temple. Jesus wanted to clear out the traders and moneychangers, but in John's Gospel he is also doing something else. When he clears the temple, Jesus is doing a prophetic action. It is as if he is sweeping away not only the temple but also the whole Old Testament sacrificial system that it stands for. He not only sweeps it away, but in John 2:21 Jesus speaks "of the temple of his body." In other words, through the Incarnation the old temple and sacrificial system is swept away to be replaced by the body of Christ. So in the first two chapters of John's Gospel Jesus takes the place of the Passover Lamb and the temple with its sacrificial system. He replaces both with himself — that is, with his body.

The Bread of Life

Jesus also fulfills another important Old Testament image with his body. In John 6 Jesus feeds the five thousand with a miraculous multiplication of bread and fish. As Moses had given the people in the wilderness flesh and bread to eat, so Jesus miraculously gives the people flesh and bread to eat. But John wants to do more than just show Jesus to be a second Moses. To understand John's meaning completely we need to remember that his Gospel was written to the early Christians, who used the fish as a symbol of Jesus himself. In the same chapter Jesus calls himself the bread of life, so the early Christians would have seen the feeding of the five thousand as a sign of Christ miraculously feeding a multitude with himself — under the symbols of bread and fish. In addition, in the same chapter the offerings of bread and flesh come together as one in Jesus.

This becomes clear after the miracle of the feeding of the five thousand — which also took place near Passover. Jesus teaches the crowds about the bread from heaven. In verses 31 through 35 of chapter 6 Jesus says the Jews had manna in the wilderness, but he — Jesus — is the true bread from heaven. He is the "bread of God . . . which comes down from heaven, and gives life to the world" (John 6:33). At this the Jews began to grumble, saying, "Who is this person? He is just Jesus, the son of Joseph. How can he say he has come down from heaven?" (cf. John 6:41-42). Then Jesus gets into a debate with them and says something truly astounding. He'd already said that he was the bread of life, and maybe his hearers understood this in a symbolic way; perhaps meaning that Jesus' teachings were nourishing and good. But now Jesus goes further. In the Old Testament the bread and the flesh offerings were always together. At the beginning of John's Gospel we hear that Jesus is the Word made flesh (cf. John 1:14). In verses 50 and 51 of chapter 6 Jesus brings the bread offering and the flesh offering together in himself and says, "This is the bread which comes down from heaven, that a man may eat of it and not die. I am the living bread which came down from heaven; if any one eats of this bread, he will live for ever." Then he says what the bread is: "The bread which I shall give for the life of the world is my flesh."

Now the Jews are genuinely aghast. "How can this man give us his flesh to eat?" (John 6:52). Maybe they simply got the wrong end of the stick. Maybe they misunderstood him. They were taking his words too literally perhaps. Earlier when Nicodemus took Jesus' words about being born again too literally Jesus corrected him. But this time Jesus doesn't correct anyone. His hearers say, "But how can this man give us his flesh to eat?" and Jesus doesn't say, "Look, I am speaking figuratively, I really mean it is my teachings that you must share in by faith." Instead he makes his point even more clear and shocking. He says solemnly, "Truly, truly, I say to you, unless you eat the flesh of the Son of man and drink his blood, you have no life in you; he who eats my flesh and drinks my blood has eternal life, and

I will raise him up at the last day. For my flesh is food indeed, and my blood is drink indeed. . . . He who eats this bread will live for ever" (John 6:53-55, 58).

Remember that after the Jewish priests sacrificed the grain and the animals, they had to eat the bread and meat in order to take part in the atonement that the sacrifice accomplished. It is also important to point out what the Jews thought about the body and the soul. We sometimes think the body and the soul are separate, as if the body were simply a container for the soul, but the Jews of Jesus' time saw it differently. For them the body and the soul could not be separated. The soul dwelled in every part of the body, and to eat the flesh of a creature was to share in both its material and spiritual life. So when Jesus says they must eat his flesh he means they must share in his life, and because he is God in the flesh this is the way to share in eternal life. He goes on to make this point in the Gospel of John when he says, "He who eats my flesh and drinks my blood has eternal life, . . . He who eats my flesh and drinks my blood abides in me, and I in him. As the living Father sent me, and I live because of the Father, so he who eats me will live because of me" (John 6:54, 56-57).

John's Gospel shows how Jesus sweeps away the Old Testament sacrificial system and replaces the temple with his body. John also shows us that Jesus is the Passover Lamb — the one "who takes away the sin of the world!" (John 1:29); the one whose flesh has to be eaten in order to share in the benefits of salvation. In John's Gospel Jesus is also the manna, the bread from heaven, which must also be eaten if one is to have eternal life. This link between the bread and Jesus' flesh is vitally important because it is through his flesh and blood that Christ was incarnate in the world. It is through his flesh and blood that the veil between matter and spirit is torn open. It is through his flesh and blood that God makes contact with us. We too are incarnate in the world. We have bodies, and for salvation to be real it has to extend in some way to our flesh and blood too. That is why he says his flesh is *real* food and his blood *real* drink (cf. John 6:55). Jesus really took flesh and blood, and to share in that reality Jesus says we must eat his flesh and drink his blood.

The link between all these strands is the Last Supper. In Luke's Gospel we see how Jesus consolidated his teaching. The night before he died, Jesus gathered the apostles together to celebrate the Passover. At the meal the Jews shared the meat from the sacrificed lamb, and they shared blessed bread and wine. As they did, they were united in their shared Jewish heritage; they were united with one another; and they were united with the God who saved them. In Luke 22 we have the account of that Passover meal, which Jesus shared with his apostles. As he takes the unleavened bread he holds it up and says solemnly, "This is my body which is given for you. Do this in remembrance of me" (Luke 22:19). Then he takes the cup and says, "This cup which is poured out for you is the new covenant in my blood" (Luke 22:20). Just as the blood of a sacrificial Lamb was poured out to seal the covenant between God and his people, so Jesus' blood will be poured out on the cross. Just as part of the Passover sacrifice was to eat the bread and lamb and drink the wine, so Jesus transfers the symbolism to himself. The wine is now his blood. The bread is now his flesh. Suddenly all the other pieces of the puzzle must have fallen into place for the apostles. This is what John meant when he called Jesus the Passover Lamb of God. This is what Jesus meant when he called himself the bread of heaven and said that they had to eat his flesh to have eternal life.

There was another level of meaning as well. When Jesus said the wine was his blood of the new covenant, he was referring back to another Old Testament passage — Exodus 24. There Moses has just received the tablet of the law from God. He scts up an altar, makes a sacrifice, and sprinkles the blood on the altar and on the people. The people promise to keep God's law and God promises in return to be their God. The blood seals the covenant that both parties have made. Then in verse 11 of Exodus 24 it says the elders of the people saw God, and they ate and drank together. This is a perfect description of what happened at the Last Supper. The apostles saw God in Jesus, and they ate and drank together.

The cross is where the whole story is leading. The next day when Jesus was taken out to die, every detail of the Old Testament images, every detail of his life on earth, and every detail of his teaching and the events at the Last Supper — every one of these details was suddenly, powerfully, and terribly fulfilled. In John's Gospel Jesus actually dies at the time when all the Passover lambs would have been killed in the temple. So there on the cross the ancient feast of Passover — by which God delivered his people from slavery — was fulfilled. There on the cross the terrible story of Abraham sacrificing his only son came to have a universal and wonderful meaning. There on the cross the sacrifice that sealed the covenant that bound God and his people came true. There on the cross the whole sacrificial system of the Jewish people suddenly took on a greater, more marvelous, and more complex meaning. There too the truths Jesus spoke at the Last Supper suddenly became clear. There his own body of flesh and blood became the sacrifice, and from now on the Passover bread and the Passover wine would have a new meaning. As he taught, they would become his body and blood — a permanent memorial of his flesh and blood that was given for the life of the world. Just as Isaac was spared death by an animal sacrifice, so Jesus gives us bread and wine to take the place of a perpetual blood sacrifice. His death was once and for all, and the bread and wine are now our commemoration and participation in that death.

The New Deal

At Jesus' death, as the ultimate victim's blood was shed, the veil in the temple was torn in two (cf. Matthew 27:51, Mark 15:38, and Luke 23:45) and the barrier between earth and heaven was demolished forever. To maintain access to this new fact, at the Last Supper Jesus instituted a new sacramental system. In Luke's Gospel Jesus commands his apostles to celebrate this new ritual meal "in remembrance of me" (Luke 22:19). This phrase, "in remembrance of me," is important because it doesn't just mean a memorial service for a dead friend. Neither does it mean simply a sign or symbol that reminds us of the dead friend. The word in Greek is *anamnesis*, which indicates a dramatic reenactment of an event in the past; a bringing into the present moment the feelings and effects of some past happening. Like the Passover, this new ritual meal was to be celebrated with solemnity as a way to make Christ's saving death alive at the present moment in a real, physical way.

The early Church understood communion in this way. While Paul was staying in Ephesus he wrote to the Corinthians about their worship practices. He orders them to maintain a decent and solemn celebration of the ritual meal he calls "the Lord's Supper." Then he expresses the formula that lies at the heart of the Eucharist to this day: "For I received from the Lord what I also delivered to you, that the Lord Jesus on the night when he was betrayed took bread, and when he had given thanks, he broke it, and said, 'This is my body which is for you. Do this in remembrance of me.' In the same way also the cup, after supper, saying, 'This cup is the new covenant in my blood. Do this, as often as you drink it, in remembrance of me.' For as often as you eat this bread and drink the cup, you proclaim the Lord's death until he comes" (1 Corinthians 11:23-26). For Paul the Lord's Supper is not only a way to remember Jesus. It is a dynamic retelling or reliving of the saving events of Christ's death. But Paul also makes the link between the Old Testament worshipers eating the flesh of the sacrifice and the sharing of the bread at the Lord's Supper. In 1 Corinthians 10:18 he points to the Old Testament worshipers and says that by eating the sacrifice they share in the altar — in other words, they join themselves with the sacrifice. A few verses before, he had said that the Christian worshipers, by eating the bread at the Lord's Supper, share in the Christian sacrifice. So Paul says, "The cup of thanksgiving which we bless, is it not a participation in the blood of Christ? The bread which we break, is it not a participation in the body of Christ?" (1 Corinthians 10:16).

Many Christians agree with all of this so far, but they understand the sharing in bread and wine to be merely a symbolic sharing in Christ's death. Certainly in the Passover and in the Old Testament sacrificial system there was a symbolic aspect, but there was a physical dimension to the ritual too. Eating the flesh of the sacrifice and the blessed bread was a vital part of the transaction. By eating and drinking, the worshipers shared physically in God's saving action. Eating the flesh was necessary for the salvation to take effect (cf. Leviticus 10:17). Jesus says the same thing in John 6 when he says that unless you eat his flesh and drink his blood you will not have life within you.

Jesus doesn't say, "You must eat the bread which is a reminder of my body." He says, "Unless you eat the flesh of the Son of man . . . you have no life in you" (John 6:53). Paul stresses the importance that the person who eats the bread acknowledges that it is the body of Christ. When Paul is addressing the Corinthians about the Lord's Supper, he warns the Corinthians not to come to the Lord's Supper unworthily. In his first letter to the Corinthians St. Paul says, "Let a man examine himself, and so eat of the bread and drink of the cup. For any one who eats and drinks without discerning the body [of the Lord] eats and drinks judgment upon himself" (1 Corinthians 11:28-29). In other words, if you eat and drink, but you do not believe that the bread and wine are the body and blood of Christ, you may be eating and drinking God's judgment, not God's blessing.

The Protestant theologians at the Reformation disagreed violently about the doctrine of the Eucharist. In different ways they all denied that the consecrated bread and wine were really and truly the body and blood of Christ. Yet this is the understanding of the Eucharist from the earliest days of the Church. The earliest writings are unanimous that the bread and wine of the communion service becomes just what Jesus said it is — his body and blood. Before the year 108 Ignatius of Antioch says, "Take great care to keep one Eucharist. For there is one flesh of our Lord Jesus Christ and one cup that unites us with his blood."[7] He says that heretics deny that the communion bread is really the body of Christ. "The Docetists [those were heretics of his day] stay away from the Eucharist and prayer, because they do not admit that the Eucharist is the flesh of our Savior Jesus Christ which suffered for our sins."[8]

The early Christian writers fervently insist that the bread and wine of communion are supernatural gifts. Through them the flesh and blood of Jesus is with us in a real way. Justin Martyr, who died in the year 165, writes, "We do not receive these gifts as ordinary food or ordinary drink. But as Jesus Christ our Savior was made flesh through the Word of God, and took flesh for our salvation, in the same way the food over which thanksgiving has been offered through the word of prayer that we have from him — the food by which our blood and flesh are nourished through its transformation — is, as we are taught, the flesh and blood of Jesus who was made flesh."[9] Irenaeus wrote to counter the heresy of his time that denied that the body was important, and said the physical could not be the channel for salvation. He links the reality of our physical salvation with the reality of Christ's body and blood really being present at communion: "Whenever then the cup that man mixes and the bread that man makes receive the word of God, the Eucharist becomes the body of Christ. . . . How then can they allege that the flesh is incapable of the gift of God, which is eternal life, seeing that the flesh is fed on the flesh and blood of the Lord and is a member of him?"[10] A few decades later Tertullian, who is known for his pithy sayings, sums it up: "The flesh feeds on the body and blood of Christ so that it may be fattened on God."[11]

The writings from these first years of the Church all agree with the New Testament, that the bread and wine of the communion service really are the body and blood of Jesus Christ. These writings show that the early Christians believed that by eating and drinking the bread and wine we have a share in Jesus' life, love, and saving work on the cross. By eating his flesh and blood we share in that eternal moment when the veil between earth and heaven is torn in two. For important theological reasons the early Christians all take Jesus' words seriously and at face value: "He who eats my flesh and drinks my blood abides in me, and I in him" (John 6:56). They listen to Christ when he lifts up the bread and says at the Last Supper: "This is my body" (Matthew 26:26; Mark 14:22; Luke 22:19). This has also been the faith of the Catholic Church down through the ages. It is a belief that is firmly based in the Scriptures and brings life and blessing to all who hold to it.

A Substantial Difference

Catholics are famous for believing that the bread and wine really become the body and blood of Christ. This is where non-Catholic Christians often disagree both with Catholics and with one another. Baptists and independent Evangelicals say the bread and wine are merely reminders of Jesus' death. Some Presbyterians believe that there is a special spiritual presence of Jesus that comes through the communion service. Lutherans believe Jesus' body and blood are "with" or "next to" the bread and wine. Many Anglicans believe there is a "real spiritual presence" of Christ that comes to the believer through partaking in communion. Catholics understand these descriptions of what happens at the Eucharist but believe it must go further than that. As Irenaeus and Justin Martyr did, we compare what happens at the Eucharist with what happened at the Incarnation. Jesus wasn't just a symbol of God or a reminder of God's presence in the world. The spirit of God wasn't just "next to" the human Jesus. Jesus didn't just "seem" to be God, nor was he God only for those who accepted him. By faith we believe the Incarnation was a historical, physical fact. Likewise by faith we believe the bread and wine really do become the body and blood of Christ.

Do we think that if we take the bread and wine and put it under a microscope we would find that it is actually human flesh and blood? No. What really happens remains a mystery, but the best description of what we believe happens is expressed in philosophical terms. It wasn't until the eleventh century that Christians began to question how this happened. Then some theologians said the presence of Christ at the Eucharist was only a spiritual presence and that the bread and wine were only symbols. After debating the matter for over two centuries the Church finally decided on a form of words to describe what happens when the bread and wine become the body and blood of Christ.

This form of words is called "transubstantiation." The word "transubstantiation" itself simply means "substance across" or "change of substance." But to know what Catholics mean by this very specific definition we have to know what the theologians some seven hundred years ago meant by the word "substance." When they said "substance," they meant almost exactly the opposite of what we think of as substance. When we say "substance," we think of physical stuff — something substantial. But when they said "substance" they meant the "essential reality" of a thing as opposed to its changing physical characteristics. So for the theologians in the thirteenth century your substance is the real you. It is your essence, or your true being. The substance of bread and wine are the essential reality of bread and wine, which might be called "bread-ness" or "wine-ness." What Catholics believe is that this essence of bread and essence of wine are transformed at the Eucharist into the essence of Jesus Christ's body and blood. A miracle happens in which the substance of the bread and wine becomes the substance of Christ. We describe what happens by saying that the body and blood of Christ are really present to us under the form, or appearance, of bread and wine.

This connects with C. S. Lewis's idea that physical things are not only the pointers to heavenly realities but can actually carry heaven in and through their physical forms. When talking about the emotion of joy and how it relates to the physical sensations a person feels, he says, "The sensation does not merely accompany, nor merely signify, diverse and opposite emotions, but becomes part of them. The emotion descends bodily, as it were, into the sensation and digests, transforms, transubstantiates it."[12]

This is what transubstantiation means — a real conversion of the bread and wine at their most basic level of existence. For all that, transubstantiation can never be more than a philosophical description of what we think happens at communion. The reality is far greater than the intellectual analysis. At the end of the day we must admit that the Eucharist, like the Incarnation, is a mystery. So we put together the scriptural words and take them for what they are — God's revelation to humanity. Jesus said, "Unless you eat the flesh of the Son of man and drink his blood, you have no life in you" (John 6:53). At the Last Supper he held up the bread and wine and said, "This is my body, this is my blood" (cf. Matthew 26:26, Mark 14:22, and Luke 22:19). Before he returned to heaven he promised his apostles that he would be with them always. Paul affirms that the bread of communion is a sharing in the body of Christ. It has been the witness of the Church down through the ages that through this Eucharistic miracle the cross of Christ is present at the heart of the Church in a real and physical way until the end of time.

The Eucharist developed from the Hebrew practice of sacrificial worship, the early Church spoke of the Eucharist as a "sacrifice," and many Christians, including Catholics, still talk of the Eucharist as a sacrifice. What can that mean when we know that the sacrifice of Christ was once for all on the cross (cf. Hebrews 10:14)? At the end of the book of Hebrews we are shown what kind of sacrifice the Eucharist is. In chapter 13, verse 15, we're told, "Through him [that is, Christ] then let us continually offer up a sacrifice of praise to God." The word "Eucharist" means "thanksgiving," so the Eucharist, or Holy Communion, is not a sacrifice of Christ over and over again. Instead it is an unending sacrifice of praise offered by the Church.

As Christ commanded, the Church — led by the apostles — comes together to offer praise and thanksgiving for the once-for-all sacrifice of Christ on the cross. There, as Paul commands, we also offer ourselves as living sacrifices to do God's will (cf. Romans 12:1-2). There, as a holy priesthood, the whole people of God — led by their local elder — call to mind the death of Jesus Christ with hearts full of praise. Just as the Jews continued to celebrate Passover, and so brought the dramatic events of the first Passover into the present moment, so at the Eucharist we bring the dramatic events of Christ's sacrifice into the present moment. We do not sacrifice Christ again. Catholic teaching is clear — just as the Bible is — that Christ's sacrifice was once for all on the cross. But we do say that the Lord's Supper "re-presents" (that is, "presents anew") Christ's once-for-all sacrifice and applies it to us at this point in time. The *Catechism* (quoting from the Council of Trent) explains it like this:

> [Christ], our Lord and God, was once and for all to offer himself to God the Father by his death on the altar of the cross, to accomplish there an everlasting redemption. But because his priesthood was not to end with his death, at the Last Supper "on the night when he was betrayed," [he wanted] to leave to his beloved spouse the Church a visible sacrifice (as the nature of man demands) by which the bloody sacrifice which he was to accomplish once for all on the cross would be re-presented, its memory perpetuated until the end of the world, and its salutary power be applied to the forgiveness of the sins we daily commit.[13]

When Catholics re-present the cross of Christ each day in the Mass, they are also re-presenting the fulfillment of the whole sacrificial history of mankind. The cross stands in the center of time and gathers into its mystery all that has gone before and all that has come after. The cross is a timeless moment in which all time is caught up and fulfilled. Within the Mass that moment when time opened up into eternity is presented to each one of Christ's faithful. There we "proclaim the Lord's death until he comes." There we participate not only in the timeless moment of the cross but in the "timeless now" of eternity.

Of course to the skeptic it seems incredible that through a form of words, a prayer, a scrap of bread, and a sip of wine, eternity should be transposed into this moment and that we can make present the very body and blood of Christ our Lord. But this skepticism is nothing new. Writing at the end of the second century, Tertullian remonstrates against those who disbelieve the simplicity and majesty of the sacraments:

> So violent are the designs of perversity for shaking faith, or even for utterly preventing its reception, that it attacks faith on the very principle on which it is based. For there is really nothing which so hardens men's minds as the contrast between the simplicity of the divine works which are seen in the act, and the magnificence which is promised in the effect. So in this matter just because there is such simplicity, such absence of display . . . in fact an absence of any costly trappings, when a man is plunged and dipped in water to the accompaniment of few words, and then rises again not much cleaner, if at all; just because of this it seems to men incredible that eternal life should be won in this manner. . . . We also marvel; but we marvel because we believe. Incredulity marvels, but does not believe.[14]

Is it so difficult to believe? We believe the stupendous fact that the Creator stepped into the world he made. Shall we deny that he does so still under the forms of bread and wine? When he walked the earth, the same Creator transformed the substance of water into the substance of wine. He multiplied the substance of bread and fish to feed the five thousand. He restored the substance of Lazarus and Jairus's daughter to their bodies when he raised them from the dead. If we believe in those miracles, why do we deny that Jesus Christ — who is with us always — might also be transforming the substance of bread and wine into his own body and blood through the instrument of a priest?

At the Eucharist that miracle of transposition that C. S. Lewis hinted at so eloquently becomes real in an objective, regular, and concrete way. Through the Eucharist the eternal reality of Christ is something we are united with, pass into, and become a part of. Just as Lewis had suggested that beautiful things might be taken up into the beauty of heaven and transmit that beauty here, so bread and wine are taken up. They absorb the body and blood of Christ and are transformed into that greater reality. The final truth is a hope beyond our greatest imaginings. If simple bread and wine can be so transposed, the tremendous truth is that our lives too may also be taken up, that day by day as we struggle to receive him, our own stubborn and confused lives might also be transformed. The miracle of transubstantiation is not limited to bread and wine. I am to become what I eat. By Christ's majestic and humble grace my own frail flesh and blood will be transformed, so together we all shall be "changed into his likeness from one degree of glory to another" (2 Corinthians 3:18).

Chapter Six Endnotes

1. C. S. Lewis, "The Weight of Glory," in *Screwtape Proposes a Toast,* London, Fount, 1986, p. 98.

2. Ibid., p. 90.

3. Ibid., p. 83.

4. Ibid., pp. 106-107.

5. W. Chatterton Dix, *Alleluia Sing to Jesus: The New English Hymnal,* Norwich, Canterbury Press, 1987, p. 601.

6. C. S. Lewis, *Letters to Malcolm: Chiefly on Prayer,* London, Fount, 1981, p. 73.

7. Henry Bettenson, *The Early Christian Fathers,* Oxford, Oxford University Press, 1969, p. 47.

8. Ibid., p. 49.

9. Ibid., p. 62.

10. Ibid., p. 97.

11. Ibid., p. 148.

12. C. S. Lewis, "Transposition," in *Screwtape Proposes a Toast,* London, Fount, 1986, p. 85.

13. *Catechism of the Catholic Church*, London, Geoffrey Chapman, 1995, para. 1366.

14. Bettenson, p. 143.

'So Great a Cloud of Witnesses'

One of the great things about our Bible church was the times of fellowship we enjoyed. Evangelical churches are strong on building up a sense of belonging, and social occasions helped us build up the community of our church. The families of the church would often meet for shared meals or life celebrations like weddings, funerals, and baby showers. Every summer we had a Sunday school picnic at which the whole church would turn up. The men had a basketball team and a softball team and the ladies had women's fellowship. There were the Boys' Brigade, Pioneer Girls, Youth Club, and Christian camp. On New Year's Eve we had a special social event with games, entertainment, plenty of food, and good times.

We were also aware that the fellowship of our church was bigger than just our particular congregation. Even though we were an independent church, we belonged to a confederation of other similar churches. Moreover, we felt part of the wider Evangelical movement and identified with Evangelicals from many other denominations whose members still held to the same essential Protestant faith. Through a network of Bible colleges and Evangelical schools we were part of a larger educational structure, and through our missionaries we were in contact with fellow Bible-believing Christians throughout the world.

Within our family we were also aware of belonging to a tradition that stretched back in time. Our ancestors were Christians who had come from Europe to the American colonies for religious freedom. Our own ancestors were Mennonites — those courageous Christians who witness so strongly and peacefully against the worldly ways of greed, war, and mindless consumption. We believed our ancestors were in heaven, and that some day we would meet our loved ones again face to face.

All Christians look to the past and remember the heroes of the faith who lived out their commitment to Jesus with extraordinary passion and zeal. In our Evangelical home we kept alive the memory of the great missionaries like the martyr Jim Elliot, Adoniram Judson, William Carey, and Hudson Taylor. In our tradition we learned about the great evangelist D. L. Moody and the hymn-writer Sankey, just as the Methodists remembered the Wesley brothers and just as the Mennonites, Lutherans, and Calvinists looked back to the heroes of the faith who founded their particular movements. In our home we were also reminded that our ancestors on both sides had all been committed Christians — godly, simple people who had always stood up for the faith in every generation. I am still proud of this heritage of faith and count my ancestors and all those Evangelical heroes of the faith as part of the "crowd of witnesses" who surround and support me today in my Christian walk.

It is a good thing to look to the past and venerate the memory of the past heroes of the faith. This natural veneration of the departed heroes of the faith has been part of the Christian story from the very beginning. It is also right and good that we see how God works within families. Looking back to our heritage in the family of the faith is not unique to Christianity. The whole history of the Old Testament is the record of God's dealings with unique individuals — men and women of faith who risked everything to obey God and follow his guidance.

The Jewish writers of the New Testament remembered their heritage of faith and referred to the heroes of the past in glowing terms. The writer of Hebrews speaks as if they are still alive and active in the life of the newly formed Christian Church. In a beautiful passage he speaks about the encouragement of being surrounded by a heavenly host: "Therefore, since we are surrounded by so great a cloud of witnesses, let us also lay aside every weight, and sin which clings so closely" (Hebrews 12:1). This verse comes right after the great list of Old Testament saints and the martyrs for the faith in the eleventh chapter of Hebrews. The word "witness" means "martyr," and the writer of the Hebrews is not actually referring to angels as the "great crowd of witnesses" but to the Old Testament martyrs and heroes of faith. The crowd of witnesses surrounds us for a particular reason: to encourage us in the faith and to point to Jesus. So the letter to the Hebrews goes on to say, "Let us run with perseverance the race that is set before us, looking to Jesus the pioneer and perfecter of our faith, who for the joy that was set before him endured the cross, despising the shame, and is seated at the right hand of the throne of God" (Hebrews 12:1-2).

The Communion of the Saints

Chapter 11 of Hebrews reads like a quick overview of the Old Testament. The author catalogues the heroes of faith to remind his audience that they belong to that great family of faith as well. For the Hebrews the family link was real and biological. They really were of the same tribe and bloodline as those heroes of the faith. The Christian Church is called the family of God because, in a way, we share the same heritage. All of us who have believed and been baptized into Christ share his inheritance. We become his brothers and sisters and therefore brothers and sisters of one another. Within the Church we share the bloodline of Jesus along with every other Christian from all the different races and languages, peoples and tribes, both those alive in the world today and all those who have lived the life of faith down through the ages.

In my Evangelical home we remembered the heroes of the faith from the past, but the Catholic understanding of the saints from the past goes further than simply remembering their good examples with thanks. We actually believe the saints from the past are our living brothers and sisters in Christ. We are all alive in Christ, but those who are dead in Christ exist in an even greater intimacy with him. They no longer "see in a mirror dimly, but then face to face" (1 Corinthians 13:12). Through Holy Communion we join in the fellowship meal and share our common kinship in Christ. The word "communion" describes how we see our relationship with those who have gone before us in the faith. The word "communion" means "universal" or "shared." We believe that we are in a real and powerful communion with those brothers and sisters who have gone before us and won the victory in Christ Jesus.

We share in this communion of the saints through our worship at the Eucharist. Catholic worship is different from non-Catholic worship in that it has traditionally focused on heaven and not on earth. Catholic worship is meant to give us a glimpse of heaven and help us to share, here on earth, in that continual worship that takes place around the throne of God. The book of Revelation is full of images of this heavenly worship, and one of the strongest images is in chapter 7, verse 9: "After this I looked, and behold, a great multitude which no man could number, from every nation, from all tribes and peoples and tongues, standing before the throne and before the Lamb, clothed in white robes, with palm branches in their hands." A few verses later we learn that this great multitude that no man can number are the glorious martyrs. At the Eucharist we remember Christ's death and bring it into the present moment, but we also remember all those who have gone before us signed with the mark of Christ.

I can remember a very holy old Anglican priest who used to love coming to church to celebrate the Eucharist early on a weekday morning. I knew attendance at this service was rather poor, and one day I asked him how many people were there. His face lit up as he said, "So many that no man could number them!" He was intensely aware of the presence of that "great crowd of witnesses," and it was through his celebration of Holy Communion that he drew close to them and felt their presence worshiping with him.

The idea that we can remember and come close to our departed saints and loved ones through the Eucharist is very ancient. From the earliest days of the Church the martyrs were remembered on the day of their death. The first Christians remembered the day of the martyr's death, and because it was the day the saint rose to new life in Christ, the early Christians called it the martyr's "birthday." They celebrated the saint's "birthday" with a special celebration of the Eucharist. This became known as the martyr's feast day. In the second century Tertullian confirms this early practice, pointing out: "We take the sacrament of the Eucharist. . . . We make oblations for the dead and for the birthdays, on the anniversaries."[1]

The first Christians celebrated the victory of the martyrs, but they also prayed for their dead loved ones at the communion service. At the catacombs in Rome there is archaeological evidence that the first Christians remembered their dead by celebrating a communion service and praying for them. Because of their holiness the Christians actually asked the martyrs to pray for their departed loved ones. An inscription from the second century at the catacombs in Rome records this practice: "Januaria, be very happy and plead for us. Paul and Peter, pray for Victor."[2] This early Christian practice is based on the earlier Jewish practice of praying for the dead. We know this was a Jewish custom from the verse in 2 Maccabees 12:44-45 where the Jews pray for the dead and offer a sacrifice for their spiritual well-being.

Many Christians have a problem with this for two reasons. First of all, they don't like the idea of praying for the dead because it sounds too much like spiritualism and séances. However, the practice is very different. In a séance the medium tries to bring a dead person back to this realm. When we pray for the dead, we are asking God to continue to give them grace to continue beyond death the journey to perfection that they began on earth. A séance tries to bring a dead person to earth. Prayers for a person who has died propel him further toward heaven.

The second objection is that once a person dies, his eternal destiny is sealed forever and praying for him won't do him any good. Catholics also believe that a person's fate is sealed at death, but we also believe that it is necessary for those destined for heaven to continue to grow in goodness and love after their earthly life is over. Our prayers don't help the dead get into heaven — they help them move into the fullest glory of heaven. I will talk about this subject more in chapter 10, but at this stage it is enough to say that praying for the dead is really no different than praying for the living. We pray here and now for our family and friends and we believe that by our prayers God will bless them, protect them, and bring them to glory. If some of our loved ones have departed from this life, we don't believe they are dead and gone forever. If they were Christians, they are alive in Christ, and our prayers for them are the same as our prayers for them while they were still alive. We ask for God's blessings and love to be poured upon them more and more.

Praying to the Saints

I was taught as a young Evangelical that Catholics prayed to saints and worshiped Mary. I wasn't surprised therefore when a Catholic friend in high school, upon hearing that I had lost my car keys, told me: "Just pray to St. Anthony." He commented in a practical sort of way: "He'll help you find them." My teachers were right! Catholics pray to saints. Later on, while I accepted the great communion of the saints and the fact that we worshiped with them, I still wasn't so sure about the idea of actually praying to saints.

Do Catholics really pray to saints? Yes and no. When a Catholic says he is praying to saints, he doesn't mean he is praying to a saint in the same way he would pray to God. He is not worshiping the saint — he is asking for his help. "Praying to saints" means "beseeching saints." By praying to saints we are asking them to pray for us. It's confusing that Catholics use the word "pray" in this context when they mean "ask." When you see it that way, it's not very different from what most Christians do all the time. All of us have known some saintly old woman who keeps a prayer list. We ask her to pray for us and for our specific needs and feel that her closeness to God makes her especially good at praying. It's the same thing with the saints. There is no such thing as a dead saint. They are alive in God and continuing their work of prayer, praise, and intercession. Some of them knew on this earth that their work would continue in heaven. St. Thérèse of Lisieux is famous for anticipating the great work she would do after her death. "I will spend my heaven doing good on earth,"[3] she wrote.

Praying to saints is therefore more precisely described as praying *with* the saints. We pray *for* our departed loved ones and *with* the saints who have paved the way for us into glory. Are we right to make such distinctions? The New Testament speaks of all Christians as saints. Why should some be better than others? The word "saint" simply means "holy one," and Catholics use the term in both ways. Like the New Testament, we refer to all Christians as "the saints of God." But from the beginning of the Church we have also recognized that some of the saints are more "saintly" than others, and that the righteous ones are also successful at prayer. James 5:16 says it is the prayer of the *righteous* person that "has great power in its effects." The martyrs, in particular, were singled out as those whose holiness was so great that they were given the grace to actually give up their lives for their Lord. Saints began to be defined as the individuals whose holiness of life or self-sacrifice in death meant they had identified so closely with the Lord Jesus that they went immediately into his presence at the time of death. Their prayers were considered especially powerful, and so it was worth asking them to pray for our needs here on earth.

As a result, Catholics recognize saints formally and ask for their prayers even today. In the twentieth century there have been more Christian martyrs than in all the other centuries put together, and the Catholic Church has recognized the great number of saints by canonizing more saints than ever before. The process of canonization, or the recognition of a saint, was informal in the early days of the Church. Around the eleventh century the Church began to establish the formal proceedings for canonization that we have today. But because the Catholic Church recognizes certain heroes of the faith formally as saints does not mean that other Christians are not saints as well. All of us are called to be saints, and there are many truly holy heroes of the faith who are known to God alone.

When the Catholic Church recognizes some Christians as heroes in the faith, she offers them to all Christians as role models. We look to the heroes of the faith as examples of ordinary people who have become extraordinary through their complete obedience to Christ's love. They show us the way forward in our own ordinary lives and encourage us to be more and more Christ-like. The vast range of the saints means there is a role model for every person and every walk of life. Patron saints are individuals who are assigned to pray and watch over people here on earth who carry on doing the same sort of work that the saint did while he or she was here on earth. So St. Joseph, for instance, is the patron saint of house hunters because while he was on earth he had to do a certain amount of house-hunting for Jesus and Mary. Because St. Francis loved animals and birds, he is the patron saint of veterinarians. Many Catholics choose their own patron, and feel close to that particular person just as we might feel close to a particular Christian friend and prayer partner here on earth. The fact that the saint is in heaven doesn't mean he or she is far away. In fact, Catholics would say that makes their saint even closer to them — not farther away.

Praying to Idols

When I first went into a Catholic cathedral in France, I can remember being shocked by what I saw. I was an Evangelical student at the time, and it was my first real encounter with Catholicism. In the dark corners of the cathedral were banks of candles and rows of people kneeling down in prayer before what I considered to be idols. It confirmed all I had been taught about Catholics. Sure enough — there they were, praying to idols!

Any non-Catholic will be struck by this at his first entrance to a Catholic church. A traditional Catholic church is full of imagery. There are carved stations of the cross, stained-glass windows, carvings on the altar and font, statues of saints in niches, paintings and crucifixes and symbols everywhere. Some Christians throw up their hands in horror because such things must be a direct contradiction of their second commandment, which warns us not to make any graven images (cf. Exodus 20:4 and Deuteronomy 5:8). It's true that the Bible forbids idolatry. The New Testament is just as adamant in its condemnation of idol worship as the Old (cf. Acts 15:20, 1 Corinthians 5:11, and 1 John 5:21). Catholic Christians are well aware of the biblical injunctions against idolatry, so it must follow that we are either blatantly disobeying the Scriptures by having statues and images in our churches or else we don't regard these things as idols.

When we look more closely at the Bible, it is clear that when God forbade idols he wasn't making a blanket condemnation of all images. We know this because later he commands Moses to fashion a bronze serpent for the people to look to for salvation (cf. Numbers 21:8-9). Furthermore, the Lord's instructions for the tabernacle included various forms of religious imagery. The Ark of the Covenant was crowned with the images of two cherubim (cf. Exodus 25:18-20), and the screens of the tabernacle were embroidered with images of angels (cf. Exodus 26:1). Solomon's temple had carvings throughout, and the huge laver was set on the back of carved bulls (cf. 1 Kings 7:25). Indeed, the descriptions of the tabernacle and temple with their rich and beautiful craftwork, carvings, and embroidered vestments sound very much like a highly decorated Catholic shrine.

It's important to distinguish between a pagan idol and a Catholic statue of a saint. A pagan idol is an image of a demon. Sometimes the idol is a beautiful figure, but more often it is some sort of bestialized human creature — maybe a man with a wolf's head or a man with wings, a bull's legs, and a lion's head.

The pagan idol is intended to be a physical channel for the demonic spirit to be summoned into the lives of the worshipers. In other words, a pagan idol is a physical way of summoning a demon. No wonder God forbade such images in the Ten Commandments. A Catholic image of a saint, however, is quite different. A statue or icon of a saint is simply a representation of a real human being who has lived on earth and served God as a hero of faith. A Catholic image is like a snapshot or portrait of a friend or family member. It's interesting that we have photographs of some modern saints like Thérèse of Lisieux and Maximilian Kolbe. No one seems to object to using their photographs to remember them, even though some Christians still object to statues and icons of saints.

The question concerning images is important because it is a controversy that is not new in the Church. In the eighth century the Church faced this problem head-on. The Eastern Church was struggling with the twin heresies of Monophysitism, which lessened the importance of Jesus' physical nature, and Manichaeism, which taught that the physical world was inherently sinful. Emperor Leo III had been brought up under these influences, and he thought the use of icons (the Greek word for images) was wrong. He also thought the use of icons was a barrier to evangelizing the Muslims and Jews. So he decided to ban icons and destroy the existing ones. The Church was immediately and bitterly divided by this interference. St. John of Damascus was a Greek monk who argued the case for icons against the iconoclasts (destroyers of icons). His argument for the use of images in Christian worship is still relevant today. John argued that since Jesus Christ — "the image of the invisible God" (Colossians 1:15) — took physical form, it was good and proper for Christians to use physical things in worship. He argued for the validity of images by saying:

The apostles saw Christ bodily, his sufferings and his miracles and they heard his words. We are double beings with a body and soul. . . . It is impossible for us to have access to the spiritual without the corporeal, while listening to audible words we hear with our corporeal ears and thus grasp spiritual things. In the same way it is through corporeal seeing that we arrive at spiritual insight.

St. John of Damascus is hinting at a deeper question here. Using images in worship is not just a matter of taste. It comes right down to what we believe about the spiritual and physical realms. Because of the Incarnation the spiritual and the physical are united forever, and our worship should reflect this truth. Tom Howard writes:

It is in the physical world that the intangible meets us. A kiss seals a courtship. The sexual act seals a marriage. A ring betokens the marriage. . . . To excise all this from piety and worship is to suggest that the gospel beckons us away from our humanity into a disembodied realm. It is to turn the incarnation into a mere doctrine. . . . The worship of God, surely, should be the place where men, angels and devils may see human flesh once more set free into all that it was created to be. To restrict that worship to sitting in pews and listening to words spoken is to narrow things down in a manner strange to the gospel. We are creatures who are made to bow, not just spiritually but with our knee bones and neck muscles. We are creatures who cry out to surge in great procession, *ad altare Dei*, not just in our hearts, but with our feet, singing great hymns with our tongues, our nostrils full of the smoke of incense.

Is it objected that this is too physical, too low down on the scale for the gospel? Noses indeed! If the objection carries the day, then we must jettison the stable and the manger, and the wine pots at Cana, and the tired feet anointed with nard, and the splinters of the cross, not to say the womb of the mother who bore God when He came to us. Too physical? What do we celebrate in our worship? It is Buddhism and Platonism and Manichaeanism that tell us to disavow our flesh and expunge everything but thoughts.[4]

Catholic worship *is* physical. It always has been, and this may be where Catholic worship shows itself to be "more Christianity" in the most practical way. When we worship God at the Eucharist, our bodies are caught up in the action. We physically get out of the house and go to church. We sprinkle holy water on our heads at the church door. We bow to acknowledge the Lord's presence when we enter the church. We kneel to pray. We stand to sing and praise. We watch the spectacle of the procession with rich vestments, candles, and crucifix. We sit to listen and learn. Then we go forward to the altar of God. We smell the incense that is wafted around the altar. We open our mouths and we eat a morsel of bread and drink a sip of wine, and under those appearances we receive the body, blood, soul, and divinity of the Lord Jesus Christ who became man for us. Afterward we may well light a candle. We may gaze at the image of those saints who have gone before us. God made us physical beings, and just as we soil both our bodies and souls in physical sin, so in Catholic worship our bodies are used to worship the One who took a body and became like us. As we do, the physical becomes the vehicle for the eternal, and the everlasting reaches through to touch us in the present moment.

People, Places, and Things

When I was working as an Anglican pastor, I often found it was the bereaved members of my congregation who, through their pain, had come to recognize how deeply interwoven the spiritual and physical dimensions of life really are. Often a widow would tell me how she felt her dead husband's presence "right there next to me — almost more real than when he was alive." Others would speak in an embarrassed way of how difficult they found it getting rid of their loved one's clothes. A widower said, "It's as if those clothes are a part of her and throwing them away is throwing away a bit of her." Through these natural emotions a deep truth is revealed. The physical and the spiritual are not separated. The spiritual dimension permeates the physical and the physical is the carrier for the eternal.

Because God came to us in physical form in the Incarnation, we also believe that God's goodness comes to us through the sacraments, and through a whole range of physical things. So in Catholic worship we not only look for God's grace through the seven formal sacraments but also through other things that we believe prayer can set apart and consecrate for a holy purpose. The priest blesses water to make it holy, and that water is used to bless us, to cleanse places that might be infected spiritually, and to cleanse other physical things spiritually. We use incense in worship, since it signifies the prayers of God's saints (cf. Revelation 8:4). We use rosary beads to give us a physical focus for prayer. We wear crosses or medals engraved with our favorite saint as a reminder of the saint's love and protection over us. We bless the images and buildings we use in worship. Just as the widower felt the physical things connected with his dead wife carried some of her in them, so we believe the physical places, people, and things of worship can be imbued with the holiness and prayers of those who use them.

In the same way, we believe the bodies of very holy people become permeated with that holiness. The supreme holiness of the saints is not just a spiritual manifestation. It transforms their bodies as well. For instance, within the Orthodox and Catholic traditions there are many well-documented cases of saints' bodies not decaying after their death. There are other stories of saints' bodies exuding a pleasing fragrance rather than corruption after they die. These miracles are reminders that the physical and the spiritual are intertwined; that what we do with our bodies affects the state of our souls and that the state of our souls can alter the state of our bodies. Because of this spiritual and physical interdependence Catholic Christians have also venerated the bodies of saints and the things they have owned. A hint of this is found in the New Testament where Paul blessed handkerchiefs, which were then circulated and which God used to help bring healing to people (cf. Acts 19:12).

Of course the veneration of relics can lead to excess and superstition. Even in the early days of the Church the leaders warned against this. Tertullian recognized some of the abuses that surrounded the veneration of relics. However, abuses should never undo right uses. At the Reformation many customs and practices that reaffirmed the link between the physical and spiritual worlds were thrown out in a sincere attempt to get rid of superstition and folk religion. As in all things, if we want more Christianity we should look carefully and see what practices and customs might be useful and use them as the Spirit leads us.

Finally, Catholics believe that places can also be made holy through centuries of worship and prayer. Just as a place can have "bad vibes" because of evil that has been practiced there, so a place can be blessed through the love, prayer, and sacrifice that go on. Our churches are holy places that we treat with respect and reverence. They are not just meeting rooms. Our homes too can become holy places if we dedicate them to God and ask him to fill them with his love, light, and grace. By dedicating places and making them holy to the Lord we can share in his work of redemption in the world. Through our prayers, love, and sacrifice we can be working to bring his redemption to the physical world in ways beyond our imagining.

Seeing the spiritual surging through the physical is a particularly Catholic way of seeing the world. It was summed up by a Catholic poet who wrote, "The world is charged with the grandeur of God. It will flame out like shining from shook foil."[5] When we see with sacramental eyes, we come to realize how important the saints really are. Suddenly they are not simply heroes of faith — they are transformed human beings. The saints surge with God's goodness to such an extent that the whole world radiates with that light and love. The transformation that God accomplished in them is a sign of the transformation and redemption of the whole created order that he has set in motion and will bring to fulfillment.

I had the privilege of meeting Mother Teresa of Calcutta once. I was in India traveling with a friend, and we wanted to visit the Missionaries of Charity and see their work. When we got to the headquarters of the order, a small bulletin board indicated that Mother Teresa was in. A little nun asked if we wanted to meet Mother Teresa. We waited a few moments and then she came through the door. She was a tiny person; with her famous wrinkled skin and big nose she was anything but physically attractive. But the power and radiance and goodness that shone from her whole being were unforgettable. Meeting that living saint was not thrilling simply because she was famous. I have met other famous people and they have shown none of that same radiance and goodness. In Mother Teresa I met one who was so filled with the same Lord Jesus whom I followed that I saw him shining through her to such a full extent that I shall never forget it.

At its heart this is why Catholics venerate the saints. In them they venerate the Lord Jesus Christ who shines through them. That is the exact emphasis in that famous passage from Hebrews 12:1-2; there it says that "we are surrounded by so great a crowd of witnesses" and that they point to "Jesus the pioneer and perfecter of our faith." When we use images of the saints in our worship, it is because we are reminding ourselves that the saints were themselves living images of the Lord Jesus. Therefore, saints and images of saints are all bound up with our love of Jesus himself. It is Jesus we see in the faces of the saints, and we venerate them because in them we can see how ordinary souls can be transformed by the power of God's amazing grace.

If such a transformation can take place in the lives of the saints, then it can also take place in me and in you. More Christianity always calls us to come "further up and further in." The lives of the saints show us that exalted state to which we can move by God's grace. In the saints we get a glimpse of all we can and shall be as Christ completes his work in us. Our love for the Lord and our love for the saints and our love for one another is caught up in our worship. In them and with them, with the whole company of earth and heaven, we join our voices in the song of unending praise, singing, "Holy, holy, holy is the Lord God of Hosts. Heaven and earth are full of his glory. Hosanna in the highest."

Chapter Seven Endnotes

1. Henry Bettenson, *The Early Christian Fathers*, Oxford, Oxford University Press, 1969, p. 148.

2. Cited in Donald Attwater and Catherine Rachel John, *Penguin Dictionary of Saints,* London, Penguin Books, 1995, p. 2.

3. John Clarke, O.C.D. (tr.), *St. Thérèse of Lisieux: Her Last Conversations,* Washington, D.C., ICS Publications, 1976, p. 102.

4. Thomas Howard, *Evangelical Is Not Enough,* San Francisco, Ignatius, 1984, pp. 36-37.

5. Gerard Manley Hopkins, "God's Grandeur," in *Faber Book of Religious Verse,* London, Faber and Faber, 1979, p. 288.

'All Generations Shall Call Me Blessed'

When an acorn falls to the ground, it sprouts and puts out a shoot. In a couple of years a tiny sapling struggles for survival. The sapling has come from the acorn but doesn't resemble the acorn. Given enough time, the sapling grows into a glorious and majestic oak tree. If you didn't know an oak came from an acorn, you would never guess they were connected. The same thing is true of a human being; from the tiniest egg and sperm a fully mature adult eventually grows. Jesus used a similar example when describing what the kingdom of God is like — it is like a mustard seed that falls into the ground from which a great tree grows for all the birds of the air to come and roost in (cf. Matthew 13:31-32).

The history of the Church shows how prophetic Jesus' parable was. The tiny seed was his body that was planted in the tomb. It rose as a glorious body and ascended into heaven. Here on earth Christ's body, the Church, has continued to grow and prosper in the world even today. The Church has grown in this organic way, and so have the beliefs of the early Church. In the first years the apostles preached Jesus' simple message of salvation, but Jesus pointed out that during his lifetime his disciples wouldn't be able to understand the full implications of who he was and what he came to accomplish. He promised that the Holy Spirit would teach his apostles all things (cf. John 16:12-13).

Guided by the Holy Spirit, St. Paul and St. John meditated on the implications of Jesus' life and work. As they meditated on the simple life of Christ, the Holy Spirit enabled them to see the true significance of who Jesus was and what he had accomplished. During his life on earth Jesus' full identity was hidden, but the New Testament authors came to understand who he really was and what he came to accomplish. The disciples' understanding of Jesus' identity grew and developed within their own lifetimes. To communicate the message, the New Testament writers used philosophical and intellectual concepts that were familiar to the people of their day to describe just who Jesus was. So St. John used a Greek philosophical concept when he said Jesus was the *logos* — the Divine Word of Creative Power that took flesh. St. Paul used another term when he said that Jesus was the "wisdom of God" in human form (cf. Ephesians 3:10).

In the first three hundred or four hundred years of Christian history the Holy Spirit continued to help the first Christians wrestle with just exactly who Jesus was and what he came to do. The early Church had to wrestle with doctrines like the Incarnation and the Trinity because they were not taught in the New Testament clearly and specifically enough to avoid confusion and wrong teaching. Sincere Christians held varied opinions about the Incarnation and the Trinity, and it was in the battles over heresies and wrong teaching that the early Church continued to refine and develop her understanding of Jesus. The Holy Spirit was not absent from these controversies. Instead he used the wrong teaching to help the Church refine the right teaching. So in 325 at the Great Council of Nicaea the Church defined the doctrine of the Incarnation as we know it. In 382 at the Council of Rome the Church finally defined which books were to go into the Bible. In 381 at the Council of Constantinople the Church defined the doctrine of the Trinity more specifically. In 451 at the Council of Chalcedon the Church rejected various heresies and defined more firmly the specific doctrines about the Incarnation.

Traditional followers of Jesus of all denominations rely on the work of these early Christians to define the beliefs about Jesus that unite all of us. The Reformers looked to these first councils of the whole Church to define the basic Christian doctrines, and all traditional Christians today still embrace the doctrines about Jesus and the Trinity that were worked out in those early years. What is sometimes forgotten is that at the same time the Holy Spirit was leading the Church to validate the canon of Scripture and fully understand the nature of the Incarnation and Trinity, the Church was also becoming clearer on other important issues. Linked with their definition on the Incarnation, the Church at this time also made some important statements about the identity and role of Jesus' mother, Mary. At the Council of Ephesus in 431 the same Church that defined the canon of Scripture, rejected certain heresies, and affirmed the full doctrine of the Incarnation also ratified a title for Mary that had already been in use for many years. At the Council of Ephesus the Church declared Mary to be *Theotokos*, which means "God-bearer" (that is, "The Mother of God"). This definition was not primarily so much an attempt to glorify Mary as it was to defend the fact that Jesus was true God and true man. The argument was that in affirming that Mary was truly and fully human, to call her "God-bearer" helped to emphasize that her son had to be true man as well as true God.

In all these areas — the definition of the canon of Scripture, the definition of the Incarnation and the Trinity, and the identity and role of Mary — the followers of Jesus were "developing doctrine." Like the acorn that becomes an oak tree, the full implications of Jesus' life grew and flourished. The first Christians knew that nothing new could be added to that basic deposit of teaching that Jesus gave to his apostles, but they also understood that the kernel of faith had to blossom and flourish as the Church faced difficult questions. The first Christians believed that the authority Jesus gave to his apostles had been handed on to their Church leaders to help them in this process of development and refinement. Irenaeus, writing around 150, had said that the apostles handed their successors the "doctrinal authority of the apostles,"[1] so with that authority the Church continues to come into a fuller understanding of the essential deposit of faith.

I begin with this explanation of the development of doctrine by the Church, because it is essential to see that all Christians actually accept the fact that doctrine has developed. If our understanding of the faith Jesus gave had not developed, we would not have the Bible as we know it. Jesus never commanded that Scriptures be written and defined. Through the guidance of the Holy Spirit the Church took the responsibility to develop the implications of Jesus' life and teaching, to write down their theology, and eventually define the canon of Scripture. Without the councils of the early Church we would not have the creeds as we know them. Without the theological work of the first Christians the doctrines of the Incarnation and the Trinity would still remain vague and implicit. Any Christian who accepts the Bible, the creeds, the Incarnation, and the Trinity therefore also accepts the possibility that our understanding of the kernel of faith that the apostles planted may develop over time by the inspiration of the Holy Spirit. The only question that remains then is to ask whether there is a cutoff date for the development of doctrine. Jesus promised that the Holy Spirit would lead us into all truth, and that the Holy Spirit would be with us to the end of time. Some Christians believe that process of development ended at a particular date. Catholics believe the Holy Spirit is still with the Church, and that while no new teaching can be given, our understanding of the deposit of faith can develop and grow in time just like the mustard seed that Jesus spoke about in his prophetic parable.

This belief is vital when we discuss the most controversial area between Catholic and non-Catholic Christians. Although the Scriptures are interwoven with archetypes of Mary, Catholics admit that there is little in the New Testament about Jesus' mother compared to the importance they place in her. Some of the things about her in the Gospels are confusing and difficult to understand. However, just as the Holy Spirit enabled the Church to understand more fully the mystery of the Incarnation and the Trinity, so during the same period of development the Church came to understand more fully the identity and role of Mary. Just as the Church came to see the types of Christ in the Old Testament, so the holy women in the Old Testament — from Eve onward — became pictures and pointers to the Virgin Mary. The earliest Christians were led to understand the importance of Mary in the plan of salvation and to call her blessed. Catholics find it odd, therefore, that many Christians turn to the early councils of the Church for true doctrine about Jesus and the Trinity, and yet they reject other teachings from those same councils about the mother of Christ.

Just as Catholic beliefs about the Incarnation are rooted in the Bible, so our beliefs about Mary are based in the Bible. As our beliefs about the Incarnation are also based in the developing understanding of the early Church, so our understanding of Mary's role is based in the prayer, meditation, and theological understanding of the very first Christians. As they pondered the mystery of the Incarnation, the Christians of the first four centuries came to also ponder the mystery of how God used a simple Jewish girl to accomplish his plan in the world. Once we accept the full impact of the doctrine of the Incarnation, it is not long before the role of Mary in the Incarnation also impresses us.

Mary and Jesus

A few years ago I was visiting the Holy Land and made a visit to Nazareth. There is a big modern church in Nazareth that is supposed to be built over the site of Mary's house. Certainly in the crypt of the church there are excavated remains of a simple first-century house. As I knelt in the crypt of the church it suddenly came home to me what a stupendous event the birth of Jesus really was. I believed in the Virgin Birth, and at this site, where the angel Gabriel visited the young virgin Mary, the full impact of the Incarnation came home to me in a real way.

The Virgin Birth is the doctrine that a simple and pure teenage girl from a village in Israel in the first century was made pregnant by a miracle. God himself chose to come into the world through the doorway of Mary. However, we believe that Jesus is true God and true man. Mary was not just a channel or conduit for the God-man. If that were the case, Jesus would be a supernatural being but not a human being. Neither do we believe that God's Son just took a human body from Mary, rather like an alien infesting a human body. Instead we believe that at the annunciation the humanity of Mary was joined with the divinity of God to conceive Jesus. God was Jesus' Father. Mary was Jesus' mother. If this is really what we believe, then just as each of us is a composite of our mother and father's genetic makeup, then Jesus was actually half Mary. Jesus shared her humanity in a literal and full way. This means he took not just a physical body like a shell but that he took on the fullness of everything human. It was this physical, mental, spiritual, and historic reality that hit me that day in Nazareth.

For centuries the Church has called Mary the "Mother of God" and this is what we mean — not that God in heaven has a mother or that Mary is some sort of goddess. Instead, since we believe that Jesus was God incarnate and Mary was his mother, we call her the Mother of God, or the God-bearer. Yet not only did Jesus take his humanity from Mary, but psychologists tell us how vitally important the months of gestation and the first few years of life are in the formation of the individual's personality. The mothering we receive makes us the sort of person we are. The foundations of our personality are determined by how much we are loved and accepted by our mother. At a very basic and profound level we learn what love is from our mother. If this is the case, then Mary was more than a sort of surrogate mother who simply carried somebody else's child (in this case God's). Mary was in that deep, permanent, and intimate relationship with Jesus from the very moment of his conception. Once all these facts about Jesus and Mary start to be considered, it becomes clear that Mary is a completely unique and wonderful human being. No other person is so close to Jesus. No other person was chosen to contribute humanity to God's Son. No other person taught him the human lesson of how to love and be loved.

These simple implications are drawn logically from the fact of the Virgin Birth. It doesn't take long to see how the first Christians soon began to honor Mary. If Jesus, as God's Son, was the perfect expression of God's love, and if he learned from his mother how to love and be loved, then his mother too must have had a special gift of grace so that Jesus might learn how to love and be loved perfectly. As they thought about the mystery

of Jesus' conception and birth, the first Christians also meditated on the event of Gabriel's visit to Mary. When Mary said to
the angel, "Let it be to me according to your word" (Luke 1:38),
the first Christian theologians saw a replay of the Garden of
Eden. As Eve had rejected God's will, Mary accepted God's will.
Because of this they began to refer to Mary as the second Eve.
Just as St. Paul had referred to Jesus as the second Adam, so
Irenaeus and Justin Martyr — writing in the early second century — referred to Mary as the second Eve. Irenaeus puts it like
this: "Eve, by her disobedience, brought death upon herself and
on all the human race: Mary, by her obedience, brought salvation."[2] A little bit later Tertullian says the same thing: "Eve had
believed the serpent; Mary believed Gabriel. That which the
one destroyed by believing, the other, by believing, set straight."[3]
It is from this basic understanding of Mary's identity that Catholics have drawn further logical conclusions about just who she
was and how she cooperated in God's plan of redemption.

Mary Immaculate

St. Paul said, "As in Adam all die, so also in Christ shall all be
made alive" (1 Corinthians 15:22). In the same epistle St. Paul
also meditated on the unity between man and woman, telling us
that "in the Lord woman is not independent of man nor man of
woman; for as woman was made from man, so man is now born
of woman. And all things are from God" (1 Corinthians 11:11-
12). The theologians of the second and third centuries understood this unity between man and woman. In God's providence,
a man was used to bring about redemption of the world, but a
woman was also used because the redemption could never have
happened without the Incarnation and the Incarnation was dependent on Mary's decision to say "yes" to God.

Before long, Christians began meditating further on the mystery of that simple Jewish girl's decision to risk her life to bear God's Son to the world. How could she have made such a decision? She must have been specially empowered by God, yet without taking away her own free choice in the matter. They saw that when the angel Gabriel came to Mary he greeted her with a special formula, "Hail, full of grace, the Lord is with you!" (Luke 1:28). The Greek wording in this verse — that is, in the *New American Bible* translation and similarly worded translations — literally means, "Rejoice, you who have been and remain filled with divine favor." The word "favor" implies an actual gift or blessing. The original language therefore says that Mary was in the past and continues to be filled with God's blessing. When the Bible was first translated from Greek into Latin, the phrase "highly favored one" was therefore rendered "full of grace."

This translation also carried the early Christians' understanding of Mary's relationship to God. Mary did not enjoy a simple measure of God's grace. She was full of God's grace and favor to a marvelous and supernatural degree. Just as we believe God's grace enables us to accept the Gospel, so we believe Mary was not only given grace, but she was *filled* with grace, to an extra measure, in order to enable her to say "yes" to God's request that she bear his Son. We believe this fullness of grace made Mary a perfect human being. By being full of God's grace she was in a state of perfect innocence just as Eve was. Mary needed to be filled with God's grace in this way for two reasons. First of all, if she was going to bear God's perfect Son she had to be a perfect mother. She had to be a perfect channel for a perfect son, but also to teach him perfect love she had first to show that perfect love in her own life.

Second of all, Mary had to live in the innocence of Eve in order to reverse Eve's wrong choice. Adam and Eve's wrong choice tainted all our choices. We are born in original sin, and one of the results of original sin is the fact that we will have an inborn inclination to choose sin. We suffer from a built-in disadvantage. Because we always have a tendency to choose wrongly, our choices cannot be totally free. Only Adam and Eve made a totally free choice, because in their first innocence they didn't suffer from that tendency to choose wrongly. In order for Mary to be the second Eve she had to be able to make a choice from that same position of innocence. Catholics believe that God, by a special intervention of grace, gave Mary that same innocence and perfection so that she could make a totally free choice without the disadvantage of original sin.

When did this freedom from the effects of original sin begin? Logic dictates that it must have been granted from the beginning of Mary's life. Therefore we believe this gift of complete innocence was given to Mary at the moment of her conception. This doctrine is called the Immaculate Conception of Mary. Although it was finally defined in the nineteenth century, it is a doctrine that has been believed by Christians from the first centuries. So St. Augustine, writing in the early fifth century, affirms the sinfulness of all. But about the Virgin Mary he writes, "Having excepted the holy Virgin Mary, concerning whom, on account of the honor of the Lord, I wish to have absolutely no question when treating of sins. For how do we know what abundance of grace for the total overcoming of sin was conferred upon her, who merited to conceive and bear him in whom there was no sin?"[4] In this way Augustine echoes his teacher Ambrose, who wrote that "from Mary, a virgin not only undefiled but a virgin whom grace had made inviolate, free of every stain of sin"[5] came forth the Son of God.

The Immaculate Conception is not the same thing as the Virgin Birth. We do not believe that Mary was born of a virgin. She was conceived and born in the natural way by her parents,

Anna and Joachim. Some people are dismayed at the idea that Mary was preserved from the stain of original sin, saying she is then on the same level as Jesus and God. Catholic teaching is clear that this is not the case. Mary needed a redeemer just like all other mortals. We believe that Mary was preserved from original sin retroactively by the redemptive work of her son on the cross. In this way she was saved with the backward action of God in time just like the saints of the Old Testament.

Saying Mary was perfect makes her sound like some sort of goddess or Wonder Woman of pop culture. This would be a misunderstanding of the true nature of Christian perfection. Perfection should be thought of as "wholeness." Mary was the perfectly fulfilled and complete person. She was totally natural and free. She was everything God created her to be — no more and no less. The wonderful thing is that this sort of holiness and perfection never seems amazing or unusual. If you've ever met a truly holy and humble person, you are aware that such a person is never remarkable in an egotistical way. Such holy individuals are simply themselves, and in being totally and utterly as God created them to be, they shine with the radiance of their Creator's image. Mary's perfection was the kind of perfection that makes her more fully human — not less. I believe this is one of the reasons why the New Testament doesn't speak more about Mary. She was a hidden soul. She was humble and holy in that unselfconscious way we see in every authentic saint. Most people probably didn't even realize what a perfect human being she was because of her naturalness, her humility, and her hiddenness. Only afterward, as the early Church reflected on her life, did Christians come to see in her the perfection that is possible for every follower of Jesus.

As part of her perfection, Catholics also believe, Mary remained a virgin for the whole of her life. To understand what this means it is important to understand how the early Christians understood virginity. We usually think of virginity in the most basic physical sense. A virgin is simply someone who has never had sexual intercourse. To praise virginity, therefore, simply means we are making a negative statement about sexual intercourse. The ancient Christians understood virginity in a much fuller sense. For them virginity was a sign of total purity and innocence. Writing in the late fourth century, St. Ambrose puts it this way, "She was a virgin not only in body but also in mind, who stained the sincerity of its disposition by no guile, who was humble in heart, grave in speech, prudent in mind, sparing of words, studious in reading, resting her hope not on uncertain riches, but on the prayer of the poor, intent on work, modest in discourse; wont to seek not man but God as the judge of her thoughts."[6]

Because a virgin was considered to be totally pure in body, mind, and spirit, a virgin bride was therefore a pure channel for the next generation. In the ancient world young girls often served in the temple as a sign of the purity of the temple itself. A virgin was therefore a sign to the early Christians of the purity each one of us should strive for, since our bodies too are meant to be temples of the Holy Spirit. The early Christians believed Mary remained a virgin because they believed it was God's will that she be an everlasting symbol of the total purity and holiness of God's servants.

The perpetual virginity of Mary was affirmed by the whole Church down through the ages, and it was a belief held to by the Reformers Calvin, Zwingli, and Luther. However, this theological understanding of Mary's virginity is also supported by the facts. Although the Gospels talk about Jesus' "brethren," the early tradition of the Church always considered them to simply be the kinsfolk of Mary — Jesus' cousins and uncles. The "brothers" of Jesus may have been sons of Joseph by an earlier marriage, but could they have been younger brothers of Jesus through the union of Mary and Joseph? The most ancient traditions of the Church have always rejected such a possibility. In the one account we have of Jesus' childhood, when he remained behind in the temple, there is no mention of younger brothers and sisters. The only characters in the story are Mary, Joseph, and Jesus. Even more telling is the fact that Jesus asked John to look after his mother from the cross. Jewish families were very strong. If Mary had other sons and daughters, they would have looked after her and John wouldn't have been needed. Catholics have therefore drawn the conclusion that the early traditions about Mary are correct, and that she remained a virgin her whole life.

Mary Is Taken Home

Mary's perfection is never something otherworldly. Neither is her holiness a characteristic that can be separated from Jesus. Instead, Mary's human perfection is the fruit of her intimate union with Jesus. Although she was kept free from the stain of original sin, Mary was preserved and kept in that perfection through her intimate bond with her son. Put very simply, Mary said "yes" to God. She literally accepted him into her life. She nurtured Jesus within her body for nine months, and then bore him to be the world's Savior. In this way Mary gives us a perfect illustration of our relationship with Christ. Like her, we must first hear the word of God and accept it into our hearts and lives. As "Mary kept all these things, pondering them in her heart" (Luke 2:19), so we must nurture Christ within our heart. As she bore him into the world, so it is our duty and calling to bear Christ to a needy world. In this way Mary is the prototype of all believers. Some writers have rightly called her the first Christian, since she was the very first person to accept Christ as her personal Savior. As the prototype of all Christians, Mary becomes the forerunner, the one who shows what wonders of transformation God can perform in anyone who submits totally to his will as Mary did.

As part of this total identification with Christ, ancient tradition in the Church taught that Mary was taken up into heaven after her earthly life was over. The formal wording is that Mary was "assumed" into heaven, and the Catholic doctrine is called the Assumption of the Blessed Virgin Mary. The Eastern Orthodox also believe in this ancient doctrine but call it the Dormition of the Blessed Virgin, or the Falling Asleep of Mary. The Bible speaks of Enoch (cf. Genesis 5:24 and Hebrews 11:5) and Elijah (cf. 2 Kings 2:1-14) who were taken up into heaven at the end of their earthly lives, and ancient Jewish tradition said Moses was also taken up into heaven at the end of his life. The Catholic belief that Mary was taken up into heaven is not based on any biblical account but on the ancient traditions of the early Church.

The tradition that Mary's body was taken up into heaven is supported by the fact that although the early Christians were careful to preserve the remains of the apostles and martyrs, there are no accounts of anyone ever preserving Mary's body or bones. Surely if early Christians venerated the bodies of all those who were close to Jesus, then if Mary's body had remained on earth they would have kept her remains in a special shrine as they did Peter's at Rome. The absence of such a shrine suggests that the ancient tradition of her body being taken up to heaven and glorified is actually true.

That Mary does enjoy an exalted place in heaven is spoken of in Scripture in the twelfth chapter of Revelation. There the visionary says that "a great portent appeared in heaven, a woman clothed with the sun, with the moon under her feet, and on her head a crown of twelve stars" (verse 1). This woman is clearly the Virgin Mary because John points out a few verses later that "she brought forth a male child, one who is to rule all the nations with a rod of iron, but her child was caught up to God and to his throne" (verse 5). If Mary was taken up into heaven, we have to be careful not to equate this belief with the ascension of Jesus. Jesus rose to heaven by his own power. Mary was "taken up into heaven." In other words, it was by the power of her son that her body was taken up. It is important that we not get too tangled up in the historical events of Mary's assumption. The meaning of this belief is that as Mary showed us the way to accept Jesus and bear him to the world, so she also shows us the fruit of our belief and trust in Jesus. By his redemptive power Mary was preserved from original sin. By that same power we too can be restored to innocence and purity. By his power Mary was preserved from sin. By that same power we can be preserved from the slavery of sin. By his power Mary was taken up to glory in heaven. By that same power we too are promised a heavenly home. In each case Mary's life shows us the way and reveals to us what Christ has done for us. In my Evangelical upbringing we were taught that the Lord would take us up to glory one day. Mary's assumption into heaven reminds us all of the hope we share that one day we shall be like him, that our mortal bodies will be made glorious bodies and that we shall, in some mysterious way, share in the resurrection of our bodies from the dead.

Mary as Co-Redeemer

Catholics sometimes speak of Mary as co-redeemer or co-mediator (mediatrix) with Christ. This is not a formal Catholic doctrine, but it is a way some Catholics have of speaking about Mary's ministry. When many non-Catholics hear this sort of language, it confirms in their mind what they already thought about Catholics — that we worship Mary and place her on an equal footing with Christ. Immediately they call to mind that verse from the New Testament, which says, "For there is one God, and there is one mediator between God and men, the man Christ Jesus" (1 Timothy 2:5). The Catholic Church would never teach something that is contrary to Scripture, so it must be that the Catholic Church means something different when she says that Mary is "co-redeemer and co-mediator."

When we speak of Mary as co-redeemer and co-mediator, we are not putting Mary on the same level as Jesus Christ. Instead we are emphasizing how united Mary's life is with that of Jesus. Remembering St. Paul's teaching that man is not independent of woman nor woman independent of man (cf. 1 Corinthians 11:11), we see that the work of Christ is inextricably integrated into the life and work of Mary. The old prophet Simeon also recognized the unity between mother and son when he met the infant Jesus in the temple. He said that Mary would share in some mysterious way in the redemption her son was to win when he said to Mary that a sword would pierce her own heart also (cf. Luke 2:35). By saying "yes" to God at the annunciation, Mary joins her will to God's will. In other words, she cooperates with God. It is in this sense that she is a co-redeemer or co-mediator. Mary is not another redeemer or another mediator. Instead we believe that she works with her son for the redemption of the world. She mediates with Christ for the salvation of souls. As such she is a model of what we should all be doing. In fact, all of us are called to be "God's fellow workers" (cf. 1 Corinthians 3:9), and St. Paul speaks of the possibility of completing "what is lacking in Christ's afflictions" through the suffering in our own lives (cf. Colossians 1:24). In such a way we believe Mary cooperates with Jesus in an intimate way for the salvation of the world. In doing so she shows the whole Church how to share in his saving work.

To cooperate is not to operate on the same level. Nor does cooperation necessarily imply equality and interdependence. I ask my eight-year-old son to cooperate with me by tidying his room. In fact, I could tidy it much more quickly and efficiently. However, I want to cooperate with him to grant him the dignity of working with me, to learn responsibility, and obedience. In the same way, Mary cooperates with God in the redemption of the world. She does so not in the same way as Christ but in a subsidiary fashion. All she does depends on all that he has done. Her example in this shows us how we can work with Christ in a similar way. We too can be filled with his Spirit and empowered for service and witness in the world.

If Mary cooperates with God, then we believe she cooperates with us too. It is one thing to talk about what Catholics believe about Mary, but any non-Catholic will observe that in this area of Catholic practice the doctrines are, in a way, secondary to the devotion. In other words, we don't simply believe certain things about Mary. We actually enjoy worshiping with Mary. We are enthusiastic about all that God has done for Mary and we are aware that she helps us in our worship, our prayers, and our Christian life. This is not to say that the beliefs about Mary are unnecessary or impossible to really hold to. It simply means that once we have learned to pray with Mary, the beliefs about her become real in a fresh and dynamic way.

The best way to express what a Catholic feels for Mary is to say that, in a way, she is our spiritual mother. As described in John 19:26-27, Mary and the apostle John stood at the foot of the cross, and at the moment of his death Jesus gave John and all of us a kind of last will and testament. He looked down from the cross and said to his mother, "Woman, behold your son!"

Then to John he said, "Behold, your mother!" His beloved disciple was to regard Mary as his own mother from that point on. Early Church tradition tells us that John looked after Mary in her earthly life and that she ended her life with him at Ephesus. As Mary becomes the mother of Jesus' disciple so we believe she becomes our spiritual mother too. St. Paul says we are adopted sons and daughters in the family of God (cf. Romans 8:23 and Galatians 4:5). We have received the spirit of sonship and are co-heirs with Christ (cf. Romans 8:15-17). If we are Christ's brothers and sisters in the Spirit, then his mother is our mother too. The intimate bond he shared with her can be ours as part of the inheritance of more Christianity. This possible relationship with Mary is shown to be a reality in Revelation 12:17, where the visionary says the woman has other offspring. They are all those who obey the commandments of God and bear witness to Jesus Christ. In other words, Mary is our mother too.

The angel Gabriel called Mary blessed (cf. Luke 1:30), Elizabeth called Mary blessed (cf. Luke 1:42), and Mary herself prophesied that "all generations" would call her blessed (cf. Luke 1:48). Catholics rejoice to be a part of that fulfillment of prophecy. We call Mary the "Blessed Virgin Mary" because in that majestic title we recognize her queenly role in the kingdom of God. We recognize in her that the humble are lifted high and that God uses the foolish things of the world to confound the mighty. Mary's life and witness is something Catholic Christians treasure and are enthusiastic about because for us Mary's life reveals the whole miraculous working of God in the world. What God did for Mary through the working of his Spirit and the redemption of his Son, he wishes to do for each one of us and for the whole world. In Mary we see the final product of our own redemption. Her perfection and glorification show us our own final perfection and glorification in Christ.

Catholics are sometimes accused of venerating Mary too highly and forgetting about Jesus. It is true that we love Mary, but we picture her in our images in a special way. In the best images Mary is always offering her son to the world. "Here he is," she seems to say. "Here is the child who is the salvation of the world." We love Mary as we love our own mother — because she is the channel of life and love. Through the sacrifice of a mother, Mary gives us Life itself — her son Jesus Christ, and her role is always and everywhere to continue to point the way to her son. At the wedding at Cana in Galilee she said, "Do whatever he tells you" (John 2:5). That is still her role. Mary bears her son to the world and points us to obedience and love for him. Our devotion to Mary is therefore never separate from our devotion to her son. Everywhere and always she takes us into a closer and more intimate relationship with him.

The Rosary

In the Middle Ages a special way of praying developed that stresses the integral part Mary plays in the Incarnation and life of Jesus. Medieval Christians rolled up rose petals into a little ball, let them dry out, then varnished them, turning them into beads. They put them on a chain or string in five batches of ten beads. As they held one of the beads in their fingers they would meditate on a particular incident from the Gospels. This meditative way of praying soon became very popular. It was linked with an already existing ancient prayer called the "Hail Mary." The words of the Hail Mary prayer are half Scripture. "Hail [Mary], full of grace, the Lord is with you!" (Luke 1:28). "Blessed are you among women, and blessed is the fruit of your womb!" (Luke 1:42). The second half of the Hail Mary prayer is an ancient form of words asking Mary to pray for us: "Holy Mary, Mother of God, pray for us now and at the hour of our death."

Catholics use this meditative way of praying to move more profoundly into the life of Christ. As we repeat the prayer we pause to meditate on the meaning of various incidents from the Gospel. Each day we pray using the five sets of rosary beads, and at each of the five sets we remember a Gospel story. The first set of stories we call the joyful mysteries. They are all about the wonder of the Incarnation. The five joyful mysteries are: the Annunciation, the Visitation of Mary to Elizabeth, the Nativity, the Presentation of Christ in the Temple, and the Finding of Jesus in the Temple. The next set of five Gospel stories is called the sorrowful mysteries, and has to do with Jesus' death and passion. They are: the Agony in the Garden, the Scourging, the Crowning with Thorns, Jesus Carrying His Cross, and the Crucifixion. The final set of stories is called the glorious mysteries. They are: the Resurrection, the Ascension, Pentecost, the Assumption of Mary into Heaven, and the Crowning of Mary as Queen of Heaven.

These are the traditional Gospel stories on which Catholics meditate using the rosary. However, the rosary is not a strict law for Catholics to follow. Many good Catholics don't use the rosary at all. On the other hand, many non-Catholics find the rosary very helpful. John Wesley prayed the rosary every day, as do many Anglicans, Lutherans, and Methodists today. The rosary is simply a devotional aid to prayer that many people find helpful. Some non-Catholics find it useful but don't particularly like the last two glorious mysteries because they are "too Marian." They substitute other glorious mysteries instead and use "the Transfiguration, the Resurrection, the Ascension, Pentecost, and the Second Coming." Still others don't use the "Hail Mary" prayer and use some other form of repetitious prayer instead.

No one needs to use the rosary, but critics of the rosary accuse Catholics of using prayers that are vain repetition (cf.

Matthew 6:7). This verse does not actually condemn repetitious prayer, indeed all prayers are repetitious to a certain extent. Psalm 136, for instance, repeats the phrase "His mercy endures forever" in every verse. The better translation for this phrase is "empty phrases" or "babbling" (*Revised Standard Version* and *New International Version* respectively). What Jesus condemns is the mindless gibberish that demon-possessed pagan worshipers indulged in. It might be true that some people turn the rosary prayers into a kind of mindless babbling, but the same criticism could be leveled at charismatic Christians speaking in tongues or any Christian who simply repeats empty (or seemingly empty) phrases in his or her prayer. However, we are talking about right uses — not abuses. The rosary, when used properly, is an aid to a profound and simple meditative way of prayer that millions of Christians find helpful and Spirit-filled.

Throughout this book I have stressed that Catholic Christianity is "more Christianity," not "mere Christianity." Time and again I have tried to show that Catholics do not believe differently than other Christians; rather, they believe *more* than other Christians. We affirm everything other Christians affirm. We simply cannot deny some of the things they deny. When it comes to the Blessed Virgin Mary, this is especially true. All traditional Christians affirm the Incarnation of our Lord Jesus Christ. We all believe he really was true God and true man. This is "mere Christianity" if you like. Catholic Christians affirm the Incarnation too, but we also pay devotion and honor to that singular and extraordinary young girl through whom the Incarnation became possible. Because of the Incarnation we honor Mary, and by honoring Mary we praise God for the Incarnation. Without her "yes" to God our Lord would not have been born. As a result we not only give thanks to God for her, but we also realize that because of her submission to God's will each one of us has a Savior.

Catholics are sometimes accused of distorting the faith with their devotion to the Blessed Virgin, but it is fair to ask whether it is not more distorted to exclude Mary from worship altogether. After all, here is a devotion and tradition that has been practiced by Christians from the very earliest days. Around the world today the vast majority of Christians honor Mary with devotion and love. Catholics, Eastern Orthodox, Anglicans, and Lutherans all have a tradition of honoring the Blessed Virgin Mary. If some Christians ask us why we venerate Mary, mightn't it be fair for us to ask why they ignore, exclude, and sometimes revile the mother of our Lord? Shouldn't we ask ourselves whether, in this matter, the vast majority of Christians — both today and down through the ages — might be right?

In solidarity with most Christians everywhere and in all times, Catholics are joyful in our veneration and homage to Mary. We are not ashamed to call her the Mother of God, because in that title we recognize her son as God incarnate. We delight to call her blessed because as we do we join with the angels and the saints who also recognized her as one who was uniquely filled with the grace of God on this earth. We are humbled to ask for her prayers and to call on her as our mother because Jesus himself gave her that role from the cross. In honoring Mary we enter a profound relationship with her son and through her prayers and love we come to know her son in a way that is more profound and intimate than we ever could have imagined.

To the non-Catholic our language about Mary often seems extreme. Our beliefs about her seem unreal and artificial. The best way to describe this is to say it is like being in love. The lover is bowled over by his emotions. Others think love has made the lover mad; made him lose his senses. But for the lover it is exactly the opposite. Love has made him see things aright for the first time. Love is the light by which he sees all things with a freshness and a beauty he had not thought possible. If others think him mad, he smiles and goes on because he has glimpsed something that has given life a deeper meaning and purpose. So it is with Mary. Just as she brought Christ into the world, so she still works to bring others close to her son. Just as she is pictured offering her son to us, so she still holds out to us the One who is Life and Love itself. We honor her because through her we have come into a deeper and fuller knowledge of him — the Love that created all things — the "Love that moves the sun and the other stars."[7]

Chapter Eight Endnotes

1. Henry Bettenson, *The Early Christian Fathers,* Oxford, Oxford University Press, 1969, p. 90.

2. Ibid., p. 74.

3. Ernest Evans, *Tertullian's Treatise on the Incarnation,* London, SPCK, 1956, p. 61.

4. John Mourant and William Collinge (trs.), *St. Augustine, Four Anti-Pelagian Writings,* Washington, D.C., The Catholic University of America Press, 1992, p. 53.

5. *Patrologiae Latinae,* vol. 5, *Santi Ambrosii, Commentary on Psalm 118,* Paris, Apud Garneir et Fratres, 1997, col. 1599.

6. H. de Romestein, *Principal Works of St. Ambrose,* Oxford, James Parker and Co., 1846, p. 374.

7. Dante, *The Divine Comedy: Paradise,* Dorothy Sayers (tr.), London, Penguin, 1976, p. 347.

Chiefly on Prayer

When I was growing up, every Wednesday evening our family went to our Bible church for a prayer meeting. After the pastor preached a short Bible message we took cards with printed prayer requests and split up into small groups. The men and boys went in one direction and the women and girls in the other. Once we'd chosen a group we'd gather in various rooms and corners of the church to pray together. I can remember praying in a group with my father and the other men of the church. Eyes squeezed tightly shut, I would listen to their long prayers for the people who were sick, for those who were bereaved, for the missionaries, and for the other churches in our fellowship. We'd pray around the circle and eventually it came to be my turn. Our prayer requests were on cards, but our prayers were never printed out. There was no liturgy. We didn't even recite the Lord's Prayer. The general opinion was that written prayers were just empty formalism. Instead we learned to talk to God naturally in our own words.

I remember those prayer meetings as special times when the grown men of our church would open themselves in prayer. They revealed a certain vulnerability, and you could see their dependence on God. It was the same in our home. Family devotions consisted of my father reading a passage from the Bible, then one of us would read a page from a booklet called *The Daily Bread*, which would comment on the Bible passage and give us something to think about. Afterward we all took turns saying a short prayer asking God for our needs and thanking him for the blessings we enjoyed. Prayer was a natural part of life. Sometimes it was boring and the adults seemed long-winded, but I can remember as a child not minding prayer meetings that much. There was something simple and pure about it that I remember to this day.

Our prayers in that form of "mere Christianity" were uncluttered with meaningless traditions, grandiose liturgies, and set words. The prayer life had a simplicity and childlike quality. For the most part prayer consisted of asking God and thanking God. Asking and thanking lie at the heart of all prayer, but prayer can consist of more than simply asking God and thanking God. Sometimes in our prayer meetings there was a silence between the prayers and in that silence contact was being made and God was giving us far more than we had dared to ask for. He was giving us the gift of his presence. One of our favorite Bible verses for prayer meetings was Jesus' promise that "where two or three are gathered in my name, there am I in the midst of them" (Matthew 18:20). I can never remember it being said, but at the heart of our prayer meetings was the assumption that through our prayers we were doing more than reciting a shopping list to God. We were making contact with the Lord. We called it a prayer meeting because we met together for prayer, but perhaps it was well-named because in prayer we were meeting with Jesus too.

This contact with the living Lord is really what prayer is all about. We are commanded to ask God for our needs, but our greatest need is for him, so at its heart prayer is asking God himself. The essence of prayer is the turning of our whole selves to find the Lord of Life, the King of our hearts, and the Creator of our whole being. Thérèse of Lisieux said, "For me, prayer is a surge of the heart; it is a simple look turned toward heaven, it is a cry of recognition and of love, embracing both trial and joy."[1] George Herbert said prayer is "God's breath in man returning to his birth . . . the heart in pilgrimage . . . a kind of tune which all things hear and fear; Heaven in ordinary . . . church-bells, beyond the stars heard, the soul's blood, the land of spices; something understood."[2]

Prayer in the Bible

The breadth and depth of prayer is shown to us from the Scriptures. Throughout the Bible story the heroes of faith have a communion with God that is intimate and real. From the very first story of Adam and Eve walking with God in the garden in the cool of the day we get a glimpse of the life of prayer. In the book of Genesis, prayer is likened to walking with God. Both Noah and Enoch were said to have "walked with God" (Genesis 5:24, 6:9). In the story of Abraham we see the great father of faith walking with God. He steps out in faith to follow God, and God establishes a covenant with him. Throughout Abraham's story, prayer is shown to be a living relationship with God. It is established in the sacrifices of the covenant and fulfilled in the promises of the covenant. The *Catechism of the Catholic Church* puts it this way, "Christian prayer is a covenant relationship between God and man in Christ. It is the action of God and of man, springing forth from both the Holy Spirit and ourselves, wholly directed to the Father, in union with the human will of the Son of God made man."[3]

In the story of Moses, other dimensions of prayer start to come alive. Moses fled to the wilderness, but God found him and called him through the burning bush (cf. Exodus 3:1-6). For Moses, prayer means not only seeking God but God seeking him. "The wonder of prayer is revealed beside the well where we come seeking water: there, Christ comes to meet every human being. It is he who first seeks us and asks us for a drink. Jesus thirsts. His asking arises from the depths of God's desire for us."[4] When God came to meet Moses at the burning bush, we are reminded that prayer is a gift from God. He first gives us the desire to pray, then enables us to pray. Therefore our prayer is always a response to God.

The burning bush is also an introduction to the "mystical" tradition of prayer. Within the mind there is a facility to apprehend a message from God given in a vivid and even frightening manner. When we speak of mystics in the Christian tradition, we don't mean mystic fortune-tellers or mediums. Instead, the mystic is one who has had a close, unforgettable, and vivid experience of God's presence. Like Moses, mystics have discovered how to listen to God as well as speak to him. Mysticism is linked with meditation, for in meditation we reflect on the Word of God and take that message to heart. Like Abraham, Moses' meditation on God's word took him further into an intimate relationship with God. God speaks to Moses face to face as a person speaks to a friend (cf. Exodus 33:11). It is from this intimacy with God that Moses becomes a great prayer warrior. He prays for Miriam's healing (cf. Numbers 12:10-13), for victory over the Amalekites (cf. Exodus 17:8-13), and for God's mercy in the face of the people's apostasy (cf. Exodus 32).

From the time of King David, the psalms began to be written down. With them the prayer life of the people of God was enriched beyond measure. The word "psalter" means "praises," and prayer as thanksgiving and supplication is nowhere more eloquently expressed than in the poetry of the psalms. "The

Psalter is the book in which the Word of God becomes man's prayer."[5] In the psalms we have the prayers of individuals and the praises of the people of God that are actually themselves inspired by God. The Jews used the psalms as their hymnbook and liturgy. The wealth of the psalms still supplies a wonderful source for the worship of the people of God today. Anyone who loves the Scriptures cannot be absolutely opposed to liturgy in practice, because the psalms themselves are liturgy, and as Scripture they are themselves inspired. In the psalms the people of God turn to God together and pour out their heart in prayer and praise. Our hymns and liturgy all hearken back to the first hymns and liturgy of the psalms. The psalms — as well as our liturgy and hymns — release us from the constant need to devise our own words of prayer and praise. Instead we can lift our hearts with words and music and blend our voices with the voices of our brothers and sisters.

Elijah is the final pioneer in the Old Testament. He stands for the prophetic tradition of prayer. Like Moses, Elijah went out to the wilderness, and on the same mountain of Horeb he was hidden in the cleft of the rock and heard the voice of God himself (cf. 1 Kings 19). Elijah typifies the monastic and contemplative life of prayer. Following in the same tradition, the prophets and finally John the Baptist and Jesus himself went out into the wilderness to seek God in solitude. Within that solitude they discovered themselves and learned to listen to contemplate God's still, small voice of love. This final expression of prayer returns to the first relationship of Adam, Noah, Enoch, and Abraham. Within the silent prayer of contemplation there is a covenant of love, and the soul learns once more to walk with God in the cool of the day.

These five traditions of prayer can be called Communion, Meditation, Intercession, Common Praise, and Contemplation.

They are grounded in the Old Testament, but they are also evident in the life of Christ. In him the Old Testament found its fulfillment, and in him the developing prayer life of the people of God finds its climax and completion. Jesus was a man of prayer, and it is from his intimate relationship with the Father that he teaches us to pray.

Jesus: Man of Prayer

As Adam walked with God in the garden, and as Noah and Enoch walked with God, so Jesus walked with God the Father in his daily life. Being one with his Father, he was in constant communion with God. In his relationship with the Father, Jesus shows us that the life of prayer is an intimate loving relationship between father and child. He is the first to call God *abba*, or "papa," that is, "father" (cf. Mark 14:36), and St. Paul tells us that we too can refer to God as "papa" (cf. Romans 8:15 and Galatians 4:6). This relationship is one in which the child rests completely in the Father's love and grace. Jesus said that we cannot come into the kingdom except as a child (cf. Mark 10:15), and the greatest of saints have reaffirmed that to live in a state of spiritual childhood is to approach that same dependent relationship that Jesus enjoyed with his Father in heaven. So Thérèse of Lisieux writes: "To be little means recognizing one's nothingness, expecting everything from the good God, as a little child expects everything from its Father."[6]

Jesus lived in this constant communion with his Father in heaven, but he also fulfills the second category of prayer in his life. Meditation is a form of prayer that uses the Word of God and allows the Holy Spirit to apply it to our lives. The Gospels show how Jesus' life was imbued with the Scriptures. Time and again he quotes the Old Testament in a fresh and startling way, showing that the Word of God had taken root in his life and that it was lodged in the depth of his being. It is good to study the Scriptures with our minds, but the psalms exhort us to hide the Word in our hearts. In the wilderness Jesus shows the fruit of his meditative prayer. He uses Scripture to drive away the devil and win the victory over evil. Meditation transforms the soul. The Word of God is living and active and "sharper than any two-edged sword" (Hebrews 4:12). It cuts to the heart and illuminates the darkest places of our being.

Jesus exhibits the third category of prayer throughout his ministry. This category is intercession. When he heals the sick, he prays for them. When he raises Lazarus, he prays for him (cf. John 11:41-44). He prays for his disciples that they will be preserved from evil. He prays for help before his baptism, transfiguration, and crucifixion. In chapter 6 of Luke's Gospel he prays for guidance in the selection of his apostles; he prays before Peter's confession of him as "the Christ, the Son of the living God" (Matthew 16:16); likewise, he prays before he sends them out on mission. Jesus' prayer of intercession is summed up in his great high priestly prayer in John 17. There he shows us what all intercession is based on. It is not simply asking God for what we need. Jesus' intercession is empowered and enlivened by the fact that he is about to lay down his life for his friends. Intercession is therefore a kind of priesthood. A priest is one who offers sacrifice. Intercession is therefore never real unless the one interceding is prepared to make the necessary sacrifices for the prayer to be fulfilled.

The fourth category of prayer is also seen clearly in Jesus' life. Jesus did not turn away from the corporate life of prayer of the Jewish people. In Luke 4 we see Jesus taking his turn at leading synagogue prayers, and throughout the Gospel we see him in the synagogue and the temple, involved in the regular, ritualistic acts of Jewish worship. The Jews of Jesus' day had a set liturgy in their worship. They used the psalms to praise God and the Scriptures to worship him. They observed the full ritual of sacrifice in the temple. Rites of worship with common words for worship were part of Jesus' structured prayer life, and through that means of prayer his own prayers were joined with the prayers of God's people.

Finally, Jesus followed the pattern of prayer established by Moses, Elijah, and the prophets. The hallmark of contemplative or mystical prayer is solitude. On the one hand Jesus took part in the corporate life of prayer. On the other hand he instructed his disciples to enter into a room and close the door and pray to God in secret (cf. Matthew 6:6). Jesus himself went out into the wilderness to fast and pray for forty days and forty nights, and throughout his ministry was constantly going off to a lonely mountainside or the wilderness to pray (cf. Mark 1:12, 1:35, 6:46; also cf. Luke 5:16). This solitary prayer includes talking to God, but more importantly, it means listening to God. As Moses and Elijah heard the voice of God in the solitude of the cave on Mount Sinai, so Jesus, going up a mountain to pray at night, must have been in contemplative communion with his Father. Contemplation is a time for listening, but it is also the purest form of adoration. In contemplation we sit in silence and simply gaze on the face of the beloved. "Adoration is homage of the spirit to the 'King of Glory.' "[7] In that rapt silence the prayer of thanksgiving is also fulfilled because the heart pours out its thanks to God for the blessing of his presence and daily provision.

Recognizing Jesus as a man of prayer, his disciples naturally asked him to teach them to pray (cf. Luke 11:1). In what is known as the Lord's Prayer, Jesus sums up all the Old Testament and the whole life of prayer. Thomas Aquinas, the great theologian of the thirteenth century, wrote: "The Lord's prayer is the most perfect of prayers. . . . In it we ask, not only for all the things we can rightly desire but also in the sequence that they should be desired. This prayer teaches us not only to ask for things, but also in what order we should ask them."[8] The Lord's Prayer is a mine of inspiration for our own prayer life, and many books have been written that plumb its depths. I don't have enough space here to speak more about it, but the essence of the Lord's Prayer is that Jesus shares it with us in order to invite us into the heart of his own prayer life. The Lord's Prayer, therefore, is not simply a form of words to be recited automatically. It is a formula given by Jesus himself that draws us into the intimate relationship he had with his Father. At its heart, the Lord's Prayer is an invitation to us to pray. It charts the territory and gives us the basic equipment to embark on the great adventure of prayer.

Catholic Tradition of Prayer

The prayer life of Jesus was complete and perfect. Within his relationship with his Father the five forms of prayer were balanced and full. Part of the reason for this is that Jesus himself was the perfectly balanced and fulfilled individual. In our own lives our personality types mean we will probably be attracted more to certain forms of prayer than others. The intellectual person may find meditation on the Word of God to come naturally while the nonintellectual will thrive on simple communion and conversation with God. The extrovert may find prayer easiest within the common tradition of worship, while the introverted person will be drawn to contemplative prayer. Whoever we are, and however we pray, we should try to expand our world and learn to pray in new and fresh ways.

The Catholic tradition of spirituality has always nurtured all these forms of prayer within the variety of her life. There are

groups or movements within the Catholic Church that special-
ize in the different forms of prayer and help the faithful to participate in the life of prayer to a greater degree. Some of these
different traditions are ancient, and some are new. Within the
Catholic Church, spirituality and the life of prayer are forever
ancient yet forever being renewed. This fullness of spirituality
and variety of prayer styles is one of the glories of the Catholic
tradition.

Coming from an Evangelical background, I knew how to
intercede and petition the Lord for prayer requests, but the other
forms of prayer were largely unknown to me. In a way, asking
the Lord for our requests was "mere prayer." As I came into the
Catholic tradition I discovered "more prayer." Within Catholicism I uncovered traditions of spirituality that feed the soul and
instruct the hungry heart in the ways of prayer. These different
ways of praying all work together to enrich the spiritual life and
bring one closer to the Lord Jesus.

How to walk with God, or commune with him in a day-to-
day relationship, has been pondered over by Christians from
the beginning. Struck by the biblical command to "pray constantly" (1 Thessalonians 5:17), spiritual writers wondered how
they could turn their whole life into a prayer. It is impossible to
be asking God for specific prayer requests every moment, but
the masters of the spiritual life developed a way of turning the
heart to God in prayer throughout the day. The Jesus Prayer is a
simple phrase that is repeated over and over again until it merges
with our breathing and lodges at the depths of our conscious-
ness. The spiritual writers based in the monasteries of Sinai and
Mount Athos in Greece first developed this technique. Almost
any phrase of Scripture that calls on God for help can be used,
but the classic phrase is, "Lord Jesus Christ, Son of God, have
mercy on me a sinner." This phrase is scriptural — combining

the hymn to Jesus in Philippians 2:6-11 and the cry of the publican and the blind man in the Gospels (cf. Mark 10:47 and Luke 18:13).

This simple form of praying reveals the heart of the Christian life. With this prayer the soul turns in repentance and calls on Jesus as Savior. This constant refrain penetrates into our lives and permeates every action and thought of our heart. The *Catechism of the Catholic Church* says this about the Jesus Prayer: "The invocation of the holy name of Jesus is the simplest way of praying always. When the holy name is repeated often by a humbly attentive heart, the prayer is not lost by heaping up empty phrases, but holds fast the Word and 'brings forth fruit with patience.' This prayer is possible 'at all times' because it is not one occupation among others but the only occupation: that of loving God, which animates and transfigures every action in Christ Jesus."[9]

The second form of prayer that I have outlined is meditation. Meditation is praying with God's Word. In meditation the mind and heart seek to understand the mystery of the Christian life. One of the most ancient Catholic traditions is that of *lectio divina* (Latin for "divine [or sacred] reading") and is popularly called spiritual reading. In *lectio divina* we read the Scriptures with an open heart. We put on one side our intellectual curiosity about the Scriptures. We eschew all kinds of speed reading. Some people who practice *lectio divina* actually trace the words with their fingers and move their lips while reading to slow themselves down. Before reading we ask the Spirit's guidance and presence. While reading we allow time to pause and reflect on what we've read. We allow time for the Spirit to speak within. In this way the "living and active" Word of God touches us on a deeper level than just our minds. The rosary is another form of meditation many Catholics find helpful. The rosary focuses their mind on certain key events of the Gospels and as they meditate on the events of Jesus' life the reality of the events moves into the inner rooms of the heart.

Another Catholic tradition that relies on meditation is the *Spiritual Exercises* of St. Ignatius Loyola. Ignatius Loyola was a Catholic priest who lived in the sixteenth century. His *Spiritual Exercises* are a method of visualizing the events of the Gospel and thereby absorbing their meaning and reality into our hearts. An Ignatian retreat is a time of guided prayer and meditation in which a person meets with a spiritual director and is taken through the *Spiritual Exercises*. Countless people, not just Catholics, have benefited from this wonderful form of prayer and meditation and have drawn closer to Christ through it.

The third form of prayer is intercession. Like all other Christians, Catholics pray for their own needs, but we also pray for the needs of our loved ones, our fellow Christians, and for the whole world. Evangelical Christians are more likely to pray extemporaneously, simply putting their requests before God in ordinary language. This is a great tradition, and one that many Catholics could learn from. Catholics are not usually very confident with extemporaneous prayer. They are not used to praying in their own words out loud, and often feel they have to use "special words" for prayer. However, intercessory prayer is a main part of Catholic prayer life. We express our own intercessions within our recitation of the Lord's Prayer or by saying formal prayers that we have memorized. Catholics also use what are called "bidding prayers," in which a worship leader will pray for a particular need and the congregation will make a response like, "Lord, hear our prayer." Bidding prayers are useful because they are planned and help us remember to pray for the things that we might otherwise forget. Catholic bidding prayers are similar to the prayer lists we had in my old Bible church.

Catholics often link their intercessory prayers with some physical action or routine of prayer. If we want to cry out to the Lord for a specific need, we will sometimes keep nine especially intense days of prayer. This is called a novena. We might link a special prayer request to a period of fasting or to some physical hardship like a pilgrimage or a vigil (staying up to pray through the night). Because the physical and spiritual are linked, we believe our prayers are intensified and our spirit strengthened when the body is made to submit to a spiritual goal.

It is in our common prayer that Catholics seem most unlike Evangelicals. From the very earliest days of the church we have used set forms and set words for worship. The word "liturgy" means "work of the people" and the liturgy is just that — it is the spiritual work of the people of God. The New Testament commands us not to forsake assembling ourselves together (cf. Hebrews 10:25). In the liturgy we sing the praise of God together, listen to the Word of God, pray for our needs, and meet Christ in the great prayer that we call the Eucharist. It is common for some non-Catholics to regard the liturgy as dead formalism. Catholics regard it in just the opposite way. Like a masterpiece of artwork or a classic piece of music or literature, the liturgy is timeless and can be repeated over and over again without becoming stale.

The liturgy is the timeless structure into which we pour our prayers, our praise, and our worship. As we use the liturgy we are not only worshiping in unison with all the other Christians present at that service, we are also united with all the other Catholics all around the world who are using the same readings and liturgy. The liturgy also unites us with all our fellow believers down through the centuries. From the Last Supper onward, Christians have followed the same basic pattern and been drawn into the mystery of the Incarnation and redemption. The liturgy is flexible in form yet established for centuries. It can be adapted for the worship of a million teenagers on pilgrimage to Rome, or celebrated by a handful of people in an attic.

In a famous passage, Gregory Dix sang the wonder and glory of the Eucharistic liturgy:

> Was ever another command so obeyed? For century after century, spreading slowly to every continent and country and among every race on earth, this action has been done, in every conceivable human circumstance. Men have found no better thing than to do this for kings at their crowning, and for criminals going to their scaffold; armies in triumph, or for a bride and bridegroom in a little country church; for a schoolboy sitting an examination, or for Columbus setting up to discover America; in thankfulness because my father did not die of pneumonia, or because the Turk was at the gates of Vienna . . . while the lions roared in the nearby amphitheater; on the beach at Dunkirk; tremulously by an old monk on the fiftieth anniversary of his vows; furtively by an exiled bishop who had hewn timber all day in a prison camp; gorgeously, for the canonization of St. Joan of Arc — one could fill many pages with the reasons why men have done this, and not tell a hundredth part of them. And best of all, week by week and month by month, on 100,000 successive Sundays, faithfully, unfailingly, across all parishes of Christendom, the pastors have done this just to make holy the common people of God.[10]

In fact, all Christians use a form for their worship. It would be impossible to invent a new style of worship every week. All of us rely on the form to help us in our week-by-week worship.

The churches that use a set liturgy recognize this and draw on the resources of two thousand years of Christian worship to enrich our own words of worship week by week. A simple form of prayers, hymns, Bible readings, and a sermon is good, but liturgy is a form of "more Christianity." It's true that liturgy sometimes takes getting used to, but that is true of virtually everything that is worthwhile. Painting a picture, playing the clarinet, learning to ski or play football — all are hard before they're easy. Prayer and worship also require effort and discipline, and we should be suspicious of any form of prayer of worship that only offers entertainment or easy inspiration.

The final form of prayer is contemplation. What is contemplative prayer? St. Teresa of Ávila says, "Contemplative prayer in my opinion is nothing else than a close sharing between friends; it means taking time frequently to be alone with him who we know loves us."[11] Contemplative prayer is different from meditation because it is more a movement of the heart than an activity of the mind. "Contemplative prayer is the poor and humble surrender to the loving will of the Father in ever deeper union with his beloved Son."[12] It is a simple, silent abiding in the presence of God. As a peasant said when asked how he prays, "I sit and look at him and he looks at me." In other words, it is the gaze of the beloved to the source of Love.

In the Catholic tradition, communities of people give their entire lives to prayer. Various orders of monks and nuns live enclosed in their convent, their whole lives devoted to a routine of prayer and worship that reaches its climax in hours of contemplative prayer. The contemplative life is nurtured in these communities of prayer and shared with the whole Church. Most monasteries and convents have a great tradition of hospitality. Anyone who wishes to can go to visit and spend time learning to pray more profoundly. Contemplative prayer is not an activity only for the spiritually elite. All of us are called to share in the contemplative life. In Catholic parish life there are times set aside for this silence and adoration. In the service of Benediction, Christ's special presence is celebrated by placing the consecrated bread on the altar. This provides a focus for contemplation and the opportunity to simply sit in silence and adore the One who gave his life for our salvation.

The life of prayer in the Catholic Church is varied and full, and I have only had space to touch on the most widely known traditions and theories of prayer. The prayer life of the Church is the most vital and important work that we do. Everything else comes from prayer, and if our efforts at mission and service are not charged with the glory of God, which we find in prayer, then they will come to nothing.

The Mission of the Church

Evangelical Christians are known for their zeal in spreading the Word of God through powerful preaching and fervent missionary activity, and in recent times Christians have come to a new awareness of how spreading the Christian message needs to be linked with ministering to the poor and needy. Throughout the world, Evangelicals work at the front line, risking their lives to set up schools and hospitals, translate the Scriptures, plant churches, and reach souls with the good news of Jesus Christ. In the last few centuries, Evangelicals have been heroic in their missionary efforts. Whole families have stepped out in faith to live in the most primitive conditions to reach tribal people with the Gospel. The Catholic Church can learn much from the Evangelicals' ability to train, fund, and support lay people engaged in missions work.

However, it is sometimes forgotten that the Catholic Church is also a great missionary church. Down through the ages the

Christian Gospel has been spread by courageous Catholic missionaries who risked their lives to reach out into new territories for Christ. In the first age the apostolic missionaries claimed great tracts of the Roman Empire for the Gospel, but in later centuries new waves of missionary effort have gone out from the Catholic Church. In the fifth and sixth centuries, missionaries from Ireland spread the Word across Britain and Northern Europe, while missionaries from Rome continued to press north. In the ninth century, the brothers Cyril and Methodius pioneered the Gospel in the lands of Eastern Europe and Russia. In the eleventh century, Cistercian monks made fresh inroads into the wilderness lands of Europe, planting monasteries and founding Christian communities. In the thirteenth and fourteenth centuries, new orders of friars followed the charismatic evangelists Francis and Dominic. In the sixteenth century, Catholic missionaries surged forward to evangelize the continents of South America and Africa, and amazing characters like St. Francis Xavier risked their lives to spread the good news in India, Malaysia, China, and Japan. In every age, Catholics have worked tirelessly to spread the Gospel, minister to the poor, and carry out the Great Commission. No other single organization has converted so many, planted more churches, or built as many schools, hospitals, universities, colleges, and clinics in the name of Jesus.

The same work goes on today. Catholic missionaries from the Third World are at the forefront of a second and third wave of missionary work. Now the indigenous peoples are sending their own missionaries into the world to continue the work of spreading the Gospel. New religious orders are springing up in the Third World as well as in Europe and the United States. Fresh approaches to missions and to the life of prayer are growing all over the Catholic world. One of the most famous examples of the new religious orders is Mother Teresa's Missionaries of Charity.

Started by a single courageous nun in the slums of Calcutta, the Missionaries of Charity are now spread worldwide. The Missionaries of Charity are a good example of the dynamic life of prayer that motivates Catholic missions. Mother Teresa was adamant that her nuns would first of all be women of prayer. At each house of the Missionaries of Charity the sisters rise at five in the morning for an hour of silent adoration. Then the day begins with the Eucharist. The nuns' labor of love for the poor is punctuated throughout the day with times of prayer and worship together. In this way their intense life of Christian witness is a kind of incarnation of the love of Jesus. First they attend to him in prayer and adoration, then he fills their lives at the Eucharist, then he ministers to the needy through their actions of love in the world.

This is the reason for prayer — to move closer and closer to union with Christ so that the world may come to know him. Jesus himself calls us to this union and prays for it to happen. In John's Gospel he prays: "I do not pray for these only, but also for those who believe in me through their word, that they may all be one; even as thou, Father, art in me, and I in thee, that they also may be in us, so that the world may believe that thou hast sent me. The glory which thou hast given me I have given to them, that they may be one even as we are one, I in them and thou in me, that they may become perfectly one, so that the world may know that thou hast sent me and hast loved them even as thou hast loved me" (John 17:20-23).

This is the reason for prayer and the motive of mission: that we may be one with Christ so that he may therefore be seen in our lives. In other words, as Christ was incarnate in the world, prayer helps him to be incarnate in our own lives, and therefore still alive in the world today. St. Teresa of Ávila famously said, "Christ has no hands but your hands, no feet but your feet, no lips but your lips." It is through the life of prayer that we live in a constant and intimate relationship with our Lord. It is that life of prayer, ever more intimate and full of the fire of love, which will finally transform these lowly bodies into his likeness. Only then as we are transformed into his likeness from glory to glory can we begin to set the world on fire with the power of his everlasting love.

Chapter Nine Endnotes

1. Thérèse of Lisieux, *Manuscrits Autobiographiques,* cited in the *Catechism of the Catholic Church*, London, Geoffrey Chapman, 1995, para. 2558 (hereafter CCC).

2. George Herbert, "Prayer," in *Faber Book of Religious Verse*, London, Faber and Faber, 1979, p. 122.

3. CCC, para. 2564.

4. Ibid., para. 2560.

5. Ibid., para. 2587.

6. Thomas N. Taylor (tr.), *Saint Thérèse of Lisieux: The Little Flower of Jesus,* New York, P. J. Kenedy, 1926, p. 295.

7. CCC, para. 2628.

8. Thomas Aquinas, *Summa Theologica,* II-III, 83, 9, cited in CCC, para. 2763.

9. CCC, para. 2668.

10. Dom Gregory Dix, *The Shape of the Liturgy,* cited in Campling and Davies, *Words for Worship,* London, Edward Arnold, 1969, p. 624.

11. St. Teresa of Jesus, *The Book of Her Life,* cited in CCC, para. 2709.

12. CCC, para. 2712.

'Further Up and Further In'

I never knew my grandfather. My mother told us the tragic story of how, when she was just sixteen, her father was walking across a bridge with her two younger brothers on a wintry day the week before Christmas. Suddenly a truck lost control on the icy surface and slid toward them. Grandfather threw himself between the truck and his sons and took the full impact. Some well-meaning passersby picked him up from the pavement, pushed him into the back of a car, and rushed him to hospital. Moving him in such an unskilled way caused internal damage. In the hospital he hovered near death for two days.

My grandmother stood by his bedside while relatives comforted the children. The doctors did all they could but informed my grandmother that his death was only a matter of time. My grandfather was a godly layman — a member of the Reformed Church, a Sunday school teacher, and a Bible student. As he lay in the hospital bed, there was nothing for my grandmother to do but pray. Then suddenly grandfather tried to sit up. His eyes opened and he looked up to the far corner of the hospital room. Grandma said his face was suddenly free of pain and radiant with the most wonderful delight.

"Don't you see them, Esther?" he cried.

She looked but could see nothing in the room.

"They're so beautiful!" he sighed, then leaned back on the pillow and was gone.

I can remember as a child in our Evangelical home hearing that true story about my grandfather's death. It is the sort of wonderful story that brings great comfort and urges us on to really believe with our hearts what we know with our heads: that the veil between heaven and earth is very thin. The story of my grandfather's death was a potent reminder that the other world was real, and that each one of us was just a heartbeat away from an eternal home that was far more wonderful than we could imagine. Heaven was "just across Jordan" and we knew we were going there when we died. The songs and sermons of our Bible Christian faith were laden with images of heaven and the promise that one day we would meet our loved ones in glory.

This hope of heaven surges through the New Testament. It is charged by Jesus' own promise that he goes to prepare a place for us, that where he is we may be too (cf. John 14:3). The writer to the Hebrews completes his song of praise for the heroes of the faith by recalling how they were on a pilgrimage to another country: "These all died in faith, not having received what was promised, but having seen it and greeted it from afar, and having acknowledged that they were strangers and exiles on the earth. For people who speak thus make it clear that they are seeking a homeland. . . . But as it is, they desire a better country, that is, a heavenly one" (Hebrews 11:13-14, 16).

St. Paul encourages the faithful with the idea that our bodies are like tents that we live in, and that God has prepared a heavenly home. He writes to the Church at Corinth, "For we know that if the earthly tent we live in is destroyed, we have a building from God, a house not made with hands, eternal in the heavens. Here indeed we groan, and long to put on our heavenly dwelling, so that by putting it on we may not be found naked. For while we are still in this tent, we sigh with anxiety; not that we would be unclothed, but that we would be further clothed, so that what is mortal may be swallowed up by life. He who has prepared us for this very thing is God, who has given us the Spirit as a guarantee. So we are always of good courage; we know that while we are at home in the body we are away from the Lord, for we walk by faith, not by sight. We are of good courage, and we would rather be away from the body and at home with the Lord" (2 Corinthians 5:1-8).

This phrase, "Absent from the body and present with the Lord," is the source for some of the beautiful language we used about death and dying. In our Evangelical tradition, if someone died we would say he was "at home with the Lord." If someone was about to die, we would comfort that person and his or her family with the reminder that "to be absent from the body was to be present with the Lord." The promise of heaven was a reality in our tradition, and we were assured that everyone who was really "saved" was headed for heaven. Our own tradition was influenced by Calvinism, so we believed in the doctrine of "eternal security." In other words, once saved, always saved. If you had truly accepted Jesus into your heart, you were guaranteed to go straight to heaven when you died.

This doctrine is a comfort to Christians, and it seems like a good counterbalance to a view of God's judgment that is too fearful. It's a good thing to look forward to heaven, and the doctrine that we are definitely going to heaven if we are saved is based in an underlying trust in God's forgiveness and the saving work of Christ on the cross. It is also based on the idea that we are called and predestined to salvation. However, there are some difficult side effects of the doctrine of eternal security. Sometimes the very thing it offers — eternal security — actually slips away from people. I've known some Evangelical Christians who constantly question whether they are really saved. If "getting saved" depends on a particular kind of religious experience, they wonder if their experience was the right one or not. Without objective signposts they wander lost on their spiritual journey.

The other problem with "eternal security" is the other extreme. Some folks who believe in eternal security seem just a little bit too "comfortable with glory." If you know you are going to heaven as soon as you die, it knocks the edge off the spiritual demands of this life. Furthermore, because there is nothing left to strive for, the overwhelming majesty of heaven remains unacknowledged. Of course there are many heroic, self-sacrificing Evangelical Christians, but eternal security sometimes makes the church seem like a rather cozy club of those who know they're saved and headed for heaven no matter what. This coziness in religion tends to cut out some of the harsher demands of the Gospel. It's all right for religion to be a crutch, just so long as it's not a cushion.

The third and most difficult side effect of the doctrine of eternal security are the implications it makes about our own decisions and actions. The logic must follow that if I am saved and going to heaven, then what I choose and do here in this life really has no effect on my final state in glory. Can it be true that my actions and decisions really don't matter? Of course we can see the effect of our decisions and actions in this life, but is there no way in which my decisions and actions matter eternally? Could God really have granted me so little freedom and responsibility? The schoolboy question to the Calvinist is always, "But what about people who get saved, then do terrible things? Are they still going to heaven the moment they die?"

In answering this question, the "more" that more Christianity has to offer is not outwardly attractive. Eternal security is a very attractive option. In the face of it, "more Christianity" can only extend Jesus' rather grim offering that "if any man would come after me, let him deny himself and take up his cross daily and follow me. For whoever would save his life will lose it; and whoever loses his life for my sake, he will save it" (Luke 9:23-24). Catholic Christianity calls us to sacrifice, discipline, devotion, and hard work. Jesus opens the door of heaven to us and gives us the grace to make the journey, but we have to set out and follow the path of life. Christianity is a serious and grueling business, and we are right to be suspicious of any creed that offers an easy road to heaven. More Christianity reminds us of Jesus' words: "Enter by the narrow gate; for the gate is wide and the way is easy, that leads to destruction, and those who enter by it are many. For the gate is narrow and the way is hard, that leads to life, and those who find it are few" (Matthew 7:13-14).

The Catholic 'Calminian'

At college the guys studying to be preachers used to argue about eternal security. The ones who were more Calvinist argued for eternal security. The ones who were more Arminian argued the more commonsense approach that a person could lose his salvation. Both sides had strong arguments. In fact, the debates were so fierce because both sides were actually partially right. It's true that we are called from before the foundation of the world to be God's elect (cf. Romans 8:29-30), but it is also true that it is possible to lose our salvation (cf. Hebrews 6:4-6). My father summed up the impression that both the Calvinists and the Arminians were right by declaring that on this issue he took the "Calminian" position.

The Calminian position is a good example of "more Christianity." It seeks to find the truth in both extremes and hold them together. It is true that the New Testament promises an eternal home to all those who repent of their sins and put their trust in Jesus. It is also true that we must persevere in the faith if we are to finally come to our heavenly home. Puzzling this one out brings us back to the mystery of how faith and actions work together. The Calminian says we do not get to heaven by our good works, but neither can we get to heaven without good works. If you prefer, the teaching of the Catholic Church is Calminian. On the one hand we are assured of heaven through faith in Jesus Christ. The *Catechism* says, "By his death and Resurrection, Jesus Christ has 'opened' heaven to us. The life of the blessed consists in the full and perfect possession of the fruits of the redemption accomplished by Christ. He makes partners in his heavenly glorification those who have believed in him and remained faithful to his will. Heaven is the blessed community of all who are perfectly incorporated into Christ."[1] On the other hand it is possible to fall out of that grace by committing some sin that, by its very nature, separates us from God's love. So the *Catechism* also teaches: "Mortal sin is a radical possibility of human freedom, as is love itself. It results in the loss of charity and the privation of sanctifying grace, that is, of the state of grace. If it is not redeemed by repentance and God's forgiveness, it causes exclusion from Christ's kingdom and the eternal death of hell, for our freedom has the power to make choices for ever, with no turning back. However, although we can judge that an act is in itself a grave offence, we must entrust judgement of persons to the justice and mercy of God."[2]

In other words, we can be confident of heaven as long as we remain in God's friendship and favor (cf. 1 John 4:17). We do this by cooperating with God's grace at work in our lives, responding daily in faith and love with our whole being. We call "mortal sin" any serious sin that leads to eternal spiritual death.

The book of Hebrews speaks of the possibility of falling into such sin (cf. Hebrews 6:4-6), and John says there is such a thing as mortal sin in his first epistle (cf. 1 John 3:15). Catholics believe it is possible to fall into a sin that takes us toward hell because God has given us freedom.

The Catholic "Calminian" takes God's mercy and grace seriously, but he also takes man's freedom seriously. For a Catholic the two do not contradict each other but work in harmony together. As a result, when it comes to heaven, Catholics speak of the "hope of heaven" rather than assuming they are going there simply because they are Catholics. In fact, the idea that we hope for heaven rather than being totally assured of our salvation is the scriptural position (cf. Romans 5:2, Ephesians 1:18, Colossians 1:5, and Titus 1:2, 3:7). The New Testament always encourages us to have hope and confidence that we are going to heaven. It never gives the utter assurance that some Evangelicals profess. When you think about it, what hope remains for the person who knows absolutely that he is going to heaven when he dies? St. Paul sums it up in Romans 8:24, "For in this hope we were saved. Now hope that is seen is not hope. For who hopes for what he sees? But if we hope for what we do not see, we wait for it with patience." In 1 Corinthians, St. Paul places hope as one of the three main virtues along with love and faith, but where is the room for hope if we know exactly where we stand at the last judgment? In saying this, the Catholic is not without hope. Indeed all his hope and trust is continually placed in his Savior Jesus Christ, knowing that without Christ he would surely fall.

Hope is the driving force within Catholic spirituality. Because we continually hope for something better, we are always striving to move further up and further into God's amazing love. A measure of uncertainty makes us aware of the mystery that lies beyond. To be in heaven is to see God face to face. Can any of us really be comfortable with such an awesome possibility? Heaven is a land of glory beyond our wildest imaginings, and hope reminds us that we still have much to learn. There is still room to grow. As St. Paul himself said: "Brethren, I do not consider that I have made it my own; but one thing I do, forgetting what lies behind and straining forward to what lies ahead, I press on toward the goal for the prize of the upward call of God in Christ Jesus" (Philippians 3:13-14). Heaven is a prize to be won. There are unplumbed mysteries of majesty that God has in store for us if we can only continue to run the race and penetrate further into that glory.

'Further Up and Further In'

In the last book of C. S. Lewis's Narnia stories, the world ends and the creatures of Narnia begin a long and joyous journey "further up and further in" to the real Narnia. As they go they continue to learn the most marvelous truths about their world, themselves, and the majestic Christ-figure, Aslan the lion. "Further up and further in!" they cry as they move into a Narnia that is far greater, far more real than the Narnia they had lived in before the end of time. Finally, after running higher and higher into the mountains of Narnia they reach a garden of paradise locked behind golden gates, and they know they are at the place where all worlds meet, at the gates of the dawn of eternity.

So it is when a Christian has hope. Hope is that sweet unhappiness that drives us to seek more and more Christianity. Hope is that awareness in our hearts that we have not yet arrived, and that each day we start a fresh journey deeper into Christ's love and goodness and purity. Hope is that quiet admission that we are imperfect, that Christ's great work of redemption is still coming to fruition in our lives. Hope is also that nagging understanding that purification is required if we are to make progress further up and further in. Hope is an awareness of the promise, but it is also an awareness of the present reality that is so far from that promise. The journey is joyful, but we must shake off all that weighs us down if we are to scale the heights of heaven.

This sense that we must still be purified settles into every heart that has approached the mountain of humility. The closer we draw to Christ, the more aware we are of our sinfulness, pride, and imperfection. There is a longing within us to be like him, and to see him as he is, but we know how far we are from that goal, and how much we still need to learn. Catholics believe that the process goes on in this life but that there are many who will be saved who die with an awful lot still to learn. Very few complete the process of purification in this life. Therefore we believe the first years after we die will be spent in a continued time of purification.

In Narnia, that onward and upward process was a joyful climb up the mountains of that new land. Another much older poet likened this process to climbing a mountain as well. Dante called his mountain "purgatory" — the place of purgation or purification. In his poem the faithful climb the mountain with a tremendous sense of joy and hope. By God's grace they help one another climb the mountain, joyfully purging the sin and darkness from their lives until at last, like Moses, they are prepared to see God face to face.

As beautiful as C. S. Lewis's fiction and the poetry of Dante are, I wouldn't want to base the idea of purgatory on them. While the full notion of purgatory was developed as the Church grew in understanding, it is based on suggestions in the New Testament. That we need to be perfect in order to enter the fullness of heaven is taught in the beatitudes, where it is the "pure in heart" who will see God (cf. Matthew 5:8). We are commanded to be perfect as our Father in heaven is perfect (cf. Matthew 5:48), and the writer of Hebrews exhorts us to pursue that perfection: "Strive for peace with all men, and for the holiness without which no one will see the Lord" (Hebrews 12:14).

That this process of purification can go on after this earthly life is over is hinted at in the Gospels when Jesus speaks of a situation in the afterlife where a reckoning will have to be made. In a parable about the judgment he encourages his hearers to take mind lest they be put into a prison not to be released "until you have paid the last penny" (Matthew 5:26). We are told in 1 Peter 3:19 that after his death Jesus went and "preached to the spirits in prison." Where were those spirits? Were they in a sort of reformatory, waiting for their purification to be complete? If so, then their earthly decisions and actions had meaning. Each person therefore had both freedom and responsibility for his decisions and actions, and what we do in this life will be included in the judgment.

In 1 Corinthians 3:10-15 St. Paul teaches about the final judgment. He says: "According to the commission of God given to me, like a skilled master builder I laid a foundation, . . . Let each man take care how he builds upon it. For no other foundation can any one lay than that which is laid, which is Jesus Christ. Now if any one builds on the foundation with gold, silver, precious stones, wood, hay, stubble — each man's work will become manifest; for the Day will disclose it, because it will be revealed with fire, and the fire will test what sort of work each one has done. If the work which any man has built on the foundation survives, he will receive a reward. If any man's work is burned up, he will suffer loss, though he himself will be saved, but only as through fire." In other words, we who have faith are built on the foundation of Christ and we are headed for heaven.

However, how we have built, or how we have spent our lives, also matters. St. Paul points out that "the fire will test what sort of work each one has done." Just after his inspiring passage on heaven in 2 Corinthians about being absent from the body and present with the Lord, Paul reminds us that there will be a judgment based on our works. "For we must all appear before the judgment seat of Christ, so that each one may receive good or evil, according to what he has done in the body" (2 Corinthians 5:10).

The New Testament is replete with passages like this one, which teach that the judgment includes an element of being tried according to our works (cf. Matthew 16:27, 25:31-46; Romans 14:12; Ephesians 6:7-8; Hebrews 10:26-27, 11:6; 2 Peter 1:10-11). Our works do not save us, but they do have a bearing on how fit we are for the ultimate purity and goodness of heaven. If we have built with worthless, sinful materials, they will need to be burned away before we can enter into heaven. If this is true, there must be a time and place after death where God's purification process continues. As such, purgatory is not a third place other than heaven and hell; instead it is like a waiting room for heaven. All those in purgatory will enter the fullness of heaven once their lessons have been learned and they are fully complete and whole in Christ.

In *The Great Divorce* C. S. Lewis takes a novel approach to the question of heaven, hell, and purgatory. In his imagination, hell is a gray, rainy town of "dingy lodging houses, small tobacconists, hoardings from which posters hung in rags, windowless warehouses, goods stations without trains, and bookshops of the sort that sell *The Works of Aristotle*."[3] It is a place where "time seemed to have paused on that dismal moment when only a few shops have lit up and it is not yet dark enough for their windows to look cheering."[4] Souls are able to leave this gray town if they wish and visit the lower levels of heaven. In his dream C. S. Lewis goes on such a journey and in heaven he asks his mentor, George MacDonald, "Is not judgement final? Is there really a way out of Hell into Heaven?"

MacDonald replies: "It depends on the way ye're using the words. If they leave that gray town behind it will not have been Hell. To any that leaves it, it is Purgatory. And perhaps ye had better not call this country Heaven. Not *Deep Heaven* ye understand. . . . Yet to those who stay here it will have been Heaven from the first. And you can call those sad streets down yonder the Valley of the Shadow of Death: but to those who remain there they will have been Hell even from the beginning."[5]

Lewis wonders, then, if people get a "second chance." MacDonald rejects this idea. Instead he explains how good and evil, when they are fully grown, are retroactive. "Not only this valley, but all their earthly past will have been Heaven to those who are saved. Not only the twilight in that town, but all their life on earth, too, will then be seen by the damned to have been Hell. . . . At the end of all things, when the sun rises here and the twilight turns to blackness down there, the Blessed will say, 'We have never lived anywhere but in Heaven,' and the Lost, 'We were always in Hell.' And both will speak truly."[6]

Lewis's imaginative treatment of heaven, hell, and purgatory is not doctrine. It is simply a writer's way of visualizing what it might be like "on the other side." Underlying his imagination is the truth that God gives us the freedom to choose his way or to choose our way, and that our choices matter eternally. God's justice will reign over all, but our choices will also be part of that judgment. Heaven and hell are both God's judgment and our choice. As C. S. Lewis has MacDonald say, "There are only two kinds of people in the end: those who say to God, "Thy will be done,' and those to whom God says, in the end,

Thy will be done.' All that are in Hell choose it. Without that self choice there could be no Hell. No soul that seriously and constantly desires joy will ever miss it. Those who seek find. To those who knock it is opened."[7]

Choosing Hell or Heaven

"We cannot be united with God unless we freely choose to love him. But we cannot love God if we sin gravely against him, against our neighbor or against ourselves: 'He who does not love remains in death. Anyone who hates his brother is a murderer, and you know that no murderer has eternal life abiding in him' [1 John 3:14-15]. Our Lord warns us that we shall be separated from him if we fail to meet the serious needs of the poor and the little ones who are his brethren [cf. Matthew 25:31-46 and 1 John 3:17]. To die in mortal sin without repenting and accepting God's merciful love means remaining separated from him for ever by our own free choice. This state of definitive self-exclusion from communion with God and the blessed is called 'hell.' "[8]

With these somber words the *Catechism* warns each one of us of the danger of hell and exhorts us, "The affirmations of Sacred Scripture and the teachings of the Church on the subject of hell are a *call to the responsibility* incumbent upon man to make use of his freedom in view of his eternal destiny. They are at the same time an urgent *call to conversion:* 'Enter by the narrow gate; for the gate is wide and the way is easy, that leads to destruction, and those who enter by it are many. For the gate is narrow and the way is hard, that leads to life, and those who find it are few.' "[9]

If hell is such a real danger, then who can be saved? Will most people who care nothing about God or who have never heard of him end up in hell? Catholics always return to the unfailing love and mercy of God, who does not want anyone to perish (cf. 2 Peter 3:9). Hell is a reality, but as C. S. Lewis holds out the hope that anyone who seriously and constantly desires joy will never miss it, so Catholics maintain the hope that many souls will finally come to glory by virtue of Christ's work on the cross. Will all those who followed other religions necessarily be hell-bound? Catholics hope not. Jesus has other sheep (cf. John 10:16) and God's loving plan of redemption is to save the whole world, not to condemn it (cf. John 3:16-17).

C. S. Lewis offers an intriguing explanation of how this might be. In his final Narnia story, *The Last Battle,* a good pagan called Emeth dies. All his life he worshiped his god called Tash and the name of Aslan (the great Christ figure) was hateful to him. For him Tash was the source of light, goodness, beauty, truth, and peace. When he got to the other side of death, he met Aslan instead, and Aslan teaches him that everything Emeth was seeking is truly fulfilled in him, and not in Tash. Aslan says, "Child, all the service thou hast done to Tash, I account as service done to me. . . . No service which is vile can be done to me, and none which is not vile can be done to him. Therefore if any man swear by Tash and keep his oath for the oath's sake, it is by me that he has truly sworn, thought he know it not, and it is I who reward him. And if any man do cruelty in my name, then, though he says the name of Aslan, it is Tash whom he serves and by Tash his deed is accepted. . . . Unless thy desire had been for me thou wouldst not have sought so long and so truly. For all find what they truly seek."[10]

The Catholic Church recognizes the goodness and truth within other religions, and while we constantly affirm that no one comes to the Father except through his Son, Jesus Christ (cf. John 14:6), we also affirm that the goodness and truth in other religions can be pointers to Christ. "The Catholic Church recognizes in other religions that search, among shadows and images, for the God who is unknown yet near, since he gives life and breath and all things, and wants all men to be saved. Thus, the Church considers all goodness and truth found in these religions as 'a preparation for the Gospel, and given by him who enlightens all men that they may at length have life.' "[11] More Christianity therefore affirms the goodness and truth in other religions while always seeking through evangelism to draw all men and women further up and further into the final goodness and truth that is Jesus Christ.

To choose him is to choose an ever-increasing freedom. "The more one does what is good, the freer one becomes. There is no true freedom except in the service of what is good and just. The choice to disobey and do evil is an abuse of freedom and leads to 'the slavery of sin.' "[12] This glorious freedom of the sons of God is a freedom to go on choosing more of Christ's goodness and truth every step of the way. The freedom to choose heaven or hell is a choice for all eternity, but it is also a choice that affects our lives here and now. Will we choose more and more of Christ, following him in freedom and truth every chance we get — or will we choose our own way? It may be that we choose our own way out of loyalty to some lesser good. As C. S. Lewis has George MacDonald say, "There is always something they insist on keeping, even at the price of misery. There is always something they prefer to joy — that is, to reality. Ye see it easily enough in a spoiled child that would sooner miss its play and its supper than say it was sorry and be friends. In adult life it has a hundred fine names — Achilles' wrath and Coriolanus' grandeur, Revenge and Injured Merit and Self-Respect and Tragic Greatness and Proper Pride."[13]

To choose more Christianity is to choose more of everything that is good and true and beautiful. It also means embracing the reality of suffering and the responsibility for our own choices — both good and bad. It is to choose a path that takes us further up and further into new dimensions of reality we never imagined. That reality, like all reality, is hard, and hard means both difficult and concrete. The journey is not easy, but as we take each step toward the reality of Christ we take a step toward that land that is reality itself.

What will heaven be like? The *Catechism* says, "This mystery of blessed communion with God and all who are in Christ is beyond all understanding and description. Scripture speaks of it in images: life, light, peace, wedding feast, wine of the kingdom, the Father's house, the heavenly Jerusalem, paradise: 'no eye has seen, nor ear heard, nor the heart of man conceived, what God has prepared for those who love him' [1 Corinthians 2:9]."[14]

C. S. Lewis loves to use the imagery of an ever-increasing reality. In *The Last Battle* the creatures of Narnia witness the end of their world. Then they are taken further up and further into a new land. But the new land looks strangely like the old, and they begin to realize that they are entering the old Narnia in its original form. It is a Narnia more ancient, more real, and more beautiful than they could have ever imagined. Lord Digory, who was there at the creation of Narnia, says of the world they knew, "That was not the real Narnia. That had a beginning and an end. It was only a shadow or a copy of the real Narnia which has always been here and always will be. . . . And of course it is different as a real thing is from a shadow or as waking life is from a dream."[15] As they penetrate this real land, they discover that the real Narnia is larger on the inside than it is on the outside. "The further up and the further in you go, the bigger everything gets. The inside is larger than the outside."[16] In the same way, here on earth the reality of Christ and his Church becomes greater, more beautiful, and more real the further we move into it.

To accept more Christianity is to accept more of Christ and to be transformed into his image. The promise is that "with unveiled face, beholding the glory of the Lord, [we] are being changed into his likeness from one degree of glory to another" (2 Corinthians 3:18). To discover him is also to discover the freedom to be our true selves, for who we really are is hidden in Christ. Therefore, to move into that deeper reality is to "arrive where we started and know the place for the first time."[17] The Greek philosophers said learning was simply a matter of remembering something we knew long ago but had forgotten. So moving further into more Christianity is like coming home. It is the completion of all that was missing and the reconciliation of all that was lost. It is the discovery of the hidden treasure and the pearl of great price. Embracing more Christianity means running on the road of the returning prodigal. It is setting our sights on another country until at last we can say with the creatures of Narnia: "I have come home at last! This is my real country! I belong here. This is the land I have been looking for all my life, though I never knew it till now."[18]

Chapter Ten Endnotes

1. *Catechism of the Catholic Church*, London, Geoffrey Chapman, 1995, para. 1026 (hereafter CCC).

2. Ibid., para. 1861.

3. C. S. Lewis, *The Great Divorce*, London, Fontana, 1988, p. 13.

4. Ibid.

5. Ibid., p. 61.

6. Ibid., p. 62.

7. Ibid., pp. 66-67.

8. CCC, para. 1033.

9. Ibid., para. 1036.

10. C. S. Lewis, *The Last Battle,* London, Harper Collins, 1992, pp. 154-155.

11. CCC, para. 843.

12. Ibid., para. 1733.

13. Lewis, *The Great Divorce,* p. 64.

14. CCC, para. 1027.

15. Lewis, *The Last Battle,* pp. 159-160.

16. Ibid., p. 169.

17. T. S. Eliot, *The Four Quartets,* London, Faber and Faber, 1979, p. 48.

18. Lewis, *The Last Battle,* p. 161.

About the Author

Dwight Longenecker, who lives in England, has four other books to his credit, including Our Sunday Visitor's *St. Benedict and St. Thérèse: The Little Rule and the Little Way.* In addition he has written for the magazines *Crisis, Envoy, This Rock, Touchstone, The Lutheran, New Covenant, The New Oxford Review, Gilbert!, St. Austin Review, Catholic World Report, Inside the Vatican,* and *The Coming Home Journal.* He also writes for most of the leading Catholic papers and magazines in Britain and Ireland. A former Anglican minister, Dwight is also an experienced public speaker and broadcaster with regular appearances on the BBC, London's Premier Radio, and EWTN. He works for the St. Barnabas Society, serves as a parish catechist and Eucharistic minister, and is a Benedictine oblate of Downside Abbey. He and his wife, Alison, have four children. He can be contacted at Dwight@Longenecker.fsnet.co.uk.

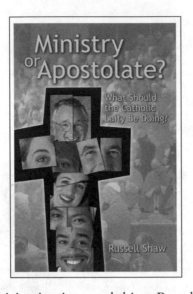

While lay participation is a good thing, Russell Shaw argues that we've forgotten the crucial distinction between *ministry* (what we do inside the Church) and *apostolate* (what we do in the secular world). We've almost completely neglected the lay apostolate, he says, and that mistake has handicapped the Church in its work of evangelizing culture. We need a new, better balance between ministry and apostolate.
0-87973-957-6 (957), paper, 128 pp.

To order from Our Sunday Visitor:
Toll free: 1-800-348-2440
E-mail: osvbooks@osv.com
Website: www.osv.com

Availability of products subject to change without notice.

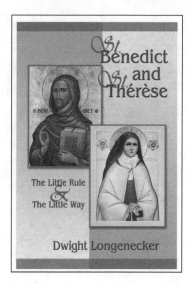

St. Benedict called his rule "a little Rule for beginners," while St. Thérèse called her way of spirituality "the little way." By bringing the two of them together, we can see how to turn our ordinary day-to-day living into an extraordinary spiritual life.

0-87973-983-5 (983), paper, 224 pp.

To order from Our Sunday Visitor:
Toll free: 1-800-348-2440
E-mail: osvbooks@osv.com
Website: www.osv.com

Availability of products subject to change without notice.

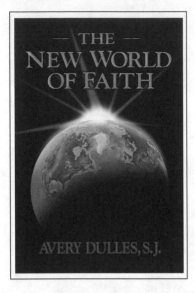

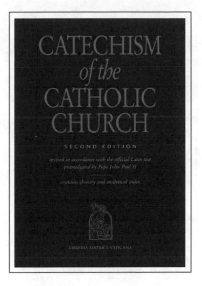

Here in one volume is the whole teaching of the Catholic Church, undiluted and uncompromised. The *Catechism* is not an *interpretation* of what Catholics believe; it *is* what Catholics believe. From animal experimentation to unemployment, it addresses all the most pressing moral questions of the modern world.

0-87973-976-2 (976), paper, 906 pp.

0-87973-977-0 (977), hardcover, 906 pp.

To order from Our Sunday Visitor:

Toll free: 1-800-348-2440

E-mail: osvbooks@osv.com

Website: www.osv.com

Availability of products subject to change without notice.

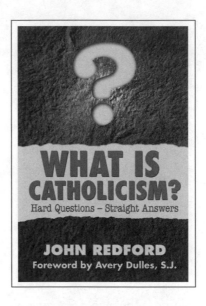

Isn't the doctrine of papal infallibility a constant embarrassment? How can a celibate priest tell married people what to do in bed? This is the book that answers such questions.
0-87973-587-2 (587), paper, 240 pp.

To order from Our Sunday Visitor:
Toll free: 1-800-348-2440
E-mail: osvbooks@osv.com
Website: www.osv.com

Availability of products subject to change without notice.

Our Sunday Visitor. . .
*Your Source for Discovering
the Riches of the Catholic Faith*

Our Sunday Visitor has an extensive line of materials for young children, teens, and adults. Our books, Bibles, booklets, CD-ROMs, audios, and videos are available in bookstores worldwide.

To receive a FREE full-line catalog or for more information, call **Our Sunday Visitor** at **1-800-348-2440**. Or write, **Our Sunday Visitor** / 200 Noll Plaza / Huntington, IN 46750.

- -

Please send me: ____A catalog
Please send me materials on:
____Apologetics and catechetics   ____Reference works
____Prayer books   ____Heritage and the saints
____The family   ____The parish
Name_____
Address_____Apt._____
City_____State_____Zip_____
Telephone (   ) _____

A29BBABP

- -

Please send a friend: ____A catalog
Please send a friend materials on:
____Apologetics and catechetics   ____Reference works
____Prayer books   ____Heritage and the saints
____The family   ____The parish
Name_____
Address_____Apt._____
City_____State_____Zip_____
Telephone (   ) _____

A29BBABP

- -

Our Sunday Visitor
200 Noll Plaza
Huntington, IN 46750
Toll free: 1-800-348-2440
E-mail: osvbooks@osv.com
Website: www.osv.com